50
YEARS

SAGE was founded in 1965 by Sara Miller McCune to support the dissemination of usable knowledge by publishing innovative and high-quality research and teaching content. Today, we publish more than 750 journals, including those of more than 300 learned societies, more than 800 new books per year, and a growing range of library products including archives, data, case studies, reports, conference highlights, and video. SAGE remains majority-owned by our founder, and on her passing will become owned by a charitable trust that secures our continued independence.

Los Angeles | London | Washington DC | New Delhi | Singapore

Tagore and the Feminine

Tagore and the Feminine
A Journey in Translations

Edited
by
MALASHRI LAL

 **SAGE** **www.sagepublications.com**
Los Angeles • London • New Delhi • Singapore • Washington DC

First published in 2015 by

SAGE Publications India Pvt Ltd
B1/I-1 Mohan Cooperative Industrial Area
Mathura Road, New Delhi 110 044, India
www.sagepub.in

SAGE Publications Inc
2455 Teller Road
Thousand Oaks, California 91320, USA

SAGE Publications Ltd
1 Oliver's Yard, 55 City Road
London EC1Y 1SP, United Kingdom

SAGE Publications Asia-Pacific Pte Ltd
3 Church Street
#10-04 Samsung Hub
Singapore 049483

Published by Vivek Mehra for SAGE Publications India Pvt Ltd, typeset in 10/12 pts Adobe Garamond Pro by RECTO Graphics, Delhi, and printed at Chaman Enterprises, New Delhi.

Library of Congress Cataloging-in-Publication Data Available

ISBN: 978-93-515-0067-4 (PB)

The SAGE Team: Supriya Das, Shreya Chakraborti, Rajib Chatterjee and Rajinder Kaur

Robey,
Shantanu
and
Kavita

CONTENTS

From *Gitanjali*

Poems

Songs

Epics and Mythology

Play

Short Stories

Essays, Lectures and Letters to the Editor

Travelogues

Epilogue

ACKNOWLEDGEMENTS

I came close to Rabindranath Tagore more through feminist theory than through my Bengali heritage. Yet the memory of my mother and aunts singing *Rabindra Sangeet* and my erudite grandmother reading out Tagore's stories late into the summer nights of Rajasthan stays vivid. As a *probashi* (non-resident) Bengali, my approach to Tagore was mediated by multiculturalism and my understanding mingled with worries about Indian feminism. Academically, it took decades before I could speak about Tagore. Now that I write about him, there are many persons to thank for giving me encouragement and confidence. My friends and Tagore scholars Aruna Chakravarti, Reba Som, Sanjukta Dasgupta, Radha Chakravarty and Shila Pain helped me through selections, my non-Bengali friends Alok Bhalla and Sukrita Paul Kumar put faith in my research ideas and enthusiasm for conferences. Shri Jowhar Sircar and Namita Gokhale gave me the institutional opportunity to work on Tagore through the programme 'Indian Literature Abroad' at the Ministry of Culture. Thanks to Tagore's 150th birth year celebrations and Indian Council for Cultural Relations (ICCR) support, I had the chance to converse with several others—Imre Bangha, William Radice, Ketaki Kushari Dyson, Alka Pande and Ana Jelnikar. To Uma Dasgupta and Sunil Gangopadhyay, I owe the impetus to carry forward my nascent views emerging from a conference in Cochin, and to *master-moshai* (my teacher) Sudhir Chanda, singer Jayati Ghosh and actor Averee Chaurey—the link they brought to the world of Tagore performance. My research assistant Soham Pain is thanked profusely for his energy and devotion to the project. I am grateful to the authors and publishers who gave permission for their work to be included here. And finally to my family—Robey, Shantanu and Kavita—far from Tagore's Bengali, but close to my work and always my devoted supporters, many thanks.

New Delhi
6 September 2014

INTRODUCTION

Malashri Lal

Rabindranath Tagore's negotiations with the feminine were deeply problematic for himself and his times, and continue to perplex his readers today. Perhaps for that reason, one tends to return repeatedly to those teasing and unforgettable portrayals in his fiction and poetry, song and philosophy. But readers have too long trusted Tagore's own rather simple ways of expressing his intuitively complex understanding of the feminine as a concept, a trope and a manifestation, and not investigated the subtexts. He said, for instance, 'There are two kinds of women, or so I've heard some pundits say. One is mostly maternal. The other is the lover.'[1] In a different mood, the gender divide is dissolved and we encounter the words, 'Our nature holds together, inseparably linked, a wilfully itinerant male, impatient of all bonds, and a shut-in home keeping female being.... The one leads us outward, the other draws us back home.' Hence, 'we are all *ardhanarishvara*: sometimes half and half, sometimes in unequal proportion'.[2] Further, we have Mrinal's famous defiance of patriarchy: 'Today having freed myself of your customs, I can live... I *shall* live, unfettered by the shelter of your feet'.[3]

This book attempts to understand Tagore's engagement with the feminine from the perspective of a contemporary reader for whom biological determinants and psychological assumptions of being *masculine* and *feminine* are questionable. Revisiting the oeuvre of Tagore through critical sensibilities nurtured by feminist theory and gender studies, it becomes possible to read Tagore in new ways since his words are multivalent, the images mercurial and the emotions brilliantly nuanced. The *contradictions* are creative, for as another iconic poet Walt Whitman said, 'Do I contradict myself?/Very well, then I contradict myself'.[4] Tagore declared in a similar vein, 'The planet which rules my life is the planet of contradiction.'[5] Without recourse to *theory* as such, Rabindranath Tagore evolved his own principles for portraying the feminine in a marvellous range of expressions. It is left to his readers to relate his literature to contemporary life.

Rabindranath entered the woman's imagination, experience and language with amazing perspicacity. If a male writer can successfully inhabit the female mindscape is a question often asked. Virginia Woolf famously declared that 'the great mind is androgynous' and cited Shakespeare and Coleridge as examples.[6] Closer to our time, Judith Butler called her book *Gender trouble* and questioned the basis of defining *sex* as biological and *gender* as sociological. Instead, she declared that gender is *performative*.[7] In other words, a person enters and explores a space of articulate desire and sexuality in specific conditions, and the ambiguous gendering is determined by that moment and the act. Hence, the manifestation of the human body is not simply biological as *male* and *female* but located in the complex impulses that drive psychological sympathies within an immediate context. Tagore's notion of *ardhanarishvara* is close to such theory. We are each, as he says, both male and female. Patriarchy, however, has conditioned us to believe that our *performativity* is according to the codifications of *male* and *female* and its concomitant binaries, *masculine* and *feminine*. Hence, we carry, from our social context, a collective burden of inherited beliefs about the home and the world, nature and nurture, beauty and intellect, and such others.

Did Tagore lean towards the *performative* idea of gender or the *normative* and traditional one? His use of androgynous principles has received scant attention partly because they occur as subtle subversions of the patriarchal norm. Androgyny is but one example of how the subject of Tagore and the feminine commands new attention. The book offers selections from Tagore's vast corpus with a perspective that seeks out references and allusions in order to highlight the debates on feminism and gender identity that remain implicit throughout his work, and are relevant today. There are surprisingly candid poems on the body and sensuality, clever play with mythology, deep empathy with rural poverty and woman's deprivation, exploration of the woman–nation equivalence and challenges to patriarchy, while also tributes to woman's familial role.

The book is constructed with the belief that in commemorating the 150th year of Rabindranath Tagore's birth we acknowledged his global and cosmopolitan identity and his contribution to intellectual history. Within that frame, his views on the feminine along with issues of gender and sexuality deserve notice for he garnered information at home and abroad, reflected on women's status and wrote in bold and sometimes radical ways. The motto of Tagore's university Visva-Bharati sees 'the world, making a home in a single nest': *Yatra visvam bhavatyekanidam*.[8] What place does the feminine hold in that world view?

Robi and childhood encounters with the feminine

Born on 7 May 1861 to Debendranath Tagore and Sarada Devi in the affluent Thakurbari of Jorasanko, Robi, the thirteenth child of his parents could not have received much individual attention. Yet, it was a populous household with many branches of the family and its many children sharing a regimented routine of education, sports, language learning, music and cultural activities. Rabindranath's *Chhelebela* captures memories of his early life until his departure for England in 1878.[9] However, written in 1940, when the poet was an elderly and lonely man, the act of recovery is fraught with difficulties of *re-memorising*, which, American writer Toni Morrison would theorise, interferes with the notion of authenticity in self-reflections.

Looking back, Tagore writes about the gender segregation in the household,

> In our family in those days, the worlds of men and women were poles apart, and so were the worlds of adults and children. In the chandelier-lit *baithakkhana*, the song-and-dance routine would be in progress; the elders would be puffing away at their *gurguris*; the women, with their caskets of *paan*, would be concealed in the dimness behind the *jharokhas*, windows with ornate filigree screens.[10]

The child Robi traverses between these worlds linking the male domain with authority and the female with indulgence. The children were largely looked after by a retinue of servants and educated by a stream of tutors, the parents being somewhat distant figures asserting presence when required. The *mother* in Tagore's account is not a sentimentalised figure, unlike in much Indian fiction, and this distancing from the maternal, except as an abstraction, tends to flow into his writing. *Boyhood days* carries a class divide, the Thakurbari women experimenting with cuisine, dress and entertainment; the underclass women such as the maid Piyari running the household. Robi's fancy is captivated by the *palki* (carriage) in which he takes imaginary journeys, has rough adventures, conquers enemies and generally emerges triumphant. The adult writer of *Boyhood days* may have introduced the palki as a literary artefact for gender debate, this hand-pulled carriage for transporting women in a hidden fashion, suggesting the epitome of a woman's veiling from public eye and many romantic tales of abduction and subterfuge being associated with it.[11] Further colouring young Robi's imagination are female ghosts, specially the *shankchunni* (malevolent female spirit, especially of a woman who died in pregnancy) who frightens women and has a weakness for fish,[12] and the intrepid folk figure, *kachi bedeni*, the snake catcher who can hack a crocodile to pieces.[13]

Sweet sixteen and the awareness of women

Robi's brother Satyendranath married Jnanadanandini, a shy, dusky little girl who quickly learnt the ways of the Thakurbari and started charting new paths for its women. She left for England with her husband, shocking the sensibilities of the community. Returning to the family home, she introduced more practical ways of eating and dressing, took to riding and going out in public without being veiled. Satyendranath, when posted to Bombay, insisted on taking his wife. Here, influenced by Parsi women, Jnanadanandini devised a sari–blouse–petticoat ensemble that has been subsequently adopted universally in India. Robi's *bouthakrun* (senior sister-in-law), Jnanadanandini, a bold experimenter, pulled her young brother-in-law out of his sheltered childhood. If she was a mentor, viewed with respect and some fear, there was to appear his muse, *notun bouthan* (new sister-in-law), Kadambari, the wife of another brother, Jyotirindranath. Born in an obscure family, she had neither pedigree nor obvious attractiveness. Yet, she acquired grace and reputation as a patron of the arts and created a terrace garden of beauty and poetry in the Jorasanko home which transformed young Robi's tastes. In *Boyhood days*, the emotions are restrained, 'Now began a new act in the drama of the second floor room, altering my life'.[14]

The literary life was aided by the women in the Tagore household. The two sisters-in-law were fond of poetry and were aesthetic homemakers. Descriptions abound about the design and accoutrements of the terrace where musical instruments were laid out, poets entertained with delicate snacks served on etched *Muradabadi* trays, fragrant flower petals arranged in water basins, and incense gently wafting in the air. In this garden, soirees attracted the family and guests with a talent for the arts. '[Jnanadanandini] trod many unfamiliar paths to engineer the advancement of Bengali women'.[15] The old gender divide of segregated spaces in Thakurbari was gone, notes Robi. And significantly, he is invited to read from texts, recite poems, sing and compose and, in general, participate in the adult world of cultural practice. He is sixteen going on seventeen, young enough to be treated casually by the women. When even younger, Robi read poems to his mother's friends and was profusely praised. As a teenager, he composes and reads his work at the gathering of poets on the terrace and there is indulgent appreciation; he writes and sings lyrics in which his cognoscenti father recognises talent. *Boyhood days*, written in hindsight, is conveniently episodic, but its ellipses suggest deliberate withdrawals. More than biography, Rabindranath's poems tell of his inner life and unfolding consciousness.

Three women and some epistolary moments

Primarily three women have been associated with Tagore: first, Kadambari Debi, the notun bouthan, who was his muse and remained so even after her mysterious death on 21 April 1884; second, his wife Mrinalini Debi (married 1883), to whom Rabindranath wrote several letters in Bengali which I have translated into English; and third, Victoria Ocampo, his Argentinean host in 1924 to whom he wrote letters all his life. On the periphery are some others such as Anna Turkhud and Ranu Adhikari.

Personal letters are often the most revealing of documents; hence, famous families do not always allow public scrutiny. Of Tagore's correspondence, the most fulsome are the letters exchanged with Victoria Ocampo, collected meticulously by Ketaki Kushari Dyson and presented with an invaluable commentary.[16] Tagore was sixty-three years old when they met, and Victoria was thirty-four. He was a celebrated poet, she an aspiring litterateur. Victoria was married to Bernando de Estrada but had left him without a formal divorce, for a lover, Julián Martínez. Tagore's accompanying secretary was the suave Leonard Elmhirst, himself engaged to be married in a few months. According to Ketaki Kushari Dyson, Victoria was reverential towards Tagore and deeply in love with him; this did not prevent her being flirtatious towards Elmhirst, who gladly reciprocated the compliment. I wish to lay emphasis on the fact that to neither of the men did Victoria mention her hidden lover Martínez, though she appears to have sobbed to them about the tragedy of her dull and disappointing married life. Victoria was married and childless but presented herself as a singular, wealthy and free European woman to Tagore and Elmhirst. Clearly in such a scenario, the categories of Wife and Beloved were excitingly mixed up. The sheaf of letters exchanged between Rabindranath and Victoria would be a Freudian psychologist's delight. She tells Elmhirst that she would like to sleep outside Tagore's door like a dog awaiting a call! Tagore, in turn, renames her *Vijaya* (victorious) and teaches her the one Bengali word that is important—*bhalobasha* or *love*.[17]

Rabindranath's relationship with Mrinalini was of a householder and a caring husband but it lacks the tense passion that showed in his letters to Ocampo even when he was over sixty. It could not have been easy to be the wife to Rabindranath. He was married in 1883 when twenty-two years old, to ten-year-old Bhabatarini, the daughter of an employee in the Tagore estates. The family went about renaming her Mrinalini, appointing tutors to rid her of her Jessore accent in Bengali and teaching her the civilities and manners of a premier household. She was also sent to Loreto School to learn English. In this makeover, Mrinalini developed her own unique personality as the mother of five children, a caregiver to all those who came asking for help, including a Punjabi *darwan* (doorman) who needed a constant supply of wheat for his chapattis. She was known for her culinary skills, improvising the exotic recipes that Rabindranath brought to her. (It is believed that he helped her cook, at times.) She assisted in the elaborate dressing up of women in the Tagore household but neglected her own appearance. One evening, when she was persuaded to wear showy earrings, she quickly covered up her ears when Tagore appeared on the scene![18]

Rabindranath wrote several letters to Mrinalini from 1890 to 1902, the year of her untimely death.[19] There was an easy familiarity between them, he addressing her as *bhai chhoto bou* or *bhai chhuti* (quite untranslatable in English), and signing off as Robi. But what did he speak about? Mostly about functional household matters: How were the children Beli and Khoka? Was the estate doing well? Had money been paid to so and so? What happened to the fifteen *ser*s (a unit of measurement in India) of ghee that had been purchased? If there is any personal note, it is to ask Mrinalini if she is taking regular walks or indulging in reading novels.

Only one letter recounting a dream expresses his physical longing for her. I have translated selections from these matrimonial epistles because of an interest in Tagore's concept of love. It would appear that he made a distinction between wifely rootedness and a beloved's freedom. Or was it also a matrix that got complicated by his notion of the East and West and the romantic freedom accorded by the West? Tagore never lectured Victoria Ocampo about wifely duties. He signed his letters to Victoria with Bhalobasha/love, an endearment he never used in his letters to Mrinalini.

Kadambari Debi's role as Rabindranath's muse has been speculated upon endlessly. In his writing, we can only find her indirectly. Their youthful attachment in the relationship of *devar–bhabi* (the husband's younger brother and the elder brother's wife) was couched in the usual rhetoric of an easy friendship rather common in joint families, but the sequence whereby Robi was first sent away from home, then suddenly married and, a few months later, Kadambari committing suicide cannot escape conjectures of a tense romantic drama.[20] Moreover, the powerful Thakurbari prohibited any public exposure and to this day the manner of Kadambari's death is not known. All letters and diaries were destroyed, the many retainers compelled into silence, the patriarch Debendranath personally preventing any leakage of news. For young Robi, Kadambari was a secret love that became apotheosised as poetry or image. *Tumi ki keboli chhobi?* (Are you just a picture?) is a famous lyric said to address the absent Kadambari. She died childless, and that could have been one of her privations. In his essays, Tagore always associated Indian women with family and mothering, though his fiction sought other idealised alternatives. Abiding by the decorum of the family, Rabindranath could never write letters to Kadambari directly. However, when he wrote from England to his family elders, he knew the letters would be read publicly and Kadambari would be a listener. By proxy, they were in communication from abroad. At home, they could be friends. The final farewell in death caused an eternal association of love with pain, bringing poignant meaning to Tagore's lines:

Sakhi, bhalobasha kare koy! Se ki keboli jatonamoy?
Se ki keboli chokher jal? Se ki keboli dukhero shvaas?

Friend, what is *love*? Is it always full of pain?
Is it all about tears? Are sighs its only breath?

Translated by **Malashri Lal**

Gender and sexuality

Love cannot be altogether in the abstract. Until recently, it has been difficult to address sexuality in the writings of Tagore because of an invisible censoring that operates upon material concerning famous men. Jawaharlal Nehru's friendships were the subject of conjecture but not brought under the pen until Stanley Wolpert published *Nehru: A tryst with destiny* (2008). After decades, a candid biography of Mahatma Gandhi could be published by Joseph Lelyveld (*Great soul: Mahatma Gandhi and his struggle with India,* 2011) though attacks persist on some of its claims. Both Nehru and Gandhi were, by and large, open about their emotions, treating expressions of love as a legitimate part of their lived experience. In a sort of parallel, Rabindranath Tagore's personal relations with women have been much speculated upon but not authentically written about. This collection on *Tagore and the feminine* will not evade the issue, but when speaking of a litterateur, one should depend on literary expression rather than social speculation.

Rabindranath Tagore was nineteen when he wrote *Kori o komal* (1880), containing rather explicit poems on physicality. The title itself bears reflection. Translating as 'Flats and sharps', the obvious reference is to musical scale, however, it would not be far-fetched to imagine a poetic subtext of amorous play, its highs and lows. Poems such as *Bibasana* (Woman unclothed), *Staun* (Breast), *Chumban* (The kiss) and *Deher milan* (Bodily union) present an acute and candid understanding of male desire in relation to the female body. A burgeoning sexuality yearns for fulfilment and far from etherealising the beloved, the young man calls out for reciprocal passion in full expectation of mutual joy. The visual quality of these poems is startling in the context of reticence often associated with Bengali *bhadralok* (gentleman) writing. The poet wishes the woman to cast off her clothes in the manner in which a person admires and is seduced by the sight of a naked Venus rising from the ocean. Her breasts are like the mounts of Sumeru glowing in the light of the sun, and her body holds the promise of quenching an eternal thirst for love.

Such a stance may be misread as the male gaze trained upon a commodified woman. However, Tagore's empathy with the woman would not permit such slippage. Read carefully, these poems attribute will and power to the woman who is in control of her sexuality and whose desire must match that of the admirer before any physical passion is expressed. The emphasis is on mutuality. At the same time, Rabindranath's words describing the female body are neither euphemistic nor evasive. In translating these poems into English, I had to be immensely careful about not demeaning the sentiments while preserving the physical and the sexual. The poem *Staun*, for instance, refers to breasts as a focus of desire as well as maternity, and expands into a mythical connection with the abode of gods. In creating such a chain of references, Tagore effects what French feminist Helene Cixous might have termed the 'Realm of the Gift',[21] for the object of desire in Tagore's version is generous, perceptive and bountiful; she determines the man's action. I do not mean to suggest that the ordinary realms of sexuality are ignored in this trajectory. Tagore is capable of portraying the erotic, the robust and the expectant in a man–woman relationship.

The Indianised context of the female body is worthy of a postscript. *Modesty*, *coyness* and *shyness* are not good equivalents for conveying the meaning of *lajjaa* which alludes to a woman's hesitation in admitting sexual attraction. There is a cultural prohibition on women showing desire. Tagore conveys the concomitants of this Indian concept or term through some remarkable vignettes using references to the *anchal*, the sari-end that should be removed from the draped body. The women in these poems are actively engaged in sexuality and from that viewpoint, Tagore is neither a voyeur nor a coercive male, but a sensitive being in a participatory act of love that was his ideal.

Tagore's androgynous imagination: Mythology revisited

To understand the feminine principle and give dignity to the woman's mind and body, a writer must be gifted with an androgynous imagination. As mentioned earlier, Tagore had said, 'We are all ardhanarishvara: sometimes half and half, sometimes in unequal proportion.' Alka Pande in her book *Ardhanarishvara the androgyne: Probing the gender within* explains, 'In the Indian context... the image of Ardhanarishvara is more a philosophical construct rather than a social or cultural expression.' She makes the further important point that 'reconciling conflicting truths... the Ardhanarishvara concept freezes the creation process at the moment of merging—emerging, between the Uncreated which is NO-THING, neither male nor female, and the Created which must have specific attributes'.[22] The import of this icon gets increasingly metaphorical with Tagore using the term to indicate gender crossings in the imaginative act of understanding and imbibing the female psyche.

Tagore entered the realms of the mythical to find icons for his androgynous imagination. The idea of a companionate romance was dear to Tagore's heart and his dance–drama *Chitrangada* (1892) was based upon this value. The original episode in the Mahabharata is altered in many details. Rabindranath embroiders the story to make Chitra (as the heroine is called in the 1913 English transcreation by Tagore himself) a dual character, the warrior, man-like person whom Arjun rejects and the luscious beauty with whom he falls madly in love. He named the two sides of Chitrangada as *kuroopaa* or *ugly* and *shuroopaa* or *beautiful*, leading to much criticism in feminist circles and problems of performance on stage. Chitrangada prays to Madan, the God of Love, to make her this alluring beauty. Tagore used the Shuroopaa image as a device for educating Arjun in higher values. Chitrangada's composite identity as the strong warrior and the seductive beauty contains the male as well as the female, and teaches a lesson to the archetypal male, Arjun, that a true partnership is above biological difference or socially constructed roles.

Why Arjun? Tagore was not a polemical writer and one would need to read into the interstices. Chitrangada's duality is closely paralleled by the Mahabharata section in which Arjun adopts the female form as Brihannala and has to cope with his male desire. In the epic, as we might recall, the Pandavas are required to undergo the thirteenth year of exile in an incognito form. Arjun, for having insulted Urvashi, is cursed to live out the year as a *kliba* which is a gender-ambiguous category in the Vedas and the Puranas. Such a person bears physical as well as emotional characteristics of both man and woman, and, hence, is an undefined *third gender* (*tritiya prakriti*). Arjun becomes Brihannala, a dance teacher with tremendous grace as well as prowess.[23]

Associated with the story of Arjun's cross-gendering is the figure of Urvashi, the alluring nymph of dawn about whom Rabindranath wrote a haunting poem admired by Edward Thompson as the 'crown (of) his first great period'.[24] According to Puranic legend, Urvashi was born full-grown from the sea, and immune to the lures of sexual appeal by her numerous admirers. She could never be wife or mother or be engaged emotionally by a single man, but she in turn could wreak havoc upon men, and even could break the concentration of sages. Arjun made the mistake of underestimating Urvashi's power, something Tagore found rather amusing as he wrote in a letter, 'Arjun had invoked his forefathers to try [and] establish a relationship with her, that was Arjun's mistake—she has no ties with anyone'. Yet, Tagore described her in the same letter as the *eternal woman*.[25] Though some critics have cited the poem *Urvashi* as the epitome of male fantasy,[26] I suggest an opposite track that she is Tagore's medium for gender questioning. Feminist discourse has convincingly shown patriarchal ideology to be located in the reproductive capabilities of women. Therein derive the codes of lineage, polygamy, *son preference*, feudal systems, rituals of initiation and other rites of passage, ashramite practices, maltreatment of widows and a lot else. It is the code which creates the story of Madhavi fated to give sons to many kings and magically turn virgin with each new partner. It is the code that guides the fates of Kunti, Gandhari, Draupadi and Sita to say the least, and Tagore wrote about all of them. Urvashi is outside this code, protected from being sexually exploited in a manner specially reserved for dependent women. She has a female body with its allurements but without its commitment to domesticated, reproductive functions. In Rabindranath Tagore's poem:

> Neither mother nor daughter are you, nor bride, Urvashi.
> Woman you are to ravish the soul of Paradise.[27]

Was androgyny easier to locate in the plenitude of Indian mythology rather than on ground reality? No. Tagore's political acumen was in place and where possible, he exercised his androgynous imagination. He was entirely aware of the exploitation of women by the hegemonic structures. In a lecture in *Personality*, he says,

> Although in the present stage of history, man is asserting his masculine supremacy and building his civilisation with stone blocks, ignoring the living principle of growth, he cannot altogether crush woman's nature into dust or into his dead building material.... It is not that woman is merely seeking her freedom of livelihood, struggling against man's monopoly of business, but against man's monopoly of civilisation where he is breaking her heart everyday and desolating her life.[28]

The feminine force and spiritualism: *Gitanjali*

In the amazing range of capacities that Tagore attributed to women, sexuality, gender identity and spiritualism formed a continuum. We can say that Tagore arrived in the Western world through *Gitanjali*. It is commonly known that the original songs and poems existed in Bengali (1910), and that one time in 1911, Tagore, while convalescing in Shelidah, took up casual translation of selected poems from *Gitanjali*, *Naibedya*, *Kheya* and *Gitimalya*, which eventually grew into a formal collection. The further narrative of how this manuscript went with Tagore to England, was lost in the underground station, retrieved dramatically and eventually found its way to W.B. Yeats and William Rothenstein, is told in pictorial detail in 'The Story of *Gitanjali*', a documentary produced by the Ministry of External Affairs.[29] Satyajit Ray's cinematic biography of Tagore also presents some memorable images.[30] I will not repeat the stories associated with the *arrival* of the *Gitanjali* text in the midst of the literary cognoscenti in London, but I would recall the significance of the English text which reached a large number through the Macmillan publication in 1913.

A series of events culminated in the award of the Nobel Prize to Rabindranath Tagore in 1913, but let me focus on Tagore's reputation in the West as an Eastern mystic from the time that W.B. Yeats wrote in his introduction to *Gitanjali*,

> I have carried the manuscript of these translations about with me for days, reading it in railway trains, or on the top of omnibuses and in restaurants, and I have often had to close it lest some stranger would see how much it moved me. These lyrics—which are in the origin, my Indians tell me, full of subtlety of rhythm, of untranslatable delicacies of colour, of metrical invention—display in their thought of a world I have dreamed of all my life long. The work of a supreme culture, they yet appear as much the growth of the common soil as the grass and the rushes.... Mr. Tagore, like the Indian civilization itself, has been content to discover the soul and surrender himself to its spontaneity.[31]

In a perceptive essay, 'The *Gitanjali* in translation: A miracle of transformation', Fakrul Alam analyses the structure of the English work and the reasons for its popularity with European readers and translators.[32]

The spiritual force portrayed in *Gitanjali* often has a feminine face and the selected poems cull out that aspect. 'She who ever had remained in the depth of my being' (No. 66) or 'In desperate hope I go and search for her' (No. 87) are encomiums to a divinity whose sign is the feminine. The images carry a long tradition of Vaishnavism, which, as Joseph T. O'Connell says in his article, 'Tracing Vaishnava Strains in Tagore', is a religio-literary strain that found easy resonance in the Tagore household.[33]

The devotion to Lord Krishna, through the medium of Chaitanya Mahaprabhu (1486–1533) is given utterance in songs and poems of *bhakti*, worship that has a secular base even as it aspires to the transcendental. Characteristically, God is addressed in terms of familiarity as a friend and companion, but also sometimes as an inscrutable and arbitrary ruler. A poet's surrender to the divine will is akin to the yearning to unite with a dear friend or lover. The Vaishnava tradition and its bhakti outpourings play wonderfully with gender as is well known in the *bhajans* (hymns) of Meera or the *dohas* of Kabir (Rabindranath translated several poems of Kabir). Indira Parthasarathy in a brief article in the *Hindu* says, 'Tagore had imbibed what was the best in Vaishnavism, besides the deep understanding he had of the other religions and philosophies.'[34]

The signature of the feminine in *Gitanjali* in the six poems selected shows Rabindranath's confident handling of the Bhakti style. If a mother is invoked in one poem, the identity of a woman slides into that of a *ragged beggar girl* in another poem. There appear vivid pictures of a youthful homemaker preparing the evening oil lamp and shading the flame with her cupped hand. The mood is that of devotion, of service. The Tagore family was not strictly Vaishnavite; they spearheaded the reformist movement of the Brahmo Samaj, Dwarakanath Tagore being one of its founding members.[35] Hence, the images of the feminine in quasi-religious Bhakti literature could be smoothly adapted to secular or social purpose. What is striking is Tagore's adoption of the female persona as a *beggar girl*, signalling his empathy with the underclass woman in several other poems and short stories such as *Durasha* (False hope). Also, *Gitanjali* alerts us to his recurrent image of the flickering light of the soul.

Woman in love

Tagore's songs and poems on the theme of love capture different moods, and perhaps it is worth pointing out that the *rasa* (aesthetic experience) theory of emotions, though not consciously adopted by Tagore, was very much a part of the intellectual Indian's repertoire of knowledge. Recently, the eminent danseuse Sonal Mansingh presented 'Nayikaa', a production of Tagore's love lyrics illustrating as she said, 'all the shades and nuances of the *Ashta-Nayikaa* genre'. She narrated and danced the

> eight situations described by traditional literature in which the woman i.e., *nayikaa* experiences love in its many dimensions: *Vasakaja*—she is decorated and fully prepared to meet the lover; *virahotkanthita*—she is pining and yearning for the beloved; *vipralabdha*—at the appointed place he is not there; *khandita*—the lover approaches much after an appointed time; she hurls harsh words at him and the lover turns away; *kalahatarita*—she is full of regrets and remorse at having sent away the beloved; *proshitabhartrika*—now the beloved has gone far away and she is counting the days for his return; *abhisarika*—she leaves home to meet the lover; *swadhinabhartrika*—the beloved returns and in their happy meeting she knows her power over him.[36]

The line of argument given by Sonal Mansingh is worth pursuing in academic research because Tagore did not make explicit reference to the traditional *nayikaa bheda* (different kinds of heroines), yet used the variations in mood throughout his own renderings of the feminine. The pensive mood of *She sits by the window* (*O janalar kachhe boshe aachhe*) or *Dream* (*Swapna*) suggests memories in which lie buried passions. This is followed by encomiums to love which explore the delicate tensions of relationship together with anxious thoughts during separation. Interestingly, Tagore's love lyrics are not in any consistent voice, male or female or of a recognisable social position and age. As though the situation commands the words, the addresser and the addressee adopt an amazing variety of attributes. For instance, *She who dwelt in secret* (*Ei sharat alor kamal bane*) is composed in a mood very different from *Krishnakali*, a tribute to a dark beauty. Associated with ecstatic joy and endless pain, love in its paradoxical intensity has, of course, been explored by writers in every country and age, but Tagore gave it a specific dimension in locating the context in turn-of-the-century Bengal, and in the marvellous opportunities for sensual and intellectual pleasure.

For me, the tender emotions of a man in love provide a fascinating counterpoint to the elaborate descriptions of women habitually associated with matters of the heart. *Last spring* (*Shesh basanta*), as the title suggests, is a poet's helpless passion in old age, an aching hopeless desire that nonetheless brings joy into his aging sensibilities. By conjecture, it was written for Victoria Ocampo. Similarly, *The image* (*Chhabi*), perhaps for Kadambari, articulates an anguished longing for the unattainable.

Woman most ordinary

There are unnamed women towards whom the poet shows compassion if not love. *Santhal girl*, set in the rural terrain of Birbhum where Tagore's dream university Shantiniketan was to be built, brings visibility to the labouring woman under the hot sun; *Sadharan meye* is an ordinary woman's plea to create the empowered woman in fiction, if not in reality. 'Make the woman about whom you are going to write victorious on my behalf,' she tells the poet in this imagined address. From such sentiments too arise Tagore's poems of female assertion, the most enduring being the climactic lyric from the dance–drama *Chitrangada* where the princess addresses Arjun on the values of a companionate marriage:

Ami Chitrangada rajendro nondini/ Nohi debi nohi shamanya nari/ Puja kori more rakhibe urdhe she nohi nohi/ Hela kori more rakhibe pichhe she nohi nohi/ Jodi parsherakho more shaunkote shompode/ Shommoti dao jodi kothin brote shohay hote/ Pabetaube tumi chinite more/ Aj shudhu kori nibedon/ Ami Chitrangada rajendro nondini.

[The princess Chitrangada I am/ Neither a goddess nor an ordinary woman/ I am not the one to be placed above and worshipped/ Nor am I the one to be neglected and cast aside. If you keep me by your side as a companion in danger and prosperity, only then will you know my worth.]

Translated by **Malashri Lal**

There could not be a stronger feminist statement on the status of women in India at the turn of the century. The original Mahabharata has Chitrangada mothering Babruvaahana and pledging to bring up a little warrior prince. Tagore minimises such mother-talk and ends his dance–drama on a crescendo of celebration of conjugal partnership. The power of the argument was such that even Jawaharlal Nehru saw Kamala's role in his life in terms of Chitrangada.[37]

Rabindranath was deeply sensitive to rural poverty and the deprivations of the people who live at the edge of survival in a minimalist sense. The idealistic expectations in setting up Shantiniketan were overlaid with the intention to bring education, practical training and work-based emoluments to the people in Birbhum district. As in his other experiments, Rabindranath adopted a philosophy of continuous learning and was able to put it on ground as early residents of the school 'Path Bhavan' would testify. Mahasweta Devi recalls the joy as well as the discipline of this unusual environment where little girls were in residence in dormitories.[38] Tagore's dilemma lay in creating a place of higher education while poverty and illiteracy marked the zone. Would this experiment lead to an intellectual island, he wondered. Thereafter came up the parallel institution, Sriniketan, where local women and men were trained in agricultural economics and rural crafts. Once again, Tagore had broken through a gender divide as Shantiniketan and Sriniketan observed no conservative segregation of women and men students. Romantic tales abound, perhaps the best known one related by Maitreyi Devi in *Na hanyate*, 1974 (*It does not die: A romance*, 1995).

Nation, nature and other feminisations

The call of the nation was deep and strident for Rabindranath's generation. The threat of the Bengal partition had roused strong passions in 1905 and resulted in the memorable novel, *Ghare baire*. *Where the mind is without fear*, a poem in *Gitanjali*, was a pennant for assertion, the song *Ekla chalo re* powered national marches and the poet was to give independent India its national anthem, *Jana gana mana*. Poetry and song could lead to polemics in the fertile imagination of Tagore and inspire an agenda for political change.

In his inimitable manner, Rabindranath engaged with the dominant icon of the national movement, the Nation identified as Mother. *The sky resounds to our mother's call (Aamraa milechhi aj maayer daake)* is a patriotic lyric from *Swadesh*. Samita Sen, in her essay, 'Motherhood and mother-craft: Gender and nationalism in Bengal', writes of 'the creation of ethicised community identities involving the identification of women with a cultur-ally and morally invested domestic domain and the projection of a multi-layered and empowered mother image'.[39] Tagore was to express as well as subvert the equations assumed in the Mother–Nation parallel, especially in his fiction. But the lyrics supported by exquisitely arranged music in his patriotic songs have convinced many that the feminine principle is the aura under which the loyal sons of the nation would pursue the path of sacrifice in honour of the Mother. Selected for this collection are verses that will open up the debates on feminising the nation: *Whosoever may abandon you (Je tomay chhare chharuk)*, *Mother, will you send your own son (Ma, ki tui porer dware pathabi)*. The post-independence generation has asked for an intellectual review of the mother–nation equivalence. I give below an arrest-ing article by feminist publisher Urvashi Butalia who converses with Tanika Sarkar, a feminist historian:

> **Urvashi**: Half a century ago our 'nation-ness'—or our nationality—was defined in opposition to another newly formed nation, Pakistan. The Indian nationalist movement mobilized thousands of women from across classes, castes, communities.
>
> **Tanika**: ... Often... it is at times when the nation comes into being through a process of struggle that women can come into their own. Women are not only incomplete subjects, but in a permanent state of homelessness. Thus the search for a homeland, which is what new nations are often about, is a search with which they deeply identify, and in which they feel involved.

But once the nation comes into being, women have little to do with how it is formulated. In India after 1947, laws were made to men's advantage; it was men (mainly upper-caste Hindu men) who put the Constitution together. When policies and plans were formulated, they made no mention of women. For Indian nationalists, some citizens were more equal than others. But then, I tell myself, Indians are not unique in this: there is hardly a place in the world where national liberation movements have meant liberation for women.[40]

I mean to return to Tagore. Towards the end of his life, he saw the clouds of war gathering over Europe. Spiritual and mystic in myriad ways, Tagore was not an escapist. As a celebrity, he was rooted in society, family, development projects, diplomacy and public events. He had witnessed personal sorrow having lost dear members of his family; he had won the Nobel Prize in 1913, and returned his Knighthood with anguish after the massacre at Jalianwallah Bagh in 1919. Sorrow and joy coexisted, he said, but one could turn to the Divinity within, the *moner manush*, to know the path of ethical action. And the message of Tagore, penned over a century ago, remains just as pertinent now, that the universe is composed of *ananda* (happiness) that can be discovered through human understanding and compassion.

The politics of the nation stayed always with Tagore, a reminder of which this collection reprints: his angry note on Katharine Mayo's *Mother India* (1937). A blockbuster account hovering with sentimentality upon a suffering India featured as a feminised nation, Mayo's fame rested upon her graphic depiction of colonial stereotypes. Rabindranath was justifiably offended and went to some length in publishing more than one version of his criticism of an outsider's condescending views. The interplay of a woman writer using negative images of the *other/native* woman, racially and metaphorically different, suggests a complex drama of identities in the woman–nation configuration. Tagore's short review does not enter the terrain too deeply but remains an interesting period piece.

The feminine in short stories

Tagore's short fiction demands attention by its own merit, and it stands within Tagore's views on the feminine expressed in his novels, poetry, drama and non-fiction as well. His ideas on feminine selfhood undergo revisions, modifications and reversals, responding to specific intellectual debates about the woman question in 19th century Bengal.

The early writings of Rabindranath show him struggling to understand the feminine. In his problematic response to one of Pandita Ramabai's lectures, he says, 'From whichever angle you may see, it is Nature's dictum that women are not meant for work other than the domestic. Had Nature's intention been otherwise, girls would have had inborn strength.'[41] Yet, at a young age, Rabindranath had composed those sensuous poems in *Kori o komal*, granting woman both physical and emotional strength. Over time, Tagore seemed to have been fascinated by the multitudinous aspects of woman as he encountered them in life and literature. At his best, Tagore abandons stereotype and envisages the roles of the two sexes as complimentary and interlinked.

Combining ideals of female empowerment from western learning with the lineage of his reformist Hindu tradition, Rabindranath created a hybrid feminism which found expression most cogently in his fiction. The novels *Ghare baire* and *Shesher kobita* are perhaps the best exponential items on the debates in his time. In the anthology, we include a range of short fiction that illustrates Tagore's delving into women's issues from a variety of perspectives. Of the twelve stories, a few are discussed here.

The plot of '*Denapaona*' clusters around the heinous custom of dowry and the repercussions on the bride who has to face the consequences. The commodification of the bride within the structure of the family is brought out in the astringent remarks, 'Even her food and clothing were neglected. If a kind neighbour expressed concern, her mother-in-law would say, "She has more than enough,"—implying that if the girl's father had paid full price she would have received full care'.[42] Tagore understands that often women themselves had been the agents of perpetuating the subjugation of women. The passage also reveals that women's oppression has not been linear and uniform throughout history and the issue of class has complicated the woman question. The originality of Tagore lies in the fact that he has not only shown the strategies of exploitation, but given an opportunity to the victim to break her silence.

'*Madhyabartini*' records the story of Hara Shundari who is initially driven by the ideal of sacrifice, only to bring about a disaster for her household. We find two women, who appear as foils to each other. While the *barren* Hara Shundari contrives a second marriage for her husband, Nibaran, so that he is not deprived of fatherhood, the young Shailabala turns out to be a pampered child who is blissfully unaware of her conjugal responsibilities. The spectre of Shailabala dominates even after her untimely death, and keeps Nibaran and Hara Shundari perpetually apart. Primarily, a story of the unexpected consequences of an error of judgement, the psychology is deep, with a sympathetic comprehension of the feminine mind.

'*Durasa*' (False hope) and '*Musalmanir galpa*' (The story of a Muslim woman), though written sixteen years apart, are bound by their common theme of the transcommunal force of love. However, while the former ends with disappointment and disillusionment for the protagonist, the other holds a promise of fulfilment. Moreover, '*Durasa*' has a layered narrative pattern, and the reader is twice removed from the Urdu-speaking protagonist, the princess of Badraon. The social backgrounds of the two women are different but their social treatment as women is similar. The decadent Muslim culture of the Nawab's household never educated women in the intricacies of Islam, and in a parallel, Kamala, a Brahmin orphan, has to face insults from the religious conservatives. The rescue for the women comes from transcommunal sources. The glamorous figure of the Brahmin, Kesarlal, inspires the Muslim princess to adopt the Hindu way of life, which was revolutionary for the times. Kamala too is a revolutionary as she relinquishes the Hindu faith and finds spiritual fulfilment in her new self as a Muslim, renamed Meherjan. '*Durasa*' is a revealing title as it reflects on the *false hope* of communal harmony. '*Musalmanir galpa*' was left as a draft by Tagore, open-ended, uncertain of its denouement.

'*Streer patra*', unlike '*Musalmanir galpa*', posits a far more direct challenge to the social institution of marriage. All the three women in the story, Mrinal, Boro Bou and Bindu, are cast into the oppressive family system through loveless marriages. The arrival of Boro Bou's orphan sister Bindu in the household marks a watershed moment and the insults she receives from her sister's in-laws propels a kinship between Mrinal and Bindu. The physicality of Bindu's yearning for Mrinal is told in resonant terms, showing Rabindranath Tagore's acknowledgement of female bonding. Bindu, when compelled to return to the mad husband and abusive mother-in-law, sets herself on fire and dies. Society is indifferent to the death of this inconsequential woman. For Mrinal, the tragedy brings home the final realisation that she cannot live under such oppressive codes for women. She must design her own liberation. Tagore's story, hypothetically written by *Mrinal* as a letter to her husband, invites comparison with Tagore's own letters, including those to his wife Mrinalini who stayed home while he roamed the world, and also bears spiritual proximity with the poem *Mukti* included in this volume.

'*Kabuliwala*', the story of an Afghan's friendship with a little girl, is included in the selection for its play upon the multiple signifiers of the untranslatable term *soshur bari* (in-laws' home), a key reference in feminised destiny. Rahmat, the Afghani trader, is released from jail after eight years. Mini has grown up and on the day of her wedding, coincidentally, the *Kabuliwala* (the man from Kabul) comes in search of his little friend who is no longer little. The father is reluctant to bring his daughter out to meet this scruffy Afghan but then relents. Mini, demure in her bridal attire, looks blankly at the Kabuliwallah, completely forgetful of the past. The Kabuli gently asks *'Khoki, tui soshur bari jabis?'* (Child, will you go to your in-laws?). Mini blushes deeply and leaves. And the Afghan sinks to the floor, suddenly aware that his own little daughter would have similarly grown up and forgotten him in the many long years he has been away. He pulls out a crumpled sheet of paper from his deep shabby pocket. We see a bereft father carrying the palm imprint of his own little child he had left behind in his mountainous homeland. In this heart-wrenching scene, Tagore reaches out in empathy to the emotions of the Kabuli, and to all little girls who must leave their childhood behind.

Public rhetoric in essays and notes

Tagore's internal debates about the meaning of the feminine can be seen in his essays. In 1925, Rabindranath responded to a curious request from Europe to explain Indian matrimonial customs to western readers. His essay titled 'The Indian ideal of marriage' was published by Count Hermann Keyserling in an anthology titled *The book of marriage: A new interpretation by twenty four leaders of contemporary thought* (1927). The Count, one may recall, had attended a musical soiree in a Tagore residence in Calcutta and left notes on the 'picturesquely folded toga' of the men and Rabindranath's 'spiritualized substance of soul'.[43] Keyserling was a rare western philosopher who wished to promote a planetary culture and recognise the values of non-western traditions. He had founded the 'School of Wisdom' in Germany in 1920, patterned on two 1,000-year-old Buddhist models. In other words, Tagore assumed that he could enter into the intricacies of Hindu domestic practice in the long essay that he was composing for Keyserling. Tagore repeated a favourite formulation: 'Woman... has two aspects—in one she is the Mother; in the other she is the Beloved.' He saw 'marriage as a state of discipline... of which the method is the control of desire', and the creation of male progeny, whereas the *beloved* remains an idealised concept, as the 'joy-giving power of woman'. The essay oscillated between the two planes of explaining Hindu *grihastha dharma* (householder's duty), including Manu's laws, various forms of marriage and duties of a householder, and on the other hand, taking flight on imaginative wings to sing the praises of Shelley's *intellectual beauty*, the ecstatic *ananda* bestowed by the beloved and the power of *Shakti*.[44]

Tagore, it would seem, was attracted to the scintillating promise of intellectual, self-determined women of whom the epitome is Labanya, the heroine of *Farewell song* which ends on that memorable note rejecting romantic love and celebrating independent womanhood:

Grieve not for me
For me there is duty, for me the universe.
My cup of life is not empty
To fill the void will ever be my pledge.[45]

Redefining the feminine

I conclude then by saying that in Tagore's oeuvre it would be untenable to maintain the western theoretical distinctions between the female, feminine and feminist as the nuances of each term slide into the other. Rabindranath's special gift for the creative arts led to constructions of the feminine that were excitingly new and contextualised in India. He reworked the old mythologies, investing them with new meaning, daring to play with some iconic tales such as those of Kunti and Gandhari in the Mahabharata. Keenly observing the predilections of women in his life and social ambit, he successfully rendered women from all classes, perhaps recognising a gendered experience that separated their world from men in a patriarchal frame. Apocryphal tales abound in relation to Tagore, a poignant one being of the severally marginalised Boshtami, *pagla khepi*, an abandoned, homeless, wandering *madwoman* who occasionally strayed into his rural abode in Birbhum. One day, Rabindranath's house attendant was throwing out flowers in a vase and placing new stems. Boshtami swooped down and picked up the wilted blooms and holding them close said they were fit for her Gods. Tagore was deeply moved by her simplicity and devotion, and learnt a lesson in frugality from a *pagli*, mad woman, he said.

Such contexts are rooted in India and one must seek an understanding of Tagore's delving into the feminine from that perspective. The concept of the *ardhanarishvara* as the androgyne identity was an extension of his sympathy with the women's cause. In his life and his works we find several examples of crossing the gender boundaries. He was *motherly* towards the little children in the Shantiniketan school after Mrinalini Devi passed away. Fascinated by the pre-pubescent stage of childhood, he wrote *Shishu, Shishu Bholanath, Post office* and *Bhanusingher padaboli*, to explore his capacity to enter maternal space. He adopted complex relations with women such as Victoria Ocampo and Ranu Adhikari, who were younger to him. Clearly, a simplified masculinity or femininity could not account for such a proliferation of gendered sympathies. Tagore was redefining the East and the West and his imagination was catching fuel from the intellectual ferment of his time and his travels. Today, perhaps it is through Rabindranath's protean self, that an aspect of the feminine in India can be mapped.

Notes and references

1. Arunava Sinha, trans., '*Dui bon* (Two sisters)', *Three women* (Noida: Random House India, 2010), p. 75.
2. Sukanta Chaudhuri, ed., *Rabindranath Tagore: Selected short stories* (New Delhi: Oxford University Press, 2000), p. 22.
3. Malashri Lal, trans., 'Streer patra'.
4. 'Song of myself', 1855, www.poetryfoundation.org
5. Sisir Das, ed., *English writings of Tagore*, vol. III (New Delhi: Sahitya Akademi, 2008 reprint), p. 676.
6. Virginia Woolf, *A room of one's own* (Peterborough, ON: Broadview Press, 2001), p. 116.
7. Judith Butler, *Gender trouble: Feminism and the subversion of identity* (New York: Routledge, 1990), p. 139.
8. http://www.visva-bharati.ac.in
9. Radha Chakravarty, trans., *Boyhood days* (Delhi: Puffin Classics, 2011).
10. *Boyhood days*, pp. 27–28.
11. Malashri Lal, *The law of the threshold* (Shimla: Indian Institute of Advanced Study, 1995).
12. *Boyhood days*, p. 27
13. *Boyhood days*, p. 16
14. *Boyhood days*, p. 74
15. Chitra Deb, *Women of the Tagore household* (New Delhi: Penguin India, 2010), p. 37.
16. Ketaki Kushari Dyson, *In your blossoming flower-garden: Rabindranath Tagore and Victoria Ocampo* (New Delhi: Sahitya Akademi, 1988).
17. Malashri Lal, 'Tagore: Impossible loves and possible ideals' (Paper presented at Sahitya Akademi seminar *English writings of Tagore*, Cochin, 24–27 February 2011).
18. Deb, *Women of the Tagore household*, p. 97.
19. Amitrasudan Bhattacharya and Aparna Bhattacharya, ed., *Bhai chhotobou: Streeke lekha Rabindranather chithi* (Kolkata: Purba, 2009).
20. See, for example, Sunil Gangopadhyay, *Pratham alo* (*First light*), trans., Aruna Chakravarti (Penguin Books, 2011). Also, Krishna Kripalani, *Rabindranath Tagore: A biography* (Calcutta: Visva-Bharati, 1980).

21. Hélène Cixous, 'The laugh of the Medusa'. *Signs* 1, no. 4 (1976): 875–93.

22. Alka Pande, *Ardhanarishvara the androgyne: Probing the gender within* (New Delhi: Rupa, 2004), pp. ix, 20.

23. *The Mahabharata*, Virata parva, sections I, ff., LXVIII.

24. Edward J. Thompson, *Rabindranath Tagore: His life and work*, rev., Kalidas Nag (Calcutta: Y.M.C.A. Publishing House, 1961).

25. The tradition that Urvashi was born from the thigh of Narayana is found in the Puranas such as *Vayu* (13.69.51) and *Vamana* (7.1-45-5). Aurobindo Ghose, *Collected poems* (Pondicherry: Sri Aurobindo Ashram, 1994). Bal Gangadhar Tilak, *Vedic chronology and vedanga jyotisha*, containing also *Chaldean and Indian vedas and other miscellaneous essays* (New Delhi: Cosmos Publications, 2004), http://www.hindurevolution.org/01/etymology_of_urvashi_and_apsaras.htm

26. Charu C. Chaudhuri, trans., *Purabi: The east in the feminine gender*, edited and introduced by Krishna Bose and Sugata Bose (London: Seagull, 2007), p. 17.

27. Sisir Das, ed., *English writings of Tagore*, vol. II (New Delhi: Sahitya Akademi, 2004), p. 249.

28. Ibid., p. 415.

29. Reba Som, *The story of Gitanjali* (documentary), 29 May 2011, www.youtube.com

30. Satyajit Ray, *Rabindranath Tagore* (documentary) (Films Division, Government of India, 1961).

31. W. B. Yeats, 'Introduction to *Gitanjali*', www.ics.uci.edu

32. Posted by Deb Banerji. Published: 6 November 2010, www.sciy.org

33. *Journal of Hindu Studies* 4, no. 2 (2011): 144–64.

34. Indira Parthasarathy, 'Anthology on Rabindranath Tagore', *Hindu*, Chennai, 19 January 2010.

35. http://en.wikipedia.org/wiki/Brahmo_Samaj

36. Sonal Mansingh, *Tagore's Naayika*, University of Delhi, programme sheet (cf. Andrea de la Dehesa, 'Classical dances of India: Theory, technique and expression', http://www.alarde.com).

37. Jawaharlal Nehru, *Discovery of India*. Cited by Reba Som, 'Chitrangada not Sita', in *In search of Sita: Revisiting mythology*, eds., Malashri Lal and Namita Gokhale (New Delhi: Penguin Books India, 2009), p. 36.

38. Malashri Lal, 'Mahasweta Devi remembers Rabindranath Tagore: Vignettes from childhood' (*Confluence*, 7 September 2011).

39. Samita Sen, *Gender & history* 5, no. 2 (1993): 231–43 (first published online on 2 April 2007).

40. Urvashi Butalia, 'Mother India', *New Internationalist*, issue no. 277, 5 March 1996.

41. Quoted in Soham Pain, 'Father and mother in one: Traditions and transgender identities in Tagore's *Chitra*', *New Academia* I, no. II (2012): 152.

42. *'Denapaona'*, in *Rabindranath Tagore: Selected short stories*, ed., William Radice (London: Penguin Books, 2005 ed.), p. 49.

43. Ketaki Kushari Dyson (New Delhi: Sahitya Akademi, 1988; reprinted 1996), p. 22.

44. Shakti is, literally, power or energy. In philosophy, especially Tantric philosophy, Shakti refers to the *creative force* and is deified in the form of Goddess. Loosely speaking, Shiva and Shakti are respectively considered to be the *transcendental* and *immanent* aspects of the Supreme Self. See Rabindranath Tagore, 'The Indian ideal of marriage', in Das, ed., *The english writings of Rabindranath Tagore*, vol. II, p. 536.

45. Rabindranath Tagore, *'Sesher kabita'* (*Farewell song*), trans., Radha Chakravarty (New Delhi: Shristi Publishers, 2005), p. 161.

Re-writing Tagore:
Translation as performance*

Radha Chakravarty

In a dramatic sequence towards the end of Rabindranath Tagore's play 'Natir Puja' (1926; translated into English as 'The Dancing Girl's Worship'), the court dancer Srimati is publicly humiliated, forced to perform before the altar where the Buddha was once worshipped, in violation of her faith in Buddhism. But she subverts the situation, casting off her costume and ornaments as she dances, to reveal beneath them, the garb of a bhikkuni, a female Buddhist ascetic. The sacrilegious becomes an expression of the sacred, as the poignant refrain of her song affirms that dance and music are the form of her worship: *Bandana mor bhangite ar sangite biraje* (my prayer resides in gesture and song). Here, the body in performance becomes a metaphor for worship. The language of devotion, in other words, is translated into body language, the language of dance. Instead of treating this translation as transparent, the lines of the song draw attention to the fact that the medium, in fact, is the message—a foregrounding of the performative as that which constitutes meaning, instead of merely transmitting something already 'there'. It is through dance that the Nati's worship comes into being.

This scene provides a useful analogue for the idea of translation as performance, which I explore in this essay, with reference to Tagore's writings.

*Reproduced with permission from *Visual Arts—The India Habitat Centre's Art Journal* (Volume 10, 2011–2012).

The idea itself is not new. The theories of Walter Benjamin and Bertolt Brecht, for instance, suggest a metaphoric link between performance as translation and translation as performance. The link between text, performance and gesture is approached by Brecht in terms of 'theatrical thought'. Benjamin in 'The Task of the Translator' (1921) questions some of the commonest assumptions about translation, which tend to be based on ideas of fidelity to the original, resemblance, or accuracy. Drawing upon these ideas, Patrick Prmavesi says: 'The various features and qualities of a performance go far beyond the rendering of a writer's intention. . . This may lead us to the theatrical nature of translation in general, to a scene of gestures that maintain and justify the exchange of signs and meanings in the 'afterlife of texts'.[1] Just as the enactment of a dramatic text involves adaptation and interpretation, so also in literary translation, the 're-presentation' of the original text in another language has a performative aspect that does not confine itself to a recovery of authorial intention. Since all interpretation involves a displacement of the original, each performance moves away from the source text, and creates something new. Translating Tagore can therefore be seen as a creative act, an act of interpretation, and in these senses, it can be understood as performative. This creative dimension of translation was apparent to Tagore. In the English *Gitanjali*, he consciously transcreated the original Bengali poems, instead of attempting literal translations in verse. In a letter to Rothenstein dated 4 April 1915, he wrote:

> My translations are frankly prose,—my aim is to make them simple with just a suggestion of rhythm to give them a touch of the lyric, avoiding all archaisms and poetical conventions.[2]

For instance, in a poem from the manuscript of *Gitanjali*, omitted from the published edition (probably as a result of Yeats' 'editing'), Tagore's use of prose bears testimony to his conviction that the spirit of the original Bengali cannot be captured in English verse:

> On the day thou breakst through this my name, my master, I shall be free and leave this phantasy of my own creation and take my place in thee.
>
> By scribbling my name over thy writing I cover thy works. I know not how further such a horror could be carried. This pride of name plucks feathers from others to decorate its own self and to drown all other music it beats its own drum. Oh, let it be utterly defeated in me and let the day come when only thy name will play in my tongue and I shall be accepted by all by my nameless recognition.[3]

But William Radice, in his re-translation of the same poem, offers a 're-enactment' in verse, as an affirmation of the musical quality of Tagore's poetry in Bengali:

> The day you wipe out
> my name, lord,
> that day I'll be free.
> I'll be reborn in you
> instead of in a dream
> made by me.
> Your writing's crossed out
> by the line
> of my name.
> How much longer
> must I carry the evil
> of that kind of fame?[4]

In the performance, the poem changes. Radice's reworking of the poem is, of course, based on his confidence in his own bilinguality, his command of the rhythms of both Bengali and English. For at the simplest level, translation involves the rewriting of a text from one language into another. Although Tagore was revered by his admirers in India as 'Gurudev', it was for his writings in English that he received world recognition and the Nobel Prize. Tagore, though, was diffident about his command of English. In the years following his short-lived, meteoric rise to international fame, he was to realise that faulty translations of his work, often published with his approval, had much to do with the eventual decline in his reputation in the world. In a letter to Sturge Moore, dated 24 May 1921, he says:

> I am convinced that I myself in my translations have done grave injustice to my own work. My English is like a frail boat—and to save it from an utter disaster I had to jettison the most part of its cargo.[5]

During Tagore's lifetime, and since his death, translations from Bengali into other Indian and world languages played a major role in sustaining Tagore's image in the public imagination; but they also, in the process of 're-presenting' or 'performing' Tagore, modified the originals and presented altered versions to the world. This is why translation needs to be understood as integral to the 'afterlife' of Tagore's texts.

The process of translation, though, involves much more than a simple linguistic transfer. Translation as performance suggests the possibility of expanding our idea of translation beyond the linguistic dimension, to consider, not only cultural translation, but also translation across genres of literature, and translation from one creative medium into another. Tagore's oeuvre, and its reception over the years and across cultures, provides extensive instances of all these ways of rethinking translation.

A common fetish in the domain of translation is the concern over faithfulness to the original. Yet Tagore himself did not believe in the reification of texts. He constantly revised, rewrote and refashioned his own work, often translating a text from one genre into another. To take a few examples, the poem 'Pujarini' becomes the play 'Natir Puja', the story 'Ekta Ashare Galpa' evolves into the play *Tasher Desh*, and some poems from *Gitanjali* have a musical version, recast as songs, undergoing a transformation of the lyrics, in the process. Contexts and readerships determine the shape of a translation. So does genre. For instance, Poem 39 in the English *Gitanjali* begins:

When the heart is hard and parched up come upon me with a shower of mercy. When grace is lost from life come with a burst of song.[6]

In Fakrul Alam's translation, the poem is rendered in verse, intended to evoke for today's readers the cadences of Tagore's poetry in modern, idiomatic English:

When life dries up
Come in a stream of mercy.
When everything graceful is covered,
Come in a shower of songs.[7]

The same poem, rendered as a song, acquires a musical aura that Alam tries to capture in his translation:

When the sap of life shrinks, seek the showers
of mercy.
When all that's lovely is hidden, come sweetly as
a song.
When work overpowers and imprisons me
Within the frontiers of the heart, O Giver of life,
tread softly![8]

Both versions by Alam, collected in the same volume *The Essential Tagore* (2011), offer the possibility of tracking the changes that occur when a text is 'translated' from one genre into another. Translation in this sense emphasizes, not the abstract reification of a sacred 'original', but a recognition of the contingent and the provisional. The mutability of texts remained, for Tagore, a source of endless creative possibility. The same consciousness, if it inhabits the activity of translation, can help us to release ourselves from the restrictive conventions demanding strict adherence to the original, in order to achieve 'fidelity', 'accuracy' and 'resemblance'.

Beyond language and genre, translation also involves a cultural transfer. When Tagore and his contemporaries translated literary texts into English for a 'foreign' audience, they often smoothened the texture of their translations by omitting cultural terms, in order to make their translations more accessible to readers abroad. Today, though, English has been appropriated by many once-colonised cultures to produce a range of variants, different 'Englishes', that are used with confidence by writers who refuse to acknowledge the dominance of so-called 'standard English'. This is also true of contemporary translations. In my own translations, for instance, I retain numerous cultural terms for which there are no English equivalents, such as kinship terms, names of seasons, items of food and clothing, and forms of address. While using modern idiomatic English, I also try to retain the flavour of the original Bengali, through careful nuancing of phrasing and vocabulary. There are no fixed rules or formulae; often, the translator must invent strategies of negotiation between cultures where no direct equivalences exist. Sukanta Chaudhuri says:

> Literary translation proceeds by a series of particular, contingent judgments, virtually a species of inspired ad hocism.[9]

Such is the creative dimension of translation; and like performance, it has much to do with the connections between context, 'performer' and audience.

Translation can also deploy the performative in ways that are political. Citing Gayatri Chakravorty Spivak, Judith Butler says:

> the practice of translation (which is something other than an assimilation to mono-lingualism) is a way of producing—performatively—another kind of 'we'—a set of connections through language that can never produce a linguistic unity.[10]

She adds:

> sometimes it is not a question of first having power and then being able
> to act; sometimes it is a question of acting, and in the acting, laying claim
> to the power one requires.

What did it mean in this sense, for Tagore to translate the *Gitanjali* poems
into English? He was unsure of his command of English, but the instinct
that prompted him to undertake this effort, was the desire to claim a place
in the international literary domain, instead of remaining confined to the
local and the regional. His act of assertion proved effective beyond expectation: Tagore's English *Gitanjali* drew the attention of noted personalities
such as Pound, Yeats and Rothenstein, brought him the Nobel Prize, and
placed him on the world literary map. According to Krishna Kripalani,
news of the award 'was received everywhere with a shock of surprise and
turned Rabindranath from an individual into a symbol—a symbol of the
West's grudging recognition of Asia's submerged potential and its imminent resurgence.'[11] The play of cultural difference here is significant, for
Tagore's triumph is read by Kripalani as a victory for Asia. Such was also
Yeats' perception of *Gitanjali*. In his Introduction, he says:

> A whole people, a whole civilization, immeasurably strange to us, seems
> to have been taken up into this imagination; and yet we are not moved
> because of its strangeness, but because we have met our own image.[12]

As Radice points out, Yeats treats Tagore's text as a symbol for the whole
of Asian civilisation, taking it to stand for the differences between cultures
of East and West, but more importantly, for the universal human values
underlying such differences. He says:

> Yeats found in the *Gitanjali* poems and in Tagore himself a symbol, a
> type, an icon. This set the tone for the way in which Tagore was regarded
> internationally throughout his post-*Gitanjali* career.[13]

In actual fact, though, *Gitanjali* does not represent the whole of Tagore's
genius, let alone the whole of Asian culture. Michael Collins argues:

> Yeats assumed that the devotional Vedantic poetry of *Gitanjali* was all
> there was to Tagore. But it was not the only Tagore. As we know, he
> also published numerous essays, philosophical works and novels, most of
> which were largely ignored by the likes of Yeats.[14]

Yeats' representation of Tagore's text, is therefore imbued with cultural politics that displace the intention and significance of the original. Yeats' subsequent change of stance towards Tagore's work is well-known. In a letter to Sir Frederick Macmillan on 28 Jan. 1917, for instance, he says:

> You probably do not know how great my revisions have been in the past. William Rothenstein will tell you how much I did for *Gitanjali* and even his MS of *The Gardener*. Of course all one wanted to do 'was to bring out the author's meaning', but that meant a continual revision of vocabulary and even more of cadence. Tagore's English was a foreigner's English.[15]

Yeats' claim over the translated versions of *Gitanjali* and *The Gardener*, and his changing attitudes towards them, demonstrate the ways in which translation displaces the authority of the original, and also the mutability and contingency of translated texts as performances. In the pre-War years when the West was hungering for a spiritual 'message' that Tagore the sage-like prophet from the East seemed to offer, Yeats found in his works something miraculous and universal. Later, as disenchantment and alienation coloured the Western mindset after the experience of the First World War, Tagore's writings seemed to lose their magic for many of his readers in those parts of the world, and Yeats' cynicism about his work reflects that transition. Changing contexts thus account in a large measure for the fluctuating international reception of Tagore's writings. If the authority of the original text is not a given, the significance of a translation is also provisional, subject to contingency.

In this sense, the idea of a single definitive translation of a literary text becomes untenable, for what seems authorised, and authoritative, today, can strike readers as stale and dated tomorrow. Translation like performance, remains premised upon the idea of repetition with difference.

Notes

1. Patrick Primavesi, 'The performance of translation: Benjamin and Brecht on the loss of small details', *TDR: The Drama Review*, 43:4 (T164, Winter 1999), 53–59, p. 54.
2. Cited in *Imperfect encounter: Letters of William Rothenstein and Rabindranath Tagore*, ed. Mary M. Lago (Cambridge, Massachusetts: Harvard University Press, 1972), 195.
3. *The essential Tagore*, ed. Fakrul Alam and Radha Chakravarty (Cambridge, Massachusetts: Harvard University Press, 2011), 257.

4. Rabindranath Tagore, *Gitanjali*, trans. William Radice (New Delhi, Penguin, 2011), 45.

5. See *Selected letters of Rabindranath Tagore*, ed. Krishna Dutta and Andrew Robinson (New Delhi: Cambridge University Press, 2005), 272–3.

6. *Gitanjali*, trans. Radice, op. cit., 27.

7. *Essential Tagore*, op. cit., 260.

8. *Essential Tagore*, 322.

9. Sukanta Chaudhuri, 'General editor's preface', *Rabindranath Tagore: Selected poems*, ed. Sukanta Chaudhuri (Oxford University Press, New Delhi: 2004), v–xi.

10. Judith Butler, 'Performativity, precarity and sexual politics', *Revista de Antropologia Iberoamericana* 4, 3 (2009), i–xiii.

11. Krishna Kripalani, *Tagore: A life* (New Delhi: NBT, 3rd edn, 1986; rept. 1997), p. 131.

12. *Gitanjali*, trans. Radice, op. cit. 169.

13. William Radice, 'Introduction' to *Gitanjali*, trans. Radice, op. cit., xv–lxxxiv.

14. Michael Collins, *Empire, nationalism and Inter-cultural dialogue: Rabindranath Tagore, writings on history, politics and society* (London: Routledge, 2011).

15. Cited in William Radice, 'Introduction', op. cit., xxvii.

Memoirs

Childhood
(from *Chhelebela*)

Chapter IX

The days passed by routinely in this way. The school would snatch away a big chunk of the midday time, and its remaining hours would spill over the morning and evening. When I entered the classroom, the benches and tables appeared to poke my mind with their unexciting elbows. Day after day they looked the same—as unyielding as ever.

I returned home at dusk. The oil lamp in the study glowed like a signal reminding me to prepare lessons for the next day. Occasionally, the man with the dancing bear visited the inner arena of our house. Also came the snake charmer to put up a show of his snakes. At times even the street magician came and brought a touch of freshness to the monotony with his performances.

The sound of their *dugdugi*, a small tabor that those mendicants played by moving it with one hand, no longer resonates at our Chitpur road. Those men perhaps have fled the land making way for the cinema, saluting it from afar. Like a type of grasshopper that imperceptibly blends its hue with the desiccated leaves, my heart too remains palely fused with the dryness of those days.

During those days there were only a few games available to us. We played marbles, or what was called bat–ball—a very distant cousin of cricket. We could as well spin tops and fly kites. All the games the boys played in the city were of such kind, demanding less hardiness. Football, that required running and bounding all over the field, still had not arrived from across the ocean. This way, my days, all of the same measure, passed by drearily encircling me in a maze of sapless fences.

Then, on one such day, the notes of the *shehnai* rang out in a classical Indian, musical mode—the Baroya tune. A new bride came in our home; thin, gold bangles on her tender, dark wrist. In the blink of an eye an opening developed in the fence, and there appeared a newcomer from the enchanted land, not known to the boundary of our familial world. I kept on circling her from afar, could not gather enough courage to reach close to her. She had taken the seat of affection, while I was just an unimportant young boy.

The house then was divided into two *mahals*, or two quarters. Men occupied the outer quarters, while the inner precincts were the space meant for women—the feudal style of the nawabs was still in practice. I still remember, Didi, my elder sister, was strolling on the upper terrace with the new bride, exchanging intimate thoughts and feelings. When I tried to get close to them, I was stopped with a stern intimidation. That marked precinct was out of bounds for boys. Again, dolefully, I must return to the shadows of the dreary existence of those old days.

When suddenly the flood of rainwater descends from distant hills, it swiftly wears away the foundations of age-old dams. The same happened with us, then. The lady of the house introduced a new set of rules. *Bouthakuran*, the new bride, was allotted the room adjoining the inner terrace. That terrace was her private domain; she had complete possession of that. The feasts served on leaf platters to celebrate the dolls' wedding took place there. On such occasions, the guest of honour would be this young lad. Bouthakuran was a good cook and she loved to invite people for meals; she found in me an eager guest to fulfil her penchant for entertainment. On return from my school, I would often find ready such delicious offerings, which she herself cooked with great care. And on the days she prepared shrimp *chorchori*, a dry dish of shrimp mixed with vegetables, and mashed it with the *panta-bhat*, an overnight water-soaked fermented-rice, with a light flavouring of green chilli, there was no end to my delight. Sometimes when she was away to visit relatives, I would notice her pair of sandals missing from their usual place outside her room. I would get annoyed and in order to pick a quarrel, I would then hide some expensive article from her room. I would argue—'Whom do you expect to mind your room when you are away? Am I your *chowkidar*, your caretaker?' She would snap with anger— 'You need not mind my room; just mind your stealing hands.'

To women of today this would seem odd. They might say, 'As if there was never a husband's younger brother or *devar* in any household but barring yours.' I do concede to the fact that what they say is correct. These days, it appears that people all of a sudden seem more mature in all respects than those days. During those days, everyone, irrespective of age, was naive at heart.

Thus began a new chapter, of my forlorn, nomadic existence, on the terrace. Into my life came touches of friendship and affection that were so humane. It was my Jyotidada, my elder brother, who enlivened this phase of my life.

Chapter XI

People in those days, almost in every household, fancied keeping caged birds. The call of the caged *koel*—the cuckoo, from some neighbouring house afflicted me the most. Bouthakuran had procured a Chinese songbird, the Shama of the thrush family. Its piercing song would rise like a fountain from underneath the cloth that cloaked the cage. There were also birds of several other varieties, their cages hung in the western veranda. A worm seller would come every morning to provide their feed; out of his bag came grasshoppers, and also *sattu*, a mixed grain flour, particularly for the barley-eating birds.

Jyotidada would answer all my arguments. However, the same cannot be expected from women. Bouthakuran once took a fancy to keep squirrels in a cage. I pointed out to her that it was being unjust on her part. Exasperated, Bouthakuran replied, 'Stop behaving like a *gurumashai*, a schoolmaster.' This was not the right answer to my argument. Instead of the war of words, I secretly released those two creatures. Of course, after that I confronted some harsh words, but I chose not to reply.

There was one thing we always quarrelled about, and that quarrel was never resolved. Let me tell you about that:

Umesh was a clever man. At a throwaway price, he would buy from the English tailoring shops the discarded silk cut pieces of different shades and combine them with pieces of net and cheap lace to make ladies garments. Taking off the paper wrapping, he would unfold the dresses with great care in front of his lady clients and would then announce: 'Behold! This is the latest fashion.' The women could not but become the captive of that magical spell. How deeply it perturbed me I cannot explain. Again and again, I would object in agitation and the reply was, 'Mind your age, you need not behave as if you are my *jethamashai*, my uncle.' I pointed out to Bouthakuran that the age-old white saree with black border, or the *Dhakai* saree, is, by far, better and a more decent option than those dresses. I wonder whether the devars of today have become speechless to comment on the georgette-draped, painted, doll-like look of their *boudi*s, sisters-in-law. Bouthakuran, clad in outfits tailored by Umesh, was surely better than that. In those days there was not so much fad for fake appearance.

I always lost in debates with Bouthakuran, because she would never counter my arguments. Also, I lost to her in chess, as she was an expert in that game.

Since we have touched upon the topic concerning Jyotidada, there is a need to add some details to introduce him properly. We must begin discussing the matters from a slightly earlier day.

Jyotidada had to travel frequently to Shelaidah to attend to the works of the *zamindari* or the estates. Once, he took me along on one such trip. Considering those conventional times, it was quite an unusual act, what people would even remark as an excessive indulgence. He must have considered this journey from home to the world outside as a kind of mobile lesson. He understood that my mind treasured to foray freely in the open air and the sky, deriving nourishment naturally from the environment. Later, when I would reach the higher classes in the school of life, I would mature into an adult in this very Shelaidah.

The old *nil-kuthi*, the indigo-house, still existed; river Padma was far away. On the ground floor was the courthouse, on the upper floor was our lodging and in front was a very large terrace. Beyond the terrace were some tall *jhau* or tamarisk trees, which, once upon a time, thrived in tandem with the business of the sahib indigo planters. Today, instead of that once-raging power of the indigo merchants exists an appalling silence. Where is the *dewan*, the messenger from hell, from the indigo-factory? Where is the band of armed footmen with belted waist and stave on their shoulders? Where has gone the banquet hall with long dining table? Where would come the sahibs riding up from the district headquarters turning nights into days with all their feasting and the whirl of ballroom dancing, their blood bubbling with the intoxication of champagne?! The pathetic cries for justice of the wretched *ryot*s, the land-tenant–peasants, would not reach the ears of their masters, whose mighty power extended far to the district prison. None of what else prevailed those days holds true today; the only facts of the past that still exist are the graves of two sahibs. Those tall tamarisks sway in the wind, and the grandchildren of the peasants of those days sometimes see the ghosts of the sahibs moving about in the dead of the night in the uninhabited garden of the indigo-factory.

I somewhat made up my mind to stay there in solitude. I stayed in a small room in the corner, my days of extensive vacation matching the vastness of the open terrace. This retreat in an unknown, distant place was like the unfathomable depth of the dark water of an ancient pond. As I heard the *bou-katha-kau* bird, the Indian nightingale, singing incessantly, stray thoughts drifted through my mind uninterruptedly. Meanwhile, poems began to fill up the pages of my notebook. Those poems, like the blossoms of the first crop of mangoes in early spring, in the month of *Magh*, have fallen away.

In those days, if a young boy—more so, if a girl—wrote a couple of cadenced lines of poetry, the connoisseurs of the country would think that as something unique, a wonder that never happened and would never be accomplished.

I have come across the names of such poetesses. Their compositions have also appeared in print. Then, those prudently expressed, chosen words in fourteen-syllable free verses declined; their names were erased and instantaneously replaced by rows of names of girls of today.

Boys are far less courageous than girls, and are much more shy. I cannot recall any young poet who composed poems then, other than me alone. One day, a nephew elder to me pointed out that words when cast in the form of fourteen-syllable take on the shape of a poem. I saw it for myself, this play of magic. The fourteen-syllable form blossomed in my hands like a lotus; all the more so, it attracted the bees to sit on it. I, thus, succeeded to prevail over the chasm that separated me from the poets, and ever since, I continued to bridge the gap.

I remember, while I was studying in the standard one year junior to the class for scholarship, Gobindababu, the superintendent, heard rumours that I wrote poems. He instructed me to continue composing, thinking that the appellation of the Normal School would get exalted. I had to write as well as recite the poem to my classmates, and had to hear them comment that the poems were for certain plagiarised. The fault-finders could not realise when later, as I matured, I became an expert at stealing ideas. Nevertheless, such stolen stuff is indeed precious.

I remember composing a poem once combining the Bengali new poetry metrical system, the fourteen-syllable *payar*, with the old form of *tripadi* poetry, expressing the grief I felt for being unable to reach up to a lotus blossom, which persistently moved beyond my reach due to the surge of the waves made by the movement of my arms as I swam. Akshyababu took me along to the houses of his relatives and made them listen to those poems. In appreciation, they remarked, 'This boy has a flair for poetry.'

Bouthakuran's reaction was completely contrary. She would never accept that I might, some day, become a writer. Rather, she would always sarcastically say that I would never be able to write like Bihari Chakraborty. Crestfallen, I would ponder that had I merited the rank even much lower than him, Bouthakuran could not have hesitated before readily dismissing her young poet–brother-in-law's aversion for women's affinity for dresses.

Jyotidada was fond of riding. There are even instances when he took Bouthakuran on horseback down the Chitpur Road for an outing to the Eden Gardens. At Shelaidah, he gave me a pony. That animal was quite sprightly. Jyotidada sent me off to Rathtala ground to take the pony for a run. I would take the pony across that rugged terrain hugging tightly on its back, to avoid falling at any moment as it galloped fast. Since Jyotidada firmly believed that I would not fall, I managed not to fall off. Later, he even took me for rides on the Calcutta streets. This time not a pony, but it was quite a temperamental horse. One day, with me on its back, it raced straight through to the courtyard where it used to get its feed of grain. From the next day, we parted company.

Jyotidada had mastered the art of rifle shooting. He longed to hunt tigers. Biswanath, the hunter, informed us one day that a tiger had been spotted in the jungles of Shelaidah. Jyotidada picked up his rifle right away and started for the hunt. To my surprise, he took me along. That there was some possibility of danger did not strike his mind at all.

Biswanath, indeed, was an expert hunter. He believed that there was no gallantry involved in shooting at a tiger from the *machaan*s or the scaffolds built high up on the trees. He would rather confront the tiger after giving it a call and only then shoot it. He never missed his target.

It was a dense forest. In such light and shade of the thickness of the forest, it was difficult for one to sight a tiger. A ladder was improvised by making notches on a robust bamboo tree. Jyotidada climbed up with the gun in his hand. I was totally unarmed; had the tiger chased, I did not even have shoes on my feet to hit it back with. Biswanath signalled to us. Jyotidada could not catch sight of anything for a long time. He kept on watching into the bushes, and at last his bespectacled eyes spotted a tiger stripe. He fired instantaneously and the bullet by chance hit the tiger's spine. It collapsed and was unable to get back to its feet. Growling furiously, it seized with the teeth whatever timbers and twigs it could reach at and thrashed its tail against the ground. As I recall the incident, I feel somewhat suspicious.

It seemed as if the tiger was waiting patiently to die, which is not in their temperament. Perhaps, its diet the previous night was craftily spiked with opium! Or else, why was it so drowsy?

On another occasion, a tiger had called in on the forests of Shelaidah. We, two brothers, mounted an elephant and began our journey in its search. On its way, the elephant uprooted sugarcanes effortlessly from the field, chewing on them, and advanced with majestic gait, undulating its back like an earthquake. We reached the forest. The elephant, pressing with its knees and tugging with its trunk, brought down the trees and hurled them down to the ground. Before this incident, I heard stories from Chamru, Biswanath's brother, about the catastrophes that occur when the tiger might leap on the back of the elephant and dig its paws in. The elephant then, along its way, trumpeting wildly through the forest, would smash the limbs, head and everything of the riders on its back against the tree trunks. That day, as we rode on the back of the elephant, that picture of crushed bones frequented my mind all the way until the end. I concealed my sense of horror to avoid embarrassment and looked all around with a daredevil attitude as if ready to attack the tiger as soon as it caught my eyes. The elephant entered into the thick of the forest. It stopped at one point on its way; the mahout did not even make an attempt to prod it further. Of the two hunting creatures, he had more faith in the tiger. That Jyotidada might injure the tiger and make it frantic must have been his greater fright. All of a sudden, the tiger sprung from the depths of the bushes like a gust of unexpected thunderstorm let loose by the clouds. Our eyes, adapted to see cats, dogs and jackals, were not ready for the sight of this enormous animal; here is a stubbly built animal, an outright physique of virility, yet it seemed so weightless. It ran through the open field, in the brightness of the midday sun. Oh! What an elegant flowing gait! The fields were bare of crop. That large, yellow, sun-bathed field was, indeed, the ideal place to watch to one's satisfaction the sight of a tiger on the run.

One more anecdote remains to be told; it may be amusing to hear. In Shelaidah, the gardener would pluck flowers and arrange them in vases. I had a flight of imagination to pen my verses with the coloured sap of the flowers. The sap that I successfully obtained, after repeated squeezing, was hardly enough to rise up to the nib of the pen. I started to think of a device for the purpose. A perforated wooden bowl and on it a pestle that could be rotated, were all that one required. A rope-tied wheel could operate that. I sought Jyotidada for my requirements. Perhaps, he laughed to himself, but that was not obvious. He ordered, and the carpenter arrived with his bits of wood. The mechanical device was created. The more I churned the flower-filled wooden bowl with the rope-tied pestle, the flowers turned into a muddy paste; no juice came out of it. Jyotidada understood that the flower juice did not rhyme with the machine-inflicted pressure; yet, he did not laugh on my face.

That was the only time in my life I ventured into engineering. There is a saying in the scriptures that there always awaits a God to humble the one who assumes to be what he is not. It seemed, at that instance, that the same divinity looked at my ventures in engineering with disdain. Since then, I stopped laying hands on machines; I even stayed away from stringing musical instruments like the sitar or the esraj.

I described in my memoir, *Jeebansmriti*, how Jyotidada competed with the Flotilla Company to run a fleet of indigenous ships in the rivers of Bengal and went bankrupt. Bouthakuran did not live long to see that collapse. Jyotidada quit his abode on the second floor of our house. In the end, he built a house on a hill in Ranchi.

Translated by **Dipannita Datta**

My life in my words
(from *Jeevansmriti*)

The chains of the rigorous regime which had bound me snapped for good when I set out from home. On my return I gained an accession of rights. In my case my very nearness had so long kept me out of mind; now that I had been out of sight I came back into view.

When I arrived it was not merely a homecoming from travel, it was also a return from my exile in the servants' quarters to my proper place in the inner apartments. Whenever the inner household assembled in my mother's room I now occupied a seat of honour. And she who was then the youngest bride[1] of our house lavished on me a wealth of affection and regard.

After my return from the hills I was the principal speaker at my mother's open-air gatherings on the roof terrace in the evenings. The temptation to become famous in the eyes of one's mother is as difficult to resist as such fame is easy to earn. While I was at the Normal School, when I first came across the information in some reader that the Sun was hundreds and thousands of times as big as the Earth, I at once disclosed it to my mother. It served to prove that he who was small to look at might yet have a considerable amount of bigness about him. I used also to recite to her scraps

[1] This is a reference to Rabindranath's sister-in-law Kadambari Devi, wife of his fifth brother Jyotirindranath (1849–1925).

of poetry used as illustrations in the chapter on prosody or rhetoric of our Bengali grammar. Now I retailed at her evening gatherings the astronomical odds and ends I had gleaned from Proctor.

But the achievement of mine which appealed most to my mother was that while the rest of the inmates of the inner apartments had to be content with Krittivasa's Bengali rendering of the Ramayana, I had been reading with my father the original of Maharshi Valmiki himself, Sanskrit metre and all. 'Read me some of that Ramayana, do!' she said, overjoyed at this news which I had given her.

My mother, unable to contain her feelings at my extraordinary exploit, wanted all to share her admiration. 'You must read this to Dwijendra (my eldest brother),' she said.

'In for it!' thought I, as I put forth all the excuses I could think of, but my mother would have none of them. She sent for my brother Dwijendra, and as soon as he arrived, greeted him with: 'Just hear Rabi read Valmiki's Ramayana; how splendidly he does it.'

❧

When my mother died I was quite a child. She had been ailing for quite a long time, and we did not even know when her malady had taken a fatal turn. She used all along to sleep on a separate bed in the same room with us. Then, in the course of her illness, she was taken for a boat trip on the river, and on her return a room on the third storey of the inner apartments was set apart for her.

On the night she died, we were fast asleep in our room downstairs. At what hour I cannot tell, our old nurse came running in weeping and crying: 'Oh my little ones, you have lost your all!' My sister-in-law[2] rebuked her and led her away, to save us the sudden shock at dead of night. Half awakened by her words, I felt my heart sink within me, but could not make out what had happened. When in the morning we were told of her death, I could not realize all that it meant for me.

As we came out into the veranda we saw my mother laid on a bedstead in the courtyard. There was nothing in her appearance which showed death to be terrible. The aspect which death wore in that morning light was as lovely as a calm and peaceful sleep, and the gulf between life and its absence was not brought home to us.

---

[2] Kadambari Devi.

Only when her body was taken out by the main gateway, and we followed the procession to the cremation ground, did a storm of grief pass through me at the thought that mother would never return by this door and take her accustomed place in the affairs of her household. The day wore on, we returned from the cremation, and as we turned into our lane I looked up at the house towards my father's rooms on the third storey. He was still in the front veranda sitting motionless in prayer.

☙❧

When, in later life, I wandered about like a madcap, at the first coming of spring, with a handful of half-blown jessamines tied in a corner of my muslin scarf, and as I stroked my forehead with the soft, rounded, tapering buds, the touch of my mother's fingers would come back to me; and I clearly realised that the tenderness which dwelt in the tips of those lovely fingers was the very same as that which blossoms every day in the purity of these jessamine buds; and that whether we know it or not, this tenderness is on the earth in boundless measure.

☙❧

Last night I dreamt that I was the same boy that I had been before my mother died. She sat in a room in a garden-house on the bank of the Ganga. I carelessly passed by without paying attention to her, when all of a sudden it flashed through my mind with an unutterable longing that my mother was there. At once I stopped and went back to her and bowing low touched her feet with my head. She held my hand, looked into my face, and said: 'You have come!'

In this great world we pass by the room where Mother sits. Her store-room is open when we want our food, our bed is ready when we must sleep. Only that touch and that voice are wanting. We are moving about, but never coming close to the personal presence, to be held by the hand and greeted: 'You have come!'

Translated by **Uma Dasgupta**
[*My life in my words* (Penguin Books India, 2006)]

Letters

To Mrinalini Debi

Masalia Ship Sept 6, 1890

Bhai Chhoto Ginni,[1] dear little wife,

The day before yesterday I sent you a letter; and I am writing another today. It seems both will reach you on the same day. What's the harm in that? Tomorrow we'll leave the ship, so I am penning this now. I'll only have the time to write again once I reach England. Don't mind please if I skip a day or two because of the disturbances of travel. It isn't too difficult to write letters while on board, but when I move around on the land (and I really have no clue as to my location at some points in time), I might lose one or two days. In all probability we reached Europe two days ago. Our ship is now making its way between Greece on the right and an island on the left. The isle appears very close—a few mountains, with houses scattered in between, and a large city at one place—I could clearly see its mansions through my binoculars. This white city, just along the sea shore, and curled into the lap of the blue mountains, looks charming. Won't you like to see it, *Chhutki*?[2] Do you know that you too will walk on this path one day? Don't you rejoice at this thought? You'll see what you haven't imagined even in your dreams. It has been a little cold for two days—not too severe— but it *does* feel cold when I sit on the deck and the breeze blows hard.

I have started wearing some of my warm clothes. I've had to quit my habit of sleeping on the deck at night. Loken suffered dreadfully from painful and swollen gums after he slept on the roof of the ship. Given the season we've come in, we'll see a mild winter, far less severe than the one we went through in Darjeeling, you remember? By the time we prepare to leave, it will probably be a little more intense. I have sent back quite a few unnecessary items of clothing and that *balaposh*[3] wrapper through *Mejbothan*.[4] Have you received them? If not, please ask for them. If they fall into the hands of Lakshmi, they'll find their way into mejbothan's cupboard. I have bought lovely material and a border for Beli and sent them through Mejbothan; you must have received them by now. A beautiful scarlet piece that will suit Beliburi; and the border too is of a new design, isn't it? Mejbothan has also given one of her special sarees to Beli, a contrast of blue and white. That too, I think, will suit Beli and Ranu well. The imaginative girl that she is, she must be very pleased to have the new cloth. Does she think of me? I don't know in what shape I'll see Khoka on my return. By then, I think he'll be speaking a few more words. In any case, I doubt he will recognise me. It might be that I'll become such a 'white man' that even you folks won't recognise me! You remember I cut my finger? It's better now. But two deep holes still remain—the wound was severe. After many days, I could bathe yesterday and the day before. On reaching Paris after tomorrow, I'll arrange for another good bath. They have places known as 'Turkish Baths', where one can wash thoroughly. You might have read about this in my account *Europe-Probashir Patra*. I am keeping good health now; I may even have gained some weight with eating three times a day on this ship. *Chhotobou*, when I return home, I want to see you healthy and happy. The carriage is now in your hands, go for regular rides instead of giving it away for the use of others. Last night, there was a performance on a makeshift stage on the roof of our ship. It was quite a mix. A woman even performed a saucy dance! So I went to bed rather late. This will be my last night on board the ship. I end my letter with kisses to all of you.

Rabi.

Translated by **Malashri Lal**

Letter No. 7

Sahajadpur
June, 1891

Dear wife, *Bhai Chhuti,*

Come now, tell me one thing. For what good reason have you never mentioned receiving the fine rich butter that I have strenuously procured for you from the best dairies of Sahajadpur, and sent in your service? I see that you are getting so many presents all the time that your sense of gratitude is quite numbed. Fifteen *sers* of pure ghee you accept every month as though it's simply the normal thing in your life, as if this was an agreement I made with you when we married! Your dear Bhola's mother is ill and bedridden. I assume that this ghee is proving useful for many people. Wonderful! The one positive thing about it is that the servants won't fall ill after stealing and consuming the ghee of such fine quality. My supply of mangoes is almost over. This time I think we had two species—one excellent, the other not bad but not particularly good either. Some rotted. Anyway, they lasted me a week. People here are surprised at my food habits. Since I don't eat rice they think I am doing a ritual penance and fasting. They cannot understand that whole wheat roti is four times more nourishing than rice. Every person who visits me raises queries about my food habits and expresses astonishment. Word has spread across Sahajadpur that I am deeply religious because I have given up eating rice. You would imagine that it's written in my horoscope that fame and a few other things will come my way without my making the least little effort!

Rabi

Translated by **Malashri Lal**

Letter No. 8

Sahajadpur
June 20, 1891

Bhai Chhuti,

Today my travels complete a month. I have seen that if there is pressure of work, I can somehow stay abroad for a month. But, after that, I begin to feel nostalgic about home. There has been quite a storm here last evening. I couldn't sleep for quite a while because of the thunder. This storm may have reached your place too. Yesterday, even during the day, there were heavy showers. The river is in a swell. The mustard fields are under water, if the water rises any more, it will come up to our garden. Wherever I look, there is some land and some water. Women are cleaning utensils and carrying on with their regular jobs despite the water in front of their homes. Keeping their modesty intact yet raising their garment a few inches above the usual level permitted in society, the women as well as the men are walking on the streets. During summer, this place has an awful scarcity of water; in the rainy season, it's just the opposite. When it rains on the third floor of our mansion, the scene is pretty much the same as here. The water stands on the verandah and bathing and cleaning of utensils can be easily done while being seated on the door-sill! If you adopted this technique in the rainy season, you'll be saved a lot of labour! Ok, now tell me, are you walking regularly on the terrace, twice a day? And are you keeping up your regular routines? I have a suspicion that you are simply sitting on the chair, reading a novel while gently swinging your legs. How is your headache now?

Rabi

Translated by **Malashri Lal**

Letter No. 16

Shelaidah
June, 1898

Bhai Chhuti,

I received your letter today, on returning from Dhaka. If things are as you say, then I should quickly wind up my assignments in Kaligram and leave for Calcutta to make the necessary arrangements. But dear *bhai*, you shouldn't worry inordinately. Try to accept all happenings with a quiet, steady and contented mind. This is the only objective I carry in my head and wish to realise in life. Not that I succeed each time; but if you too could keep such equanimity, then, perhaps we could be supported by our combined efforts and I too could find some peace of mind. Of course, you are much younger than me, your experience of life still limited; and your nature is, in a sense, more peaceful, restrained and patient than mine. Therefore, your need to stay out of mental turmoil is considerably less. But some time or another, crises surface in everyone's life; then patience and contentment prove useful. One realises that small losses and obstacles, hurt and pain which often disturb and paralyse our thoughts are actually nothing. To love and impart good and perform one's duty towards others with sweetness and pleasure—these apart, let whatever happen, and whenever. Life is too short, joys and sorrows are always ephemeral. Harm, hurt, deprivation—these are things which are difficult to take lightly, but if not taken so, the burden of life grows insufferable, and high ideals become impossible to retain. If I can't make that happen, if I spend day after day without satisfaction, without peace, if all of life is spent in tackling small adversities, then life is wasted. Tranquility, renunciation, selfless love and disinterested action— these are the markers of life's success. If you find contentment in yourself, and also spread comfort to others, then your achievement is greater than that of an empress's! *Bhai Chhuti*, the moment you allow the mind to fuss over small matters it gets scattered in all directions. Most of our sorrows are self-created. Please don't get irritated because I seem to be giving you a verbose and serious lecture. You cannot imagine with what intensity I am writing these words. My love for you, my respect for you and an easy assurance of mutual help stand steadfastly before me. Such peace and happiness is the greatest gift in the world, and in its presence the small disappointments of everyday life seem immaterial—these days such a realisation comes to me as a significant achievement.

The passionate relation of man and woman in youth has a driving energy, but perhaps you know from your own experience that a mature and steady flow of love comes only when a man and woman have experienced the vicissitudes of this great world together. That is when a deep, quiet and wordless play of love begins. An expanding household gradually pushes away the outer world. As this household grows there is an increasing isolation for the couple. At a time when the demands of a family surround them on all sides, the man and wife are pushed into proximity. There is nothing more beautiful than the human soul; whenever it comes up close, whenever it touches you at first-hand, in a face-to-face acquaintance, deep love takes its origin. Then there is no illusion, there is no need for deification of the other; union and separation does not raise any storms. Whether near from far, there is a deep joy and serene confidence of mutual support in danger and distress, prosperity and achievement. I know that you have felt distress because of me, but I also think that somewhere in the future happiness will be gained from this too. Forgiveness in love, and acceptance of the sorrow brings more joy than easy gratification and wish fulfilment. These days I have only one wish, that our lives be pure and simple, our surroundings tranquil and blissful, our household be free of pomp and be directed towards good, may our needs be few, our purpose lofty, our efforts selfless and may our service to our country be a higher goal than the work we do for ourselves. Even if our children move away from these ideals and distance themselves from us, may we, till the end, pass our lives in grace, recognising each other's humanity and being helpmates and support for our tired and world-weary souls. This is the reason why I am eager take you away from the lifeless shrines of self-interest in Calcutta and bring you to the solitude of rural Bengal. There, one cannot get away from the thoughts of profit and loss, self and the other. Constantly tormented by trivial matters, finally you cast away your ideals into a thousand pieces. Here, little is enough, and you never mistake falsehood for truth. Here, it isn't so difficult to remember the dictum: 'Joy and sorrow, like and dislike, attainment and failure, accept everything with an expansive heart'.

Your Rabi

Pramatha, Suren and a Gujarati friend of Pramatha's, are in Shelaidah.

Translated by **Malashri Lal**

Letter No. 33

Santiniketan
July 20, 1901

Bhai Chhuti,

I have come back after leaving Bela at her in-laws'. It's not as grave a situation as you had imagined from afar. Bela is quite delighted and there is no doubt that she is enjoying her new life. Now we aren't so important for her. It occurs to me that a girl immediately after marriage must have the opportunity to enter a state of complete and exclusive connection with her husband, detached from any link with her parents. If parents are around, such a bond is obstructed. The tastes and habits of a girl's family are bound to be different from that of her in-laws, even where this is slight. With parents around, a girl can never completely forget the practices of her natal home and surrender to the habits of her spousal family and mingle with them. If one can't help giving away a daughter, why hold her back? In this context, the girl's happiness and wellbeing are the supreme concern. Looking to our own joys and sorrows, why should we burden her with thoughts of us when she already has to bear the burden of adapting to her husband's home? Believing that Bela is quite happy, please try to still the pain you feel on this separation from her. Had we continued to stay with the two of them even after their wedding, I believe the result wouldn't have been pleasant. Because Bela lives at a distance from us, the affections will endure, always. When they visit us during the pujas, or we visit their house, we'll experience a joy that is deep and new. In all forms of love, there must be some separation and some freedom. The consequence of taking over each other's life can never be beneficial. If Rani goes far after her marriage, it'll be a good thing. Of course, for the first two years she must remain with us, but as soon as she comes of age, it will be necessary to send her away for her own good. In our household, the education, taste, habits, language and manners are different from all other Bengali families; therefore, it's especially necessary for the daughters of our family to move a little far after their marriage. Otherwise, the tiny irritations of everyday life will build up and interfere with the respect and dependence they must feel towards a husband. Rani's nature is such that her demeanor will improve if she is separated from her parental home. Should she stay close to us, her old associations will never be severed. Just think of yourself. Had I established myself in Phooltala after our marriage, your nature and manners would have been different.

We would have entirely given up thoughts of own life and worried only about our children. They haven't been born for the sake of our happiness though their wellbeing and success should be our only joy. All through yesterday, memories of Bela's childhood kept flashing upon my mind. How carefully I brought her up, personally! How she used to play naughtily among the bolsters, and how, if she caught sight of a boy her age, she would jump on him. She used to be such a greedy but good-hearted child. I used to bathe her at our Park Street house, and while at Darjeeling, I would raise her from sleep at night and feed her warm milk. Memories return of those days when I first understood my immense love for her. But she doesn't know all this, and better so. May she associate herself with her household without any sorrow, may she find fulfilment in life through devotion, love, affection and expression of conjugal duty. Let us have nothing to regret.

Today, having reached Santiniketan, the abode of peace, I am engulfed in an ocean of peace. How important such visits are can hardly be understood at a distance. It seems as though my solitary self, encircled by infinity of space, breeze and light, is lying restfully in the lap of a primeval Mother, sucking nectar from her.

Your ____.

Translated by **Malashri Lal**

Letter No. 34

Kushtia
On way to Shelaidah
1901

Bhai Chhuti,

I have reached Kushtia. On one matter I feel absolutely hopeless. I met my brother-in-law, but couldn't meet his son! The entire town of Kushtia appears highly relieved after sending him off to his mother's place at Kashi. His cot and bedding are there all the same, his soiled garments are hanging from the stand, but the person isn't anywhere! Alas!

Your mother is suffering from something akin to rheumatism. She was fine in Shelaidah but rheumatism has caught her in Kushtia. The glowing face and plump form of your Kinuram is a source of joy. He keeps coming here intending to talk about something, hangs around, but seeing me busy with my letters, he goes back with a heavy heart.

I am waiting for the steamer and shall leave for Shelaidah in the afternoon.

Who has the key to the almirah that contains my books in the new house in Calcutta? I need a few of those books.

Late midnight a heavy storm and showers hit Calcutta. You could call it a 'preparation' for my journey! The last three to four days haven't seen a drop of rain here. The sun is scorching, the heat isn't mild either. When I reach Shelaidah, I shall find that the breeze there is filled with the stench of rotten jute.

I have given the turnips to your mother, and to Satya as well. Manisha and the others must have reached Bolpur by now. All of you must be very busy. Are you travelling a lot? Jagannath has sent garments, fruits and sweets for you through Manisha and her group. Right?

Today's meal was unforgettable. Your mother was adamant. She insistently fed me fish curry after many days. But the truth is I did not like the taste. I have hired a Brahmin at the rate of one rupee per day, and brought him with me. Because my stay will be brief, I had to hire him at such an exorbitant rate. Tell me, how could I eat the stuff prepared by Bipin, being a Brahmin myself?

Please keep a watch so that there isn't the slightest lapse in Rathi's lessons.

Here I take leave, with...

Your Rabi

Translated by **Malashri Lal**

Kaligram
On the way to Shelaidah
1901

Bhai Chhuti,

Finally I am here, having faced many dangers on route. At first, there was an adverse wind for two days in which the boat could not move.... Later when it sailed gently, it was caught in a marsh. You know, a marsh is like the sea—a vast expanse of water on all sides with patches of paddy fields rising occasionally through it. No space for cows to graze, no place for people to move; they can only travel by boat or canoe from one island to another. When you live in a place like Bolpur such a scene can hardly be imagined. All around float strands of *kalmi*[5] moss, stray lotus and their stalk peep in between; they mingle to create a typical smell. Black cormorants streak through the water, fish-baiting kites hover overhead. During the evening when peace descends over the vast, endless expanse of water, a strange desolation catches the heart. Sea waves carry a resonance, waters have music; here there is no such sound. Just a silent void, and in it a sailing boat with its gently swishing oars. Over this when moonlight descends, I feel I am stationed in a desolate realm of death. Extinguishing the lamp, I draw my chair near the window, and sit silently in the moonlight, and the tranquility of this vast body of water possesses my heart. The day before yesterday, within this marsh, the Western sky was overcast with thick clouds presaging a storm. Fortunately the boat was within a paddy field, so it could cast anchor and hold itself to the earth below the water. When the storm died down, we set sail once more, but destiny was such that within a short distance we met with another sudden storm. Luckily we were at another safe point. Had it been otherwise, I don't know where the boat would have been flung by the wind. Reaching here, I was told that I have to report to the High Court on Monday. Therefore, I must leave tomorrow. Amidst the thousand tasks in Calcutta, it would be difficult to write to you, that's why I am writing now. My health has benefited from the compulsory solitude of the last few days in the silent expanse of water. I have realised that if my wretched, broken health is to be mended, I should surrender to the quiet, comforting lap of water. As I am writing these lines, another storm is brewing. Topsi is creating a racket when pulling at the anchor. I think I might hear from you once I reach Calcutta.

Your Rabi.

Translated by **Malashri Lal**

Letter No. 36

Shelaidah
1902

Bhai Chhuti,

In Shelaidah the mind is restless. That which one has to surrender appears all the more splendid—such is our attachment. Memories of both joy and sorrow are linked to Shelaidah but the happy ones appear magnified. But Shelaidah is not in such a good condition now. Everything is soaked in dew, fog remains till eight o'clock, and it's chilling after evening sets in; the water in the wells and ponds is disgusting and malaria rules everywhere. We have chosen the right moment to quit Shelaidah, or else we would have been in trouble with our ailing children. Bolpur is far cleaner and healthier than this. But innumerable roses are blooming here. They are large and superb. The fragrance of acacia pervades the air. Like an old friend, the place Shelaidah sends you a few of her acacias.

Have you received the *moog*,[6] molasses and books which were sent from here? All the supply of moog is for the school. The *chhola*[7] will be sent once it grows.

I want to prepare Rathi for a higher life—for which discipline, restraint and austerity are necessary. The more he practices self-discipline without swerving the least, the more he will emerge a truer man. From our early childhood, we have only focused on self-gratification. The outcome is that we grant more importance to our trivial desires than to lofty ideas, great truths, humanity and even love and wellbeing. We are not prepared to give up self-gratification under any circumstances or for the sake of any person or anything. We are not ready to curb our trivial desires by the slightest, even if it means shirking duties, breaking vows or inflicting hurt on our loved ones. To allow one's desires to triumph every time is practically to invite self-defeat, to kill one's higher humanity before a diminished self. This is no joy but a vanity. Perhaps we can't remedy the past. Therefore, I want to let go my children and offer them up to a benign God for their wellbeing. May He free them from the pride of wealth, keenness of desire, flow of instinct and lures of the world, and may He bedeck them with goodness and indomitable courage. This is my prayer. May we restrain our desires and participate in God's law or dharma, instead of trying to rival it by asserting our vanity. If I am unsuccessful even in this effort, my entire life would appear fruitless.

Rabi

Translated by **Malashri Lal**

From Amitrasudan Bhattacharya and Aparna Bhattacharya, eds, *Bhai Chhotobou: Streeke Lekha Rabindranather Chithi* (Kolkata: Purba, 2009).

Notes

1. *Chhoto Ginni* is a vocative that refers to the junior/youngest wife in a household. Tagore's wife was the youngest during that time in the Tagore household; therefore, this vocative is used. Other variants are *Chhotobou* and *Bhai Chhuti*. *Bhai* here means 'dear'.
2. 'Little girl'. A colloquial for a young woman.
3. Quilt.
4. Mejbothan is a variant of *mejo* (middle) + *bouthaan* (a vocative for one's brother's wife). So it means, 'middle sister-in-law'.
5. Swamp cabbage.
6. Gram seed.
7. Chickpeas

To Victoria Ocampo

Tagore to Ocampo

[The following undated communication must be Tagore's first letter to Ocampo, written just a few days after he came to live at Miralrío. In Ocampo's *Autobiografía IV* (1982) the date for this letter is mistakenly given as October 1924. That cannot be correct, of course, as Tagore did not even reach Buenos Aires till 6 November. This letter could be the same as the 'letter of apology' from Tagore that Elmhirst mentions having carried to Ocampo on Friday, 14 November 1924 (in the document entitled 'The Argentine Adventure' preserved in the Elmhirst Records Office). The apology was apparently for some failure in communication the previous night, referred to as the 'iceberg night'.]

[San Isidro, 14? November 1924]

Last night when I offered you my thanks for what is ordinarily termed as hospitality I hoped that you could feel that what I said was much less than what I had meant.

It will be difficult for you fully to realise what an immense burden of loneliness I carry about me, the burden that has specially been imposed upon my life by my sudden and extraordinary fame. I am like an unfortunate country where on an inauspicious day a coal mine has been discovered with the result that its flowers are neglected, its forests cut down and it is laid bare to the pitiless gaze of a host of treasure-seekers. My market price has risen high and my personal value has been obscured. This value I seek to realise with an aching desire which constantly pursues me. This can be had only from a woman's love and I have been hoping for a long time that I do deserve it.

I feel today that this precious gift has come to me from you and that you are able to prize me for what I am and not for what I contain. This has made me so glad and yet I know that I have come to that period of my life when in my travel across a desert I need my supply of water more than ever before but I neither have the means nor strength to carry it and therefore can only thank my good fortune when it is offered to me and then take my leave.

Sri-Rabindranath-Thakur[1]

Tagore to Ocampo

[This letter was written on board the *Giulio Cesare*, on the ship's notepaper, and was posted from Rio de Janeiro.]

Jan. 5. 1925

Vijoya, under a grey sky my days are repeated in rhymes that are monotonous, like a perpetual telling of beads. I pass most part of my day and a great part of my night deeply buried in your armchair which, at last, has explained to me the lyrical meaning of the poem of Baudelaire that I read with you. I had hoped that I should be able to do some writing while crossing the interval between two shores—but the wind has veered and my manuscript book lies idle, its virgin pages looking like the sandy beach of a distant island unexplored. My day is divided into 2/3rd part of sleep and 1/3rd part of reading. I am completamente surrounded by a deep atmosphere of laziness as befits a human male in an ideal condition of life. In these two days I have been able to understand why Chinamen must smoke opium in order to realise intensely for a few moments the profound

---

[1] Signed in Bengali script. For typographical convenience Tagore's Bengali signatures have been romanized throughout.

dignity of the male, his natural birthright of inutile passiveness of which he is forcibly deprived the rest of his waking hours. The modern human females are never tired of accusing us of violence and tyranny, they do not know that it is a perverse expression of our inherent contemplative placidness repressed and tortured through the compelling necessity—for us to be the useful members of society. The Spanish Philosopher was right when he said that it was women who civilised us, and thus they have made our life burdensome, have imposed upon us missions which are not ours. We have taken our revenge, made them more decorative than useful, turned them into a hothouse where forced sentiments are cultivated, prized for their ravishing colours and perfume of sickly passion. Life has its necessities, but Mind must have its leisure;—women who are the guardian spirits of life are allowed leisure and men who, at their best, are philosophers, lovers of ideas, are made to toil for supplying necessaries of life and overfeeding the race. The modern feminists want to compete with men in an open field of work;—but that will have the effect of accelerating men's energy, and their fire of ferocity will rage with a greater intensity. The only satisfactory solution will be to remove them altogether from the region of usefulness, to let the lure of the unnecessary set them free in the realm of the unknown. They are natural savages who love to roam alone in the wilderness of thoughts and dreams. But you want civilisation for your progeny, that they may be secure from all injuries and privations. And therefore you lassoe [*sic*] these wild creatures and try to train them for domestic needs which are the needs of society. The antisocial beings are captured by the social beings, but the adjustments are not properly made and most of the works which are yours we are compelled to with the mistaken notion that you are not fit for them and in return saddle you with a leisure which only makes you restless. I only wish you could see how greatly Leonard has improved since he has got his leisure on this ship (not shiiiiip). He has suddenly turned an astronomer, haunting the upper deck, waiting for the chance of meeting some star of the first magnitude belonging to the southern hemisphere. You know, human males as secretaries are inefficient, but as astronomers they know how to make their opportunities rich and shining. I suppose you know that also for me astronomy has a great attraction, but being a poet I have my chart of stars in my memory which I can study even when I am confined in my cabin. I have been advised never to joke with a woman but I am afraid that some of the observations in this letter show signs of frivolity. You will excuse me when you know that a man who is not a prophet and yet who is treated as a prophet must give vent to his fit of laughter even at the risk of misunderst[and]ing.

Sri-Rabindranath-Thakur

Telegram: Tagore to Ocampo

[This telegram, preserved in the Ocampo archives at Buenos Aires, was sent from Calcutta and was received at Buenos Aires on 27 February 1925.]

Arrived love from

Rabindra

Tagore to Ocampo

[Since the telegram we have just looked at (document 21) was sent from Calcutta and reached Buenos Aires on 27 February, it is likely that the following letter was also written from Calcutta.]

[Calcutta?] Feb. 27. 1925

Dear Vijaya

There are some animals which feign death in order to save themselves from the danger of death. I am advised by doctors to follow their example must never move, never talk, never meet people—in fact, behave in every way as if I am dead. Therefore I shall completely have to surrender myself to your easy chair which has followed me from shore to shore. Thus I shall be saving my energy with a miserly care till I leave India once again for Italy next May the first. My cabin has been secured or? the same boat 'Cracovia' which has brought me to India. I hope that by that time I shall have strength enough to carry out my plan and sail for the shore where the people are expecting me with all their wealth of welcome.

The other day I met with a remarkable French woman who has been travelling in Thibet for some years and who has been able to love the people.[1] She asked my opinion about La Nacion[,] the Editor having asked for some contribution from her. I assured her of the respectability of the paper have referred her to you. You are likely to receive a letter from her.

I am writing this letter against the prohibition of the doctor who has advised me to keep to my reclining position on an easy chair and never to sit at the desk to do any writing. I am allowed to dictate but I take the risk of writing to you personally and lose a fraction of my vitality much more readily than sending my message to you through somebody else's handwriting.

My bhalobasa[2] [.]

Sri-Rabindranath-Thakur[3]

The name and address of the French lady:
Madame Alexandra David-Neel
c/o The French Consul
Colombo Ceylon

---

[1] Alexandra David-Neel (1868–1969), intrepid French explorer who travelled extensively in Asia and devoted many years of her life to the study of Tibetan customs, doctrines, philosophy etc. Fluent in all the Tibetan dialects, she lived in Tibet for many years, gained the confidence of the principal lamas, and even adopted an ordained lama as her son. Among her many books are *Initiations lamaïques, Voyage d'une parisienne à Lhassa, Parmi les mystiques et les magiciens du Tibet, Les enseignements secrets dans les sectes bouddhistes tibétaines* etc.

[2] Bengali for love.

[3] Signed in Bengali script.

Tagore to Ocampo

Santiniketan

March 4. 1925[1]

Dear Vijaya

I am writing this, reclining on your armchair, which, I am afraid, will keep me within its enclosure much longer than what I calculated. I am much worse than I was when you saw me and I am certain it will not be possible for me to leave India before August. I have asked my son to cancel my passage this summer.

I am sending you some of my short stories, translations of which[,] I hope[,] will be acceptable for La Nación.[2] If not, make any use you like, for they have not yet been published.

I suppose, you have, by this time, heard from Italian sources how cordially I was received there. This has been a further inducement for me for seeking my European home somewhere in Italy. I hope Elmhirst has been successful in cho[o]sing a suitable place. Have you heard from him?

I must close my letter here—my body refuses to work[.]

Bhalobasa[3][.]

Sri-Rabindranath-Thakur[4]

[1] I find in the 'Chronicle of Eighty Years' prepared by Prabhat-Kumar Mukhopadhyaya and Kshitis Roy and appended to the Tagore Centenary Volume of 1961 that 4 March 1925 was the day of the death, at Ranchi, of Rabindranath's elder brother Jyotirindranath Tagore. Had he received the news when he wrote this letter? On this day Tagore also wrote to Elmhirst: 'I have just received a letter from Vijaya which makes me feel sad. I know love is precious in this world and yet helplessly to allow it to be wasted hurts me deeply. Now that I am away from Vijaya the pressure of her gift no longer oppresses, my mind—I only feel the beauty of it, and the intense cry of her pain from across our endless separation seems to burn like a star—I do hope her offering which finds no adequate value in return may not be an unmixed loss for her and that this divine music of love's suffering may modulate her nature into a harmony which has its own eternal worth.' (Quoted from the typed copy of the letter kept in the Rabindra Bhavana archives, Santiniketan; the original is in the Elmhirst Records Office at Dartington.)

[2] Some of these short stories were published in the *Natión*.

[3] Bengali for love.

[4] Signed in Bengali script.

Ocampo to Tagore

San Isidro. March 31. 1925.

Dear Gurudev:

This is a business letter and I feel it is more difficult to write than if it were a literary one[.] (Bad literature is so easy[.])

Yesterday, after receiving your letter from Bombay, I went to la [*sic*] Nación and had a long talk with Mitre.[1]

Yes, Elmhirst had arranged the money should reach you through him. But as you are anxious to get it 'regularly and without much circumlocution', we have decided, with Mitre, that drafts will be sent straight to me and that I will immediat[e]ly forward them straight to you, as I am more likely to know your whereabouts than the Nación's[2] people.

Regarding what you write to me: 'I have some misgivings about the continuity of my relationship with La Nación etc etc'[,] you must rub that off your mind. Mitre said to me that he was *most anxious* to keep you *always* as a collaborator because so many readers here are interested in your thoughts and personality.

Mitre said, too, that he would only be able to publish one article by month (*occasionally* two)[3] as it had been *first* arranged with Elmhirst, owing to the quantity of rubbish they must squeeze in this paper from each part of the world... (of course he did not use the word rubbish, but I find it is the right one).

Mitre said also that la [*sic*] Nación wanted *only* writings that had not been already published in other papers, or books, or magazines. He was very particular about this point. He said *an exception* had been made with you while you were staying here, but that now they could only publish *original articles*.[4] He repeated several times that he wanted very much to keep you

---

[1] Jorge Mitre of *La Nación*. *La Nación* was founded by Bartolomé Mitre in 1870 and is still controlled by the Mitre family.

[2] There is no accent on the *o* in the MS here. Quite possibly, the word had become anglicized in her mind at that point because of the article 'the' put before it by her.

[3] The edge of the sheet is torn after the first two letters of this word, but the context makes it easy to fill in the gap.

[4] This insistence on original articles in a newspaper some thousands of miles away from an illustrious foreign author's home base is somewhat cheeky, normally, in such circumstances a newspaper or magazine is happy simply to publish reprints

as a collaborator because such a lot of people were anxious to follow your thoughts.

I have here 2 of your articles, one published in 'The modern review [*sic*]' (The fourfold way of India); the other in 'The Visva Bharati Quarterly'. What shall I do about them?

I want to post this letter immediat[e]ly because a *sheeeep* is sailing this morning. I will write to you this week about other matters.[5]

You need not hurry too much about sending new writings because *four* of your articles have not yet been published ('To the Child', 'The Giant Killer', 'Judgment', and the lecture on *Xmas*)[.][6]

I always remember you with *all my love*[.]

Vijaya.

Mr. Danvila sends his best regards and Fany is always talking about you and asking me to *give*[7] you her love[.]

---

or translations. It is also very ironical. Most of what Tagore wrote was written first in Bengali: in the case of creative writing almost always so, and articles too were likely to spring from talks given to Santiniketan audiences. Tagore could scarcely give up his right to publish something in Bengali first, and to appear in the *Nación* at all, such material would have to pass through two layers of translation. The *Nación* was in no position to check the accuracy of the first stage of the translation, or indeed to verify if something had been first published in Bengali or not. Perhaps Mitre simply meant: 'not published in English anywhere?' But the insistence remains ironical, as no translator of the *Nación* could translate directly from the Bengali and would have to be provided with an English text to translate from.

[5] But it would seem that she did not get round to it.

[6] At least two of these appeared in the *Nación:* see the Appendix to this book.

[7] Underlined twice in the MS.

Tagore to Ocampo

[Written on Visvabharati/Santiniketan notepaper, this letter was presumably written from Santiniketan. An envelope sent from Santiniketan on 5 August 1925 has survived in the Buenos Aires archives and probably goes with this letter.]

August. 2. 1925

Dear Vijaya

My weakness has not yet forsaken me. I am asked to keep still, and I am only too willing to do so, but there are others who in their dealings with me are guided by a motive which has an object contrary to mine. My time in this country is constantly pelted with petty claims by numerous individuals, each of whom believes that he is the only one who deserves to be attended to. There is no escape from them unless I run away from India.[1] Roma[i]n Rolland has thought of a sanitorium[2] near his own place in Switzerland where he will arrange to intern me as long as doctor advises. Our steamer sailing on the 15th August will reach Genoa somewhere about the beginning of September. I wish you could be there to welcome me. But I suppose it is not going to happen.[3] Now that I have vast stretches of leisure chiefly

---

[1] But even when he was ill, or at least convalescent, in Argentina, he insisted on seeing the streams of visitors who called on him at Miralrío! Ocampo and Elmhirst had a job to keep him from exhausting himself.

[2] *Sic.* Tagore's misspelling seems to be a cross between *sanitarium* and *sanatorium,* both of which are endorsed by the dictionary.

[3] He is still hoping against hope to meet her in Europe in September, though the plan to stay in an Italian villa seems to have been abandoned in favour of a sanatorium in Switzerland to be arranged by Romain Rolland. In mid-July he had cabled to Elmhirst: 'Intend staying very quietly in Europe to regain health Rolland already arranged sanatorium Switzerland which I wish to try. Overjoyed possibility meeting you.' (Copy of the telegram kept in the Rabindra Bhavana archives.) Had Tagore received any cable from Ocampo informing him of her plans? I have not found any such cable, but I have seen a cable from Elmhirst to Tagore in the Rabindra Bhavana archives, received in Santiniketan on 5 June 1925, which says: 'Shall proceed with Victoria over Italian villa on receipt ***in news your coming please confirm love'. There is also a letter from him to Tagore, dated 7 June 1925, which says: 'I only have rumour indirectly that you are better & still hoping to come to Europe in August. So I've cabled Victoria to know whether she is willing to rent for you the villa I chose,– option of purchase later if needed & I'm writing the

employed in cultivating dreams a swarm of details from my memory of San Isidro repeatedly comes to hum and hover around my thoughts. You express regret in your letter that I could not continue my stay at that beautiful house near the river till the end of summer,—you do not know how often I wish I could do so.[4] It was some lure of duty which drove me from that sweet corner with its inspiration for seemingly futile idling; but today I discover that my basket, while I was there, was being daily filled with shy flowers of poems that thrive under the shade of lazy hours. I can assure you, most of them will remain fresh long after the time when the laboriously built towers of my beneficent deeds will crumble into oblivion. Very few people will know that they ought also to thank you for this gift of lyrics which I am about to offer to them,[5] My bhalobasa[6]

Rabindranath Tagore

Italian agent to hold on till I get news from you both. Is that all right?' But I have not seen this cable of Elmhirst's to Ocampo, nor Ocampo's reply, if she sent any. I do not know what came of these cable exchanges. Was it just Tagore's continuing bad health which caused the villa plan to be put aside in favour of a sanatorium, or was it also some inability of Ocampo's to proceed with the original plan? And if that inability existed, was it just financial (as hinted in *Autobiografía IV*), or also connected with her forthcoming appearance, on 29 August 1925, in *Le Roi David* under the direction of Anserrnet? Or was it due to an even more complex tangle of events and circumstances, including a reluctance on the part of Julián Martínez to let her go away? Anyway, nothing came of these plans of Tagore to visit Europe in the autumn of 1925. They had to be cancelled.

[4] He is referring to her letter of 19 May 1925. Writing to Elmhirst on 4 October 1925, he refers to the same letter of Ocampo's: 'Some time ago I got a letter from Vijaya bewailing the evil fate which wrenched me away from her protection and wrecked my health. She wished I had spent South American summer months in San Isidro. Occasionally in weak-moment[s] I also indulge in such regrets which are foolish— for nobody can ever have the chance to be sure of the comparative desirability of the have-been and the would-have-been. Only thing in this case on which I can dwell with certain joy is the amazing fact that there is someone in this world for whom the mere fact that I exist could have an ultimate value.' (Quoted from the copy of the letter in the Rabindra Bhavana archives.)

[5] He was clearly getting *Purabi* ready for the press.

[6] This word is written in Bengali script and is followed by the Bengali sign for the full stop.

Tagore to Ocampo

Calcutta Oct. 29. 1925

Dear Vijaya

I do not[1] like to talk about my illness which has become a bore in its endless monotony. I am wearily waiting for the summer to come when I shall make another attempt to visit Europe in order to get proper medical treatment.

I am sending to you a Bengali book of poems which I wish I could place in your hand personally.[2] I have dedicated it to you though you will never be able to know what it contains.[3] A large number of poems in this book were written while I was in San Isidro.[4] My readers who will understand these poems will never know who my Vijaya is with whom they are associated.[5] I hope this book will have the chance of a longer time with you than its author had. Bhalobasa[6]

Sri-Rabindranath-Thakur[7]

[1] The two components are separated but joined by a pen-stroke.

[2] *Purabi*, of course. Unfortunately, those in charge of the Ocampo archives at Buenos Aires were unable to locate for me this very first copy of *Purabi* sent by Tagore to Ocampo. I saw a copy of the second impression of the first edition, which must have been sent much later, because it has the following inscription in Tagore's hand: 'To/ Vijaya/ with love/ Rabindranath/ July 30/ 1940'. I also saw a copy of this same imprint (2nd impression of the 1st edition) presented to Ocampo by Kalidas Nag 'with the fraternal greetings/ of the PEN. Club, Bengal, Calcutta' on 15 September 1936.

[3] During Tagore's lifetime Ocampo knew three of the *Purabi* poems, 'Atithi', 'Ashanka', and 'Kankal', in his own re-created English versions. A few more were translated for her many years later by Kshitis Roy. But it is true that Ocampo ended her days without gaining an adequate knowledge of what the book contained.

[4] 21 of the *Purabi* poems were written while Tagore was in San Isidro; 2 were written at Chapadmalal; 4 more were written on board the *Giulio Cesare;* the last poem of the book was ostensibly written in Milan. Further details on this subject are given in the main body of this book.

[5] Some hope he had! Perhaps in October 1925 not many of his readers understood the association, but it must have been apparent to members of his entourage in the thirties.

[6] Written in Bengali script.

[7] Signed in Bengali script.

29. Tagore to Ocampo

Calcutta Nov. 12. 1925

Dear Vijaya

I hope you have got my book by this time as well as my letter accompanying it.

I feel banished into an isolation of ill health, sort of a lonely island full of dim shadows and muffled sounds, in the midst of a babbling and rushing stream of life. The value of one's physical existence becomes small when one's activities are repressed. This is the time when [one's] mind has a longing for somebody to whom one's living presence is precious for its own sake.

I am almost certain that I shall be able to come to Europe next March. Is it possible for you to come and meet me there?[1] Bhalobasa[2]

Sri-Rabindranath-Thakur[3]

Tagore to Ocampo

Santiniketan. Bengal
India
Dec. 30, 1925.

Dear Vijaya

Your cablegram has made me glad. Last year it was about this time that I was in San Isidro and I still vividly remember the early morning light on the massed groups of strange flowers, blue and red, in your garden, and the constant play of colours on the great river which I was never tired of watching from my solitary window. Often I have a twinge of regret in my

---

[1] Witness how anxious he still was to meet her again, one year after the original encounter. Note that this letter was written exactly a year after the composition of 'Bideshi phul', the first poem he wrote as her guest in Miralrío (on 12 November 1924).

[2] In Bengali script.

[3] Signed in Bengali script.

mind that I did not stay longer under your tender ministration and escape all kinds of strain that have wearied [me] and made me weak.

I have been trying to secure accom[m]odation in some steamer sailing for Europe. My intention was to start sometime next March, but I am informed that all the berths are fully engaged till May. I am feeling anxious to have a change in some quiet spot in Europe and be under proper medical treatment. Romain Rolland has arranged for a sanatorium in Switzerland near his own place which I hope will not be too expensive.

I had a letter from Elmhirst lately—he is happy and in the expectation of a newcomer in his home. Bhalobasa

Sri-Rabindranath-Thakur

Tagore to Ocampo

11th March 1929

Dear Vijaya

After repeated hesitations I have at last started on my voyage to the West. This time it is through one of its northernmost entrances—Canada. I got an invitation to an Educational Conference to be held in Vancouver in the beginning of April. From there I shall go to Los Angeles and spend six weeks in the university there in lecturing and in other futilities.[1] History has been repeating itself and since our steamer left Bombay I have been suffering from a mild attack of influenza and my life in this cabin has become a stale copy of my life I experienced on the steamer that took me to Bueonos [sic] Ayres years ago. Unfortunately history leaves out of its copy some of the most important details when chooses to repeat itself. But the gap was filled up my mind all the more strongly because it was left blank in the outer picture. Our memory is dotted with dreams—some rich moments that are not washed away by the flood of casual events but are captured in

---

[1] On Tagore's 1929 trip to Canada and the U.S.A. see Kripalani, *Rabindranath Tagore*, 2nd edition, pp. 361–363. His lectures at Victoria and Vancouver attracted large, appreciative audiences, but insulting, treatment received from the U.S. immigration authorities caused him to cancel his programme and leave the country precipitately.

the depth of our experience, growing greener every day and harbouring our songbirds in its perfumed shades.[2]

With bhalobasa[3]

Rabindranath Tagore

My address till the end of June C/o American Express & Company, Los Angeles, U.S.A.[4]

---

[2] Note that his nostalgia for Victoria Ocampo had not dimmed a bit.
[3] In Bengali script.
[4] But he left in a hurry. See note no. 1.

Ocampo to Tagore

[Note that this letter comes after a four-year-gap in the correspondence. It was written en route to Europe on board the *Cap Arcona,* which belonged to a German shipping company called the 'Hamburg-Südamerikanische Dampfschifffahrts-Gesellschaft', on a picture postcard showing the ship. The card bears a German stamp. The letter begins on the reverse of the picture, but continues on the picture itself.]

Dear Gurudev—

I am back in France again;[1] at least I hope to be there on the 21 of this month. I hope too I shall go to England & see Leonard.[2] How are you & how is everything around you? I always think about you, though I do not write.[3]

---

[1] She might have given Tagore the impression that this was her first visit to Europe since 1930, but she had visited Europe every year. (See Carlos Adam, 'Bio-bibliografía de Victoria Ocampo', *Sur,* no. 346, January–June 1980, p. 139.) She had heard Gandhi speak in Paris in 1931.
[2] She did visit Elmhirst at Dartington Hall. An entry made in the Visitors' Book at Dartington on 5 July 1934 shows that Victoria Ocampo was there with her sister Angélica Ocampo and their cousin Josefina Dorado.
[3] Her last communication, unless letters have been lost, had been, as we have seen, in June 1930.

Please, dear Gurudev, if you can write just one word, send it: Avenue Malakoff 27. Paris. It shall be so welcomed.

Love from

Vijaya.
Atlantic Ocean

June 1934 Fany[4] sends her love.

[4] Her old nurse, Fani, of course.

48. Tagore to Ocampo

[This undated letter, written on the notepaper of Tagore's Santiniketan residential complex, Uttarayan, has been dated by the Rabindra Bhavana archivists as having been written on 9 July 1934. I found the matching envelope at Buenos Aires: addressed to Avenue Malakoff 27, Paris, and bearing an air mail sticker, it has the postmark of the Calcutta G.P.O., dated 10 July 1934. From the biographical chronology compiled by Mukhopadhyaya and Roy and appended to the Sahitya Akademi *Tagore Centenary Volume* one would guess that Tagore was in Santiniketan between 28 June and 14 July (see—p. 496 of that volume); so it is possible that the letter was written in Santiniketan but posted by someone else from Calcutta.]

[9? July 1934.]

Dear Vijaya

Lately I have tried to find your address but failed.[1] Often I have wished to meet you once again, but I am afraid the chance is growing more and more remote. This very morning in my letter to Elmhirst[2] I wrote about

[1] How Tagore could have allowed himself to be without Ocampo's address (or how Ocampo could have allowed Tagore to be without her address) is a mystery to me!

[2] Elmhirst quotes from this letter of Tagore's to him in his essay 'Personal Memories of Tagore' (Sahitya Akademi *Tagore Centenary Volume*, p. 23), but there he makes the mistake of thinking that the letter was written in 1930. Tagore had not dated that letter to Elmhirst as he has not dated this letter to Ocampo. But as this letter makes clear, both letters were written on the same day.

one Christmas morning in the beautiful garden in Argentina where you so kindly sheltered me and a shadow of sadness still hangs over my mind to know that those days belong to an irrevocable past. It is a strange coincidence that your card unexpectedly reached me just after I had sent that letter, reminiscent of your loving care, to Leonard.

Last month I had an adventure in Ceylon where I took with me some of our singers and girl students from our institution. We gave some performances which had lyrical appeal and the success was far beyond our expectation.[3] If the expenses were not too heavy for us I could confidently take them over to Paris and I believe that the French audience would have been pleased to see something which is genuinely oriental and full of exotic beauty.[4]

With all my heart I wish you could include India in your extensive programme of travels and visit me in my own place in Santiniketan. Why should it be impossible? From the middle of November to the end of the year you will find the climate delightful and you know I shall do my best to make you comfortable.

I am sending you a latest photograph of mine taken in Ceylon and I hope it will reach your hand.[5]

With my bhalobasa[6]

Rabindranath Tagore

---

[3] On Tagore's tour of Ceylon in May–June 1934 see the Sahitya Akademi *Tagore Centenary Volume*, p. 496 and Kripalani's biography of Tagore, 2nd edition, p. 402. The performances of *Shapmochan* by the dancers and singers of Santiniketan were much appreciated.

[4] Was Tagore perhaps hoping that Ocampo could be his impresario in Paris in this field, just as she had introduced his drawings and paintings to Paris viewers four years ago?

[5] The photograph was apparently sent by sea mail, while the letter itself was sent by air mail. The envelope in which the letter travelled bears the added inscription (which could be in somebody else's hand): The photo is being sent by ordinary mail.

[6] This word is in Bengali script.

49. Ocampo to Tagore

[This letter is written on the notepaper of *Sur,* bearing the printed address: Calle Viamonte N. 548, Buenos Aires.]

[Buenos Aires]

Dear Gurudev—

I have been thinking so much about you and wishing I could see you.
Kalidas Nag & Mrs. Sophia Wadia were here for P.E.N. Club.[1] And I can[']t hear about India or meet Indian people without thinking of you because you are & always will be India to me. Love from

Victoria
Octobre[2] 3/36

❧

[1] Mrs. Sophia Wadia (1901–1986) was the official delegate from the Bombay P.E.N. Centre and Nag was the official delegate from the Calcutta P.E.N. Centre at the International P.E.N. Congress held at Buenos Aires in 1936. It had been hoped that the conference would be an amicable gathering of intellectuals from different parts of the world, but against the backdrop of growing fascism and the Spanish Civil War just beginning, it turned out to be rather different: The P.E.N. Club meeting was explosive. It contained leading fascists like the former Futurist Filippo Marinetti and the poet Giuseppe Ungaretti; victims of German racist policies, like the Austrian Stefan Zweig and the German Emil Ludwig (who would later be published in *Sur*), and liberal French writers such as Maritain, Jules Romains and Benjamin Crémieux, who was of Jewish origin. Marinetti publicly attacked Ocampo and there were many confused and heated debates. The intellectuals of *Sur* were faced not with a universal brotherhood of like-minded writers, but with the bitter consequences of a world torn and divided' (John King, *Sur and Argentine Culture, 1931–1970,* Oxford University doctoral thesis, 1982, p. 114.) There are also some pertinent reminiscences about the conference in José Bianco's essay 'Victoria', published in the Mexican magazine *Vuelta* (no. 53, vol. 5, April 1981, pp. 4–6). Bianco recalls that as the exchanges between Marinetti and Ocampo got sharper and sharper, the official Indian delegate tried to mediate between them, the delegate being 'a very pretty woman, with a red dot between the eyebrows, who always turned up decked out in very luxurious saris'. This must have been Mrs. Wadia. Apparently she exhorted the delegates in theatrical French to keep calm and refrain from being harsh to each other.

[2] This hastily written word *could* be interpreted as 'October', but knowing the ways of Ocampo's English spelling, I am more inclined to interpret it as I have presented it (the French form).

50. Tagore to Ocampo

[This letter, written on the notepaper of Uttarayan, was posted from Santiniketan; there is an envelope at Buenos Aires, directed to the Viamonte address of Ocampo's magazine and bearing a Santiniketan postmark of 20 October 1936.]

[Santiniketan] 19/10/36

Dear Vijaya

Very sweet of you to remember me. Dr Kalidas Nag came to see me when he was about to leave for Argentina and I felt a real grievance against your people for not asking me to come. I assure you I would have responded at once if they had done it.

Let me still cherish the hope of finding the chance to cross the sea and meet you once again before my days are over. Love from

Rabindranath

Tagore to Ocampo

[This is the only letter of Tagore to Ocampo of which I have not seen the original. When I was at Buenos Aires, this letter was missing from its place in the file where Tagore's letters are kept, though the matching envelope was there. The letter had apparently been mislaid and could not be located. I hope it will be located one day; until then the xeroxed copy preserved in the Rabindra Bhavana archives is the closest semblance. Written on the note paper of Uttarayan, the letter was addressed to Ocampo's Paris address of 31 Rue Raynouard etc. and sent by air mail from Santiniketan on 15 March 1939.]

[Santiniketan] 14/3/39

Dear Vijaya

How often I feel that your nearness which once was so untram[m]elled and close, now that it has receded into a hopeless distance[,] has come poignantly closer to me, its gifts disclosing value that teases the mind by its rarity. Unfortunately the paths that accidentally had reached some preciousness can never be retraced and when the heart longs to own it back[, it] realises that it is lost for ever. The picture of that building near the great river where you housed us in strange surroundings with its cactus beds that lent their grotesque gestures to the atmosphere of an exotic remoteness, often comes to my vision with an invitation from across an impossible barrier. There are some experiences which are like treasure islands detached from the continent of the immediate life, their charts ever remaining vaguely deciphered—and my Argentine episode is one of them. Possibly you know that the memory of those sunny days and tender care has been encircled by some of my verses—the best of their kind—the fugitives are made captive, and they will remain[,] I am sure, though unvisited by you, separated by an alien language.[1]

With dearest love
Rabindranath Tagore

[This is a selective collection. Any reference to documents cited in the foot-notes refers to the original source below.]

From Ketaki Kushari Dyson [*In Your Blossoming Flower-Garden: Rabindranath Tagore and Victoria Ocampo* (New Delhi: Sahitya Akademi, 1988)]

[1] Note that Tagore has not answered a single query of Ocampo's. He says nothing about writing for *Sur*, going to a religious congress in Paris, the differences between Gandhi and himself—or the visit from the Sieyes couple that never mate-rialized. He talks only about the original encounter between Ocampo and himself in Argentina, which he now sees like one looks at a great work of art in a gallery, framed, precious, and full of meanings. And he concludes by triumphantly reiterat-ing the artist's confidence in his own art, in his own poems in which he has immor-talized that encounter, though written in a language not accessible to the woman who inspired them (a circumstance scarcely relevant to a poet). Like Shakespeare he hopes that 'in black ink' his love 'may still shine bright', and hopes also perhaps that 'thou in this shall find thy monument,/ When tyrants' crests and tombs of brass are spent.' (See Shakespeare's sonnets nos. LXV and CVII.)

To Indira Devi Chaudhurani, Sarojini Naidu, Maria Montessori and Margaret Sanger

1. To Indira Devi Chaudhurani (Tagore)

[Though he was born and brought up in Calcutta, and earned his initial celebrity there, Rabindranath never liked the city. As he grew older, and Calcutta itself became larger and more commercial, his antipathy turned to detestation and he spent less and less time there. In the early 1920s, he wrote:

Calcutta is an upstart town with no depth of sentiment in her face and in her manners. It may truly be said about her genesis: In the beginning was the spirit of the Shop, which uttered through its megaphone, 'Let there be the Office!' and there was Calcutta. She brought with her no dower of distinction, no majesty of noble or romantic origin; she never gathered around her any great historical associations, any annals of brave sufferings, or memory of mighty deeds.[1]

This letter shows Tagore's dislike of Calcutta in an amusing and novel form, a dream, but incorporating a favourite preoccupation of his: education. He had a low opinion of all the educational institutions of

[1] *Creative Unity* (London, 1922), p. 116.

Calcutta—and indeed Bengal as a whole—having himself attended several of them, including St Xavier's College.²]

Shahzadpur, [Rajshahi, Bangladesh]
[June 1891]

[Bibi/Bob?]

Last night I had an extraordinary dream. The whole of Calcutta was enveloped by some formidable but peculiar power, the houses rendered only dimly visible by a dense dark mist, through which strange doings could be glimpsed. I was on my way down Park Street in a hackney carriage, and as I passed St Xavier's College I found it to be growing rapidly with its top fast vanishing into darkness and fog. I came to know that a band of men had come to town who could, if properly paid, perform many such magical tricks. When I reached our house at Jorasanko, I found the magicians had got there too. They were ugly-looking fellows, Mongolian in features, with wispy moustaches and a few long hairs sticking out of their chins. They had the power to make people, as well as houses, grow. All the ladies in our house were keen to become taller, and the magicians sprinkled some powder on their heads and they promptly shot up. I could only mutter: 'This is most extraordinary—just like a dream!' Then someone proposed that our house should be made to expand. Our visitors agreed, and as preparation they quickly demolished some portions. Dismantling done, they demanded money, or else they would not go on. Kunja Sarkar [the cashier] was aghast; how could payment be made before the job was completed? The magicians became wild. They twisted the building into a stupendous tangle, so that half of some occupants was set into the brickwork and the other half was left sticking out. It was a diabolical business. I said to my eldest brother: 'Just look at the mess we're in. We'd better start praying to God for help!' I went into the corridor and concentrated on praying. When I had finished I thought I would go and reprimand these creatures in the name of the God—but though my heart was bursting, no words came out of my throat. Then I woke up—I am not sure when. A curious dream, wasn't it? Calcutta entirely under the control of Satan: everything in it inflating tremendously in size and prosperity with his help, while enveloped in an infernal fog.

² RT attended St Xavier's for two-and-a-half months in 1875, an experience he describes in *My Reminiscences,* pp. 84–6/*RR*, XVII, pp. 328–9.

One aspect was rather funny: with the whole city to choose from, why single out the Jesuit college for special satanic attention?...

The schoolmasters of the English school in Shahzadpur paid me a courtesy call yesterday. They showed no sign of leaving, even though I could not find a word to say. Every five minutes or so I managed a question, to which they offered the briefest of replies; and then I sat like a dunce, twirling my pen and scratching my head. At last I ventured a query about the crops, but being schoolmasters they knew nothing of this subject whatsoever. About their pupils I had already asked everything I could think of, so I had to start over again: 'How many boys had they in the school?' One said eighty, another a hundred and seventy-five. I hoped that this might provoke an argument, but no, they settled their difference. Why, an hour and a half later, they should have decided to take their leave, is hard to know. They might just as well have gone an hour earlier or, for that matter, twelve hours later. They seemed not to follow any rule but to rely on blind fate.

[Uncle Rabi?]

Source: MS copy at Rabindra Bhavan, Shantiniketan; letter published in *CPB*, pp. 51–53.

2. To Indira Devi Chaudhurani (Tagore)

[As a short-story writer (and indeed as a painter), Tagore has a particular gift for portraying women. One of his most touching stories, 'Shamapti' ('The Conclusion'), was based on the village girl he describes in this letter. As he reminisced to an Indian interviewer in 1936:]

She was quite wild and extraordinary. There was nobody to restrain her freedom. She used to watch me every day from a distance and sometimes she brought a child with her and with finger pointed towards me she used to show me to the child. Day after day she came. Then one day she didn't come. That day I overheard the talk of the village women who had come to fetch water from the river. They were discussing with anxiety about the fate of that girl, who was now to go to her mother-in-law's house. 'She is quite wild. She doesn't know how to behave. What will happen to her!' they said. The next day I saw a small boat on the river. The poor girl was forced to go aboard. The whole scene was full of sadness and pathos. One of her girl companions was shedding tears stealthily, while others were persuading and encouraging her not to be afraid. The boat disappeared. It gave me the setting for a story named 'The End'.[1]

Shahzadpur, [Rajshahi, Bangladesh]
4 July 1891

[Bibi/Bob?]

There is a boat moored at our ghat, and on the bank in front of it is a crowd of village women… It looks as if someone is going to embark and the others have come to see her off. Infants, veiled faces and grey hairs are all present together in large number. One girl attracts my attention more than the rest. She must be twelve or so, but the fullness of her figure could let her pass for fourteen or fifteen. Her face is fine—very dark, yet very pretty—and her hair is cropped like a boy's; it goes well with her simple, frank and alert expression. She holds a child in her arms and stands staring at me with unabashed curiosity and certainly no lack of candour or intelligence in her eyes… In fact her entire face and body are pleasing to look at, as if they contained not a hint of silliness, crookedness or imperfection. Her half-boyish, half-girlish look is singularly appealing, a novel blend that combines an air of unconscious independence with feminine sweetness. That such women existed in the villages of Bengal I had never imagined, Apparently none of her family is much troubled by bashfulness. One of them has let her hair down and stands in the sun combing out the knots with her fingers while conversing with another on board at the top of her voice. I learn that she has only this daughter, no son, and that the girl is a dimwit who doesn't know how to behave or talk or even the difference between family and strangers…

---

[1] 'Discourse on short stories', *Forward*, Calcutta, 23 Feb. 1936 (interview in Shantiniketan with a group of visiting writers). According to Naresh Chandra Chakravarty of Shahzadpur, the girl was the daughter of a well-known local businessman, Gopal Shaha (Paul, *Rabijibani*, III, p. 279). 'Shamapti' ('The Conclusion') was published some two years after this letter in *Sadhana*, Ashwin–Kartik 1300 [Oct.–Dec. 1893]; a recent translation appears in *Selected Short Stories* (Krishna Dutta and Mary Lago trans.; London, 1991), pp. 80–102. Satyajit Ray filmed the story in 1961, with Aparna Das Gupta (later Aparna Sen), as the tomboy Mrinmayi, acting in her first film role.

I learn, too, that because her husband Gopal's son-in-law has turned out badly, now this daughter doesn't want to go to him.

At last, when it is time to start, I see my short-cropped, plump-bodied, gold-bangled damsel with the guileless radiant face being led towards the boat with much commotion; but she refuses to get on board. With a great deal of effort, they eventually cajole her into the boat. I grasp that she is being returned from her parents' to her husband's home. As the boat casts off, each woman and girl stands on the ghat following it with her gaze, one or two slowly wiping their eyes with the loose end of their saris. A small girl with her hair tightly knotted clings to the neck of an older woman and quietly, weeps on her shoulder. Perhaps she has just lost a darling *didimani* who joined her in playing with dolls and also cuffed her when she was naughty.[2] The morning sun and the riverbank seem deeply melancholic. The whole morning feels bereft of hope like the sound of a mournful ragini, and the world, for all its beauty, seems full of pain to me... The life history of this unknown girl has become intimately familiar.

The floating away of a boat on a stream adds pathos to the moment of farewell—it is so like death. Those who watch wipe their eyes and return to their lives, while the one who floats away becomes invisible. True, the grief wears off, perhaps sooner than we expect, the feeling is transitory, while the forgetting is permanent. But if we pause for an instant, we can see that it is the pain that is real, and not the oblivion. Separation and death remind man clearly from time to time that grief is terribly true. They make us aware that we can remain untroubled only by remaining ignorant; that anxiety and grief are the world's true realities. No one lives on, nothing survives—so stark is this truth that we humans suppress our realisation of it, along with our grief—and if and when we do call it to mind, it deeply perplexes us that not only do we ourselves not live on, neither do we live on in the minds of others. We are totally obliterated from both the outer and the inner world. There cannot be any music suitable for man's condition, whether now or eternally, except the mournful raginis of our country.

[Uncle Rabi?]

Source: MS copy at Rabindra Bhavan, Shantiniketan; letter published in *CPB*, pp. 53–55.

---

[2] *Didimani*: literally, 'jewel of an elder sister'.

3. To Sarojini Naidu (Chattopadhyay)

[In late November 1933, Sarojini Naidu organised a Tagore week in Bombay, with performances of his plays by the students of Shantiniketan and an exhibition of his paintings in the town hall. His previous visits to Bombay had not been particularly fruitful, but this was a success, because of the inimitable charm of his hostess. Although she had long since given up poetry for politics, she remained poetic in her approach to politics, which appealed to Tagore, and was close to many of the Congress leaders; thus she was an ideal conduit for Rabindranath into the public life of Bombay.

This letter was by way of a thank you to Naidu, before Tagore left Bombay.]

Esplanade House, Waudby Road, Bombay, (India]
3 December 1933

Dear Sarojini,

You are great. Once I thought that you were as frivolous as I am. I still hope I was not wrong—but there is another side of your character, and I repeat once again that you are great. You have helped me as none else could have done but what is still more important to me is that I have come close to you and known you. You have amazing gifts which would have made me envious but I have loved you and that has saved me. I am afraid my language sounds absurdly sentimental, but I do not care. I expose myself to your delightful laughter, for I know it cannot be unkind to me. Please do not doubt my sincerity when I say that from this trip I carry back the memory of an experience which will be precious to me.

Ever yours,

Rabindranath Tagore

Source: MS copy at Rabindra Bhavan, Shantiniketan; letter published in *VBN.*

4. To Maria Montessori

[Tagore first came in contact with Maria Montessori, the Italian educator, on his American tour in 1916. Ten years later, she wrote to him to enquire of the potential for the Montessori system in India: 'I feel that your people have achieved a higher degree of capability for feeling and sentiment than the Europeans, and I am certain that my ideas which are founded only on love for the children would find a good welcome in the hearts of the Indian people'.

Rabindranath, a great admirer of Montessori, responds in kind.]

Santiniketan, [West Bengal, India]
3 February 1926

Dear Dr Maria Montessori

I read with much pleasure your last letter for which I express to you my sincere thanks. As far as I know, the Montessori method is widely read and studied not only in some of the big cities of India but also in out of the way places; the method is, however, not so extensively followed in practice largely owing to the handicap imposed by the officialised system of education prevalent in the country. The enthusiasm and admiration felt for your work have induced a few private individuals of means to institute small experiments which are conducted with success on lines recommended by you.

With all good wishes,
Yours very sincerely

Rabindranath Tagore

Source: MS copy at Rabindra Bhavan, Shantiniketan.

5. To Margaret Sanger[1]

[In August 1925, Tagore received a letter from Margaret Sanger, the American pioneer of the birth control movement. Mahatma Gandhi had just issued a statement in *Young India* supporting birth control but opposing artificial methods: Sanger hoped that Tagore would counter this with his own statement. 'You have travelled all over this earth, and you have observed the joys and sorrows and miseries of the world, and we take it for granted that with your international outlook on life and human society you cannot but feel friendly towards birth control.'[2] Tagore's reply, which follows, was printed in Sanger's *Birth Control Review,* with her editorial comment: 'Rabindranath Tagore has placed himself on the opposite side from the great ascetic.']

Santiniketan, [West Bengal, India]
30 September 1925

Dear Margaret Sanger

I am of opinion that the birth control movement is a great movement not only because it will save women from enforced and undesirable maternity, but because it will help the cause of peace by lessening the number of surplus population of a country, scrambling for food and space outside its own rightful limits. In a hunger-stricken country like India it is a cruel crime thoughtlessly to bring more children into existence than could properly be taken care of, causing endless sufferings to them and imposing a degrading condition upon the whole family. It is evident that the utter helplessness of a growing poverty very rarely acts as a check controlling the burden of overpopulation. It proves that in this case nature's urging gets the better of the severe warning that comes from the providence of civilised social life. Therefore, I believe, that to wait till the moral sense of man becomes a great deal more powerful than it is now and till then to allow countless generations of children to suffer privations and ultimately death for no fault of their own is a great social injustice which should not

---

[1] Margaret Sanger (1879–1966): founder of the birth control movement in the USA. She visited RT at Shantiniketan in Dec. 1935.
[2] Sanger to RT, 12 Aug. 1925, *VBQ, 1,* 1985, p. 13.

be tolerated. I feel grateful for the cause you have made your own and for which you have suffered.[3]

I am eagerly waiting for the literature that has been sent to me according to your letter and I have asked our secretary to send you our Visva-Bharati journal in exchange for your *Birth Control Review*.[4]

Sincerely yours,

Rabindranath Tagore

Source: MS copy at Rabindra Bhavan, Shantiniketan; letter published in *Birth Control Review,* Dec. 1925.

From Krishna Dutta and Andrew Robinson, eds, *Selected letters of Rabindranath Tagore* (Cambridge: Cambridge University Press, 1997).

[3] Leonard Elmhirst provided RT with books by Havelock Ellis, Marie Stopes and Margaret Sanger in Argentina in 1924. 'He is going to try and introduce the idea [of birth control] in our own dispensary and among his own women folk as a beginning' (Elmhirst to Dorothy Straight, 25 Dec. 1924 [Dartington]).

[4] RT meant *Visva-Bharati Quarterly,* which Sanger had requested in her letter.

From Gitanjali

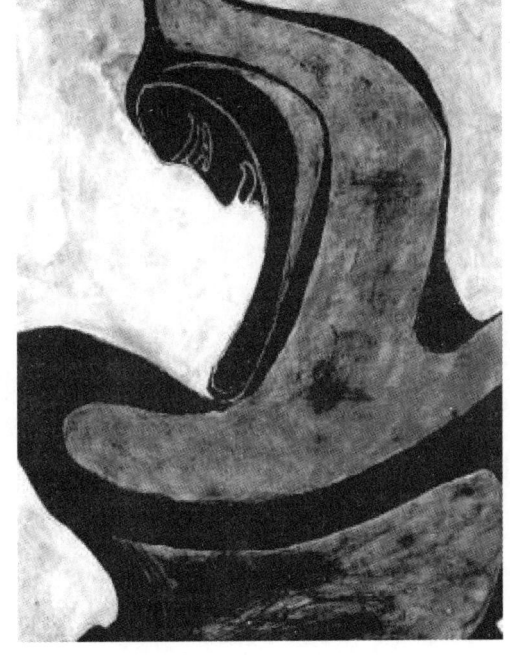

8

The child who is decked with prince's robes and who has jewelled chains round his neck loses all pleasure in his play; his dress hampers him at every step.

In fear that it may be frayed, or stained with dust he keeps himself from the world, and is afraid even to move.

Mother, it is no gain, thy bondage of finery, if it keep one shut off from the healthful dust of the earth, if it rob one of the right of entrance to the great fair of common human life.

41

Where dost thou stand behind them all, my lover, hiding thyself in the shadows? They push thee and pass thee by on the dusty road, taking thee for naught. I wait here weary hours spreading my offerings for thee, while passers by come and take my flowers, one by one, and my basket is nearly empty.

The morning time is past, and the noon. In the shade of evening my eyes are drowsy with sleep. Men going home glance at me and smile and fill me with shame. I sit like a beggar maid, drawing my skirt over my face, and when they ask me, what it is I want, I drop my eyes and answer them not.

Oh, how, indeed, could I tell them that for thee I wait, and that thou hast promised to come. How could I utter for shame that I keep for my dowry this poverty. Ah, I hug this pride in the secret of my heart.

I sit on the grass and gaze upon the sky and dream of the sudden splendour of thy coming—all the lights ablaze, golden pennons flying over thy car, and they at the roadside standing agape, when they see thee come down from thy seat to raise me from the dust, and set at thy side this ragged beggar girl a-tremble with shame and pride, like a creeper in a summer breeze.

But time glides on and still no sound of the wheels of thy chariot. Many a procession passes by with noise and shouts and glamour of glory. Is it only thou who wouldst stand in the shadow silent and behind them all? And only I who would wait and weep and wear out my heart in vain longing?

52

I thought I should ask of thee but I dared not the rose wreath thou hadst on thy neck. Thus I waited for the morning, when thou didst depart, to find a few fragments on the bed. And like a beggar I searched in the dawn only for a stray petal or two.

Ah me, what is it I find? What token left of thy love? It is no flower, no spices, no vase of perfumed water. It is thy mighty sword, flashing as a flame, heavy as a bolt of thunder. The young light of morning comes through the window and spreads itself upon thy bed. The morning bird twitters and asks, 'Woman, what hast thou got?' No, it is no flower, nor spices, nor vase of perfumed water it is thy dreadful sword.

I sit and muse in wonder, what gift is this of thine. I can find no place where to hide it. I am ashamed to wear it, frail as I am, and it hurts me when I press it to my bosom. Yet shall I bear in my heart this honour of the burden of pain, this gift of thine.

From now there shall be no fear left for me in this world, and thou shalt be victorious in all my strife. Thou hast left death for my companion and I shall crown him with my life. Thy sword is with me to cut asunder my bonds, and there shall be no fear left for me in the world.

From now I leave off all petty decorations. Lord of my heart, no more shall there be for me waiting and weeping in corners, no more coyness and sweetness of demeanour. Thou hast given me thy sword for adornment. No more doll's decorations for me!

64

On the slope of the desolate river among tall grasses I asked her, 'Maiden, where do you go shading your lamp with your mantle? My house is all dark and lonesome—lend me your light!' She raised her dark eyes for a moment and looked at my face through the dusk. 'I have come to the river,' she said, 'to float my lamp on the stream when the daylight wanes in the west.' I stood alone among tall grasses and watched the timid flame of her lamp uselessly drifting in the tide.

In the silence of gathering night I asked her, 'Maiden, your lights are all lit—then where do you go with your lamp? My house is all dark and lonesome,—lend me your light.' She raised her dark eyes on my face and stood for a moment doubtful. 'I have come,' she said at last, 'to dedicate my lamp to the sky.' I stood and watched her light uselessly burning in the void.

In the moonless gloom of midnight I asked her, 'Maiden, what is your quest holding the lamp near your heart? My house is all dark and lonesome,—lend me your light.' She stopped for a minute and thought and gazed at my face in the dark. 'I have brought my light,' she said, 'to join the carnival of lamps.' I stood and watched her little lamp uselessly lost among lights.

66

She who ever had remained in the depth of my being, in the twilight of gleams and of glimpses; she who never opened her veils in the morning light, will be my last gift to thee, my God, folded in my final song.

Words have wooed yet failed to win her; persuasion has stretched to her its eager arms in vain.

I have roamed from country to country keeping her in the core of my heart, and around her have risen and fallen the growth and decay of my life.

Over my thoughts and actions, my slumbers and dreams, she reigned yet dwelled alone and apart. Many a man knocked at my door and asked for her and turned away in despair.

There was none in the world who ever saw her face to face, and she remained in her loneliness waiting for thy recognition.

87

In desperate hope I go and search for her in all the comers of my room; I find her not.

My house is small and what once has gone from it can never be regained.

But infinite is thy mansion, my lord, and seeking her I have come to thy door.

I stand under the golden canopy of thine evening sky and I lift my eager eyes to thy face.

I have come to the brink of eternity from which nothing can vanish—no hope, no happiness, no vision of a face seen through tears.

Oh, dip my emptied life into that ocean, plunge it into the deepest fullness. Let me for once feel that lost sweet touch in the allness of the universe.

From *The English writings of Rabindranath Tagore* (New Delhi: Sahitya Akademi, 2004).

Poems

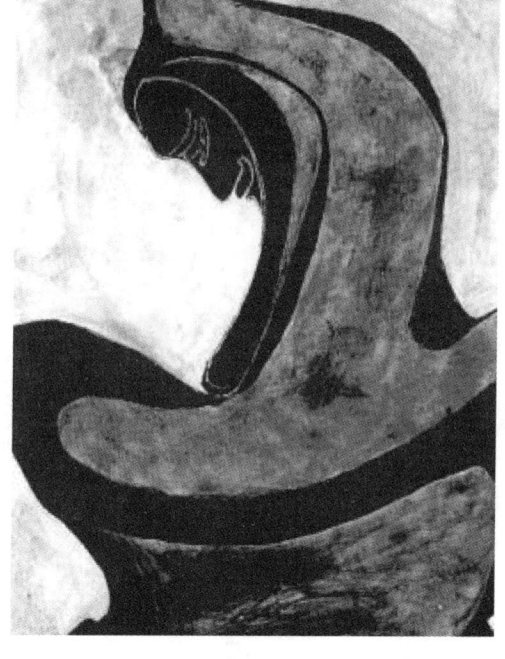

Bodily union
(*Deher milan*)

My being in every part yearns for yours
The hearts' union beckons the union of our bodies.
My possessed self, overcome by desire
Yearns to cover you with passion.
Towards you, my eyes turn
My lips wish to melt into your lips.
My thirsty heart cries out piteously
Asking to adore you with all its senses.
The heart hidden in the lake of the body,
Sorrowfully calls to the shores of life.
Today let my desperate senses caress you,
Let me lose myself in the mysteries of the body.
Allow my body and soul at all times
To merge, unite, with all parts of you.

Translated by **Malashri Lal**

Woman unclothed
(*Bibashana*)

Cast off your clothing, remove the sari-end
Wear only the ornament of your nude self
Like a nymph divine, draped in light.
Your body in full bloom, tender,
A carnival of life in youth and sweetness.
Stand proudly alone in this wondrous world.
Let moonlight caress every crevice of your body
Let gentle breeze play with your curves.
Surrender to the infinite blue
Like the stars, nude in nature.
The God of Love may hide his face amid clothing
Seeing unclothed your splendid body.
Let gentle dawn approach the human world
See unabashed, unclothed body in its pristine purity.

Translated by **Malashri Lal**

Breasts
(*Staun*)

Woman's love is gentle and tender
Blossoming in youth in spring-time

Unfolded in space; with fragrance
Turning mad the impatient heart.
Her soul's softness, rising in ripples,
Overflows the banks of desire.
What call of the flute
Beckons her bashful heart to manifest in the world of love,
Stopping, startled, in the realm of light,
Shyly veiling herself with the sari-end?
The music of love lies ripe within
Heaving and falling to the pulse beat.
Behold the lotus-seat of mother Lakshmi,
Behold the sanctum of a woman's heart.

2

This indeed is the sacred Sumeru
A golden mountain, haunt of the Gods;
The good woman's breast, with heavenly wonder
Has brought glory to the human world.
The infant sun rises at dawn from this mount,
The tired sun in the evening sets there,
The gods that stay awake through the night
Reside in its unblemished twin peaks;
Its nectar flowing from the source of eternal love
Nourishes the lips of the world.
Watching over a calmly sleeping earth
Gathering the unending faith of a helpless world
From the earth, touching the heavens,
This is the refuge of Man, the child of God.

Translated by **Malashri Lal**

The kiss
(*Chumban*)

The language of lips is coded at the corners,
Twin hearts partaking of each other.
Leaving home in unbounded love
Their pilgrimage ends in the confluence of a kiss.
Twin waves rise to the rules of love
They break and unite in the lips.
In wild longing they desire each other
The body's limits tested in their touch.
Songs of love are cast in gentle alphabets
Punctuated by the trembling of a kiss.
With flowers plucked from the boughs of the lips
String a garland at home, together.
This is the sweet union of two pairs of lips
This is the smiling hue of a bridal bed.

Translated by **Malashri Lal**

Elder sister
(*Didi*)

Hacking away the mud by the riverbed,
Are workers from the west, trying to build a kiln.
Their little girl runs often to the shore,

Laden with utensils, plates, bowls
To scour them a hundred times. Her bangles ringing against the brass vessels
She scurries all day.
Her tiny brother, shaven head, mud-spattered, naked,
Like a pet animal, follows her,
Waits further at the sister's command,
Patiently. A full pitcher on her head,
Brass vessels in her left hand, trudges the girl
Pulling the child with her other hand.
She is the eternal mother,
Weighed with work, she is the little girl, the aged little sister.

Translated by **Malashri Lal**

Dream
(*Swapna*)

A long, long way away
in a dream-world, in the city of Ujjain,
by River Shipra I once went to find
my first love
from a previous life of mine.

Lodhra-pollen on her face,
dalliance-lotus in her hand,
kunda-buds perched on her ears,
kurubaks pinned to her hair;
on her slim body
a red cloth waist-knot-bound;
ankle-bells making a
faint ringing sound.

On a spring day
I wandered far,
figuring out my way.

In the Shiva-temple
in solemn tones just then
the evening service
began to resound.
Above the empty
shopping arcades gleamed
on darkened buildings
the last of the evening sun.

At last I reached
by a narrow winding road
my love's house,
secluded and remote.

Conch-shell and wheel were
painted on her door.
On either side stood a
young kadamba tree—
growing like sons.
A carved lion,
majestic and proud,
sat above the white
columns of the gate.

All her pet doves
returned to their dovecot.
Her peacock slept,
perched on a golden rod.
At such a time
a lighted lamp in her hand,
slowly, slowly
my Malavika came down.

She appeared outside the door,
above the stairs,
like a goddess of evening

holding the evening star.
Her saffron-scented limbs
and incensed hair
shed all over me
gusts of their restless breath.
Her drapery, slightly slipped,
by chance revealed
tracery of sandal
painted on her left breast.

Like a statue she stood
in that quiet evening
when the humming city was mute.
Seeing me, my love
slowly, ever so slowly
put her lamp down,
came before me,
put her hand in mine,
and without words
asked with her tender eyes,
'Hope you're well, my friend?'

I looked at her face,
tried to speak,
but found no words.
That language was lost to us:
we tried so hard
to recall each other's name,
but couldn't remember.

We thought so hard
as we gazed at each other,
and the tears streamed from
our unflickering eyes.

We thought so hard
by that door
beneath a tree!
And I don't know when
under what pretext

her soft hand slid into my
right hand like a bird
of evening seeking its nest,
and slowly her face
like a drooping lotus
came to rest on my breast.

Keen with yearning,
they mingled quietly—
her breath and my breath.

Night's darkness swallowed
the city of Ujjain.
The wild wind blew out
the lamp left by the door.
In the Shiva-temple
on River Shipra's bank
the evening service
came to an abrupt end.

Translated by **Ketaki Kushari Dyson** [*I Won't Let You Go: Selected Poems of Rabindranath Tagore* (Penguin India, 2010)]

When the ocean of creation
(*Kon kshane srijaner samudramanthane*)

When the ocean of Creation was churned,
Rose two women,
Leaving their repose beneath the fathomless deep.
What moment was that?

One was Urvashi, the charming,
Empress of the world of desires,
The nymph celestial.
The auspicious Lakshmi was the other,
The mother of the world, no doubt,
The Goddess divine.

One disrupts penance;
Filling the wine-glass of spring
With the flaming sap of laughter,
She steals our hearts,
And to the tune of sleepless youth,
Disperses them with both hands
Over the efflorescent trance of spring,
Over *palashes* and roses painted red.

The other restores you,
To desires drenched in tearful dew,
To the wholeness of the fruitful, golden peace
Of the dewy season.
Her elegance unwavering,
Tinged with the nectar of smile benign,
Harks you back
To the benison of the macrocosm.
Gently traces your path
Back to the holy confluence of life and death,
The sacred abode of the Infinite.

Translated by **Soham Pain**

Freedom
(*Mukti*)

Let the doctor say what he wants,
Do keep the windows open
Near my bedside—let the breeze touch my body
Medicines?—My days of having medicines are over
Bitter, strong, I have had so many medicines in my life
Through so many days, from time to time
To remain alive, seems to be a disease;
So much *ayurveda* and *mustiyoga*
But a little carelessness, terrible results.
This is good, this is bad, having to obey everything what others say
With downcast eyes and veiled head
I have spent twenty-two years in your house
That's why both at home and without
Everyone says I am *Lakshmi, Sati*
An extremely good woman!

I had come into this family as a nine-year-old girl
Since then I have been pacing the long corridor of this family
Living according to the desires of others, I have dragged on
Till I have reached the end of the road.
My happiness and sorrow
There was no time to think about those.
Whether this life is good or bad, or something else
When could I understand that, or think about the past or future.

In a tired monotonous strain
The wheels of labour keep on turning
For twenty-two years I have been tied to that same wheel
Blinded and dazed by the turns
I don't know who I am, I don't know about this vast earth
What meaning it may contain

I haven't heard the messages of men
That resonates in the strings of the *veena* of the timeless universe. I just know
To cook and then to eat, and again to eat and then to cook
For twenty-two years I have been tied to the same wheel.
I now feel that wheel—seems almost to have stopped;
Let it stop. Why medicines again?

For twenty-two years the spring season visited the forest floor
The fragrant intoxicating southern breeze
Swayed the hearts of the earth and waters;
Spring yelled out, 'Open, open the doors'
But truly when spring would come and go I just did not know
Perhaps secretly my heart
Was swayed by springtime; perhaps as I did my work within the home
Suddenly it would cause me to make mistakes; perhaps my soul resonated
With the pain of previous births; oblivious of reason, in sorrow or joy
Perhaps my soul awaited eagerly someone's footsteps
In the bewildering springtime.
You would return from office, then during the evenings
You would go out to play chess in the locality.
No point thinking about all that
Why is it that today I feel such momentous longings in my heart?

This is the first time after twenty-two years
That spring has entered my room
As I look through the window at the sky
Happiness rises in my heart every moment—
I am a woman, I am a queen
My song is twined with the veena of the moonbeams of the sleepless moon
Without me the rising of the evening star would be of no use
The blossoming of flowers in the garden would be of no use too.

For twenty-two years
I felt imprisoned infinitely within your house, yet I was not sad about that
My days were spent with an inert mind, if I live longer this will just go on
All my relatives praise me as Lakshmi
In this life it seems this is my greatest glory—
To be praised by others as I remain in a corner of the house!
Today at last

When I am free of all these chains
Life and death have united in the immense limitless ocean
Where is it that disappears
The walls of the kitchen storehouse
Like surf on the waters.

At last it seems for the first time the strains
Of a wedding flute are heard between the earth and sky
Wasted has been my twenty-two years in the room's dusty corner
The one who has beckoned me to the marital death bed
He awaits me at the door as a supplicant, he is not just an owner
He will never ignore me.
He desires from me
The deep and secret nectar that lies within me
In the midst of the planets and stars
He gazes at my face with steadfast eyes
Sweet world, I am a sweet woman
Sweet death, O my eternal beggar!
Open, open the door
Let me drift away from the hopeless twenty-two years into the sea of infinity.

Translated by **Sanjukta Dasgupta**

Getting lost
(*Hariye jaoa*)

My little daughter
As she heard her friends calling her
She went down the steps to the ground floor
As it was dark, she took frightened hesitant steps downwards

I was on the terrace
In a spring night with a sky full of stars
Suddenly hearing my daughter's cry
I rushed to find out—
As she was going down the stairs
The wind had blown off the light of her lamp
I asked, 'What's the matter, Bami?'
She cried out from below. 'I am lost'

In the spring night with a sky full of stars
I went back to the terrace again
As I looked at the sky I felt
There too was a girl like my Bami
She was trying to protect with her blue sari-end
The light of her lamp as she walked slowly, alone
If abruptly the light had been snuffed out, if it had stopped all of a sudden
The entire sky would have resonated with her cry, 'I am lost'.

Translated by **Sanjukta Dasgupta**

Remembering
(*Mone pora*)

I cannot remember my mother,
only sometimes in the midst of my play
a tune seems to hover over my playthings,
the tune of some song that she used to
hum while rocking my cradle.

I cannot remember my mother,
but when in the early autumn morning
the smell of the *shiuli*[1] flowers floats in the air,
the scent of the morning service in the
temple comes to me as the scent
of my mother.

I cannot remember my mother,
only when from my bedroom window
I send my eyes into the blue of the distant sky,
I feel that the stillness of my mother's
gaze on my face
has spread all over the sky.

Translated by **Uma Dasgupta** [*My life in my words*
(Penguin Books India, 2006)]

Last spring
(*Shesh basanta*, from *Purabi*)

Before the day passes away
This my hope to fulfilment bring,
Let us for this once together go
Gathering the flowers of Spring.
April will come to your garden time and again,
From you I would beseech only one of them.

Daytime has gone in vain,
I didn't heed so long,

---

[1] A fragrant autumnal flower.

In a flash in the evening light
I see in your eyes my time is gone.
And so like a miser, hesitant and eager, I count
My last days of the end of Spring, one by one.
Have no fear, in your flowering garden
Needless I will not linger, and when
Bidding farewell at the end of day
I will not cast a look behind.

I will not look to your eyes hoping for
pitiful tears
To keep the memory green for ever in
my mind.

Do not turn away, listen, O listen,
The sun hasn't yet gone down;
There is yet time, and time to elude
You need have no apprehension.
Let the afternoon glow fall from behind
the leaves
On your dark hair and let it for some time
more glisten.

Laugh a sweet and loud laughter
In an unkind and causeless cheer
Startling the timid here
On the wild bank of the lake with fear.
I will not remind you of your forgotten troth,
And make your fleeting feet go slower.

Go away thereafter, with hasty tread
Trampling the fallen leaves,
When homing birds with meaningless chatter
Disturb the evening's peace.
Far away in the dusk darkened by the bamboo
grove shade

With the dying twilight music your figure will
fade.

When the night will darken
Take your seat on the window sill;
For ever I will leave, down the path below
And beloved, we will not meet again.
Throw away the Mallika garland strung
together at dawn,
That will be your caressing touch, that will be
your farewell song.

Translated by **Charu Chowdhury**
[*Purabi: The east in its feminine gender* (London: Seagull Books, 2007)]

The image
(*Chhabi*, from *Balaka*)

Are you only an image, only on canvas
painted?
Those far off nebulae
That crowd into their nest in the sky,
Those pilgrims unto the dark—

Journeying day and night, with torches
of light,
Are you not as real as they are?
An image only are you?

Why do you stand still among all forever
moving?
Join the travellers, you who has no road
to travel.

Why do you keep so far aloof
Behind a curtain of stillness eternal
From all among whom forever you live?
Its grey scarf fluttering, the dust rides on
the wind;
In summer it strips the widowed earth of all
her jewels
And clothes her with ascetic's saffron robe,
And in Springtime dawn when she meets her
lord,
It adorns her limbs in designs of flowers and
leaves.

This dust—even this dust is real
And this grass—suppliant before the universe;
No rest they know and so real are they all.
But you are still, you are painted,
Alas, only an image are you.

Once along this road, you walked by our side,
Your bosom heaved with your breath,
And in every limb of yours
In many a dance and many a song
Your soul did create new and fresh rhythms of
its own
In tune with the rhythm of the spheres.

Alas, how long ago it was!
How real were you in my life and in
my vision!
It was you who painted the world around in
my eyes

In forms of rapture, in tints of grace.
And on that dawn,
It was you in whom the song of this universe
Was incarnate.

Travelling together along the road,
You stepped aside behind the veil of night;

And thereafter, in happiness and in sorrow
I move on and on, forever.

Ebb and tide of dark and light flow in the sea
of the sky,
On either side the road, in silent steps,
Flowers march on in pageants of
brilliant colours,
And jingling the music of death,
The wild spring of life rushes on in
thousand streams.
The call of the unknown takes me from far
to far;
I am enthralled by the love of the road,
But you stand still just where you
stepped aside,
Beyond the moon and the sun and the stars,
Beyond them all, painted you are,
And only an image are you.

What empty words of the poet are these?
Only an image are you?
No, no, you are not a mere image.
Who says you are still,
Who says you are imprisoned within bonds
of lines
In silenced moaning?

If your joy had come to an end,
The river would have lost its flow and lost
its waves
And the cloud would have shed its golden hue;
If the shade of your lustrous hair
Had been lost from this universe,
Then, long long ago, the shade of the
Madhabi copse
Swaying and murmuring in the restless wind
Would have been a thing of dream.

Did I forget you?
You have taken abode at the root of my life,
And so I forget.
Unmindful I go along the road,
Did I not forget the flowers, do I not forget
the stars?
Yet, they sweeten the breath of my life,

And fill with music the forgetful void.
Not to remember is not—to forget,
For, from the heart of oblivion
You have sent a quiver through my blood.
You are not before my eyes,
It is within their depth that you live.
And so, today, you are the green of the
green earth,
And the blue of the blue sky,
And in you my world has found its heart's
desire.
I do not know and nobody knows—
It is your music that I sing in my songs
And it is you who is the poet in the
poet's mind.
Not a likeness, not a painting,
Not a mere image are you.

I gained you one distant morning
And then in the night you I lost;
And since, in darkness and unseen,
It is you whom I ever and ever regain.
Not a painting you are, not an image are you.

Translated by **Charu Chowdhury**
[*Purabi: The east in its feminine gender* (London: Seagull Books, 2007)]

The guest
(*Atithi*)

My days of sojourn have you filled, woman,
With nectar sweet; how easily you made your own,
A distant traveller; just as in the evening sky, with ease,
Stars unknown from the heavens with their placid tender smiles
Greeted me; at these desolate casements
When I stood alone and gazed at the southern sky
A voice of light in harmonious note from above struck deep in my heart.
A voice profound said, 'We know you, know you well.
From the bosom of darkness, the earth took you over to her own.
Our guest you are, the eternal guest of the realm of the bright.'
You glanced at my face like those stars, auspicious woman,
And in a similar voice did say, 'I know you, know you well.'
I know not the language you speak, but your music have I heard,
'Poet, you are the guest of love, the eternal guest of mine'.

Translated by **Soham Pain**

Woman empowered
(*Sabala*)

Why should you not let woman empowered be
With right to conquer her own destiny,

O Lord?
Why must I sit and watch beside the road
With lowered head, in tired patient wait
For the day ordained by fate
To grant my hopes? Why should I gaze in space?
Why should I not by my own powers trace
Fulfillment's path?
My questing chariot why should I not drive forth,
Checking the turbulent horses with firm rein?
Why should I not win
With faith invincible
From the fortress of the inaccessible
The prize of my endeavor, with my life
Staked in dire strife?

Robed as a bride, I will not make my way
To the wedding-chamber, ankle bells at play:
Make me fearless with the valor of love.
One day I shall receive
The wedding-garland from a hero's hand:
Will that holy hour not extend
Beyond one solitary dim twilight?
I will not let him once forget
My lustrous rigor: no abject
Submission is worthy of his respect.
I will put by
The cloak of my weak-spirited modesty.
I shall meet him beside the raging sea:
The breakers' roar will fling the call of victory
At our union, to the horizon's breast.
My veil aside I'll cast
And say to him, 'In heaven or on earth,
You alone are mine.' The ocean birds
Will raise a roar, flailing the west wind in their flight
As they surmise their track by the Seven Sages' light.

Leave me speechless, O Lord:
I hear a furious veena playing in my blood.

When I have scaled life's most exalted hour,
From my voice let there shower
Life's finest utterance
Pouring down unrestrained.
And what I cannot in my words impart,
Let my love apprehend within his heart.
If then my time should cease,
In the still sea of silence let that flow find peace.

Translated by **Sukanta Chaudhuri**
[Fakrul Alam and Radha Chakravarty, ed.,
The essential Tagore (Santiniketan: Visva-Bharati, 2011)]

Ordinary woman
(*Sadharan meye*)

I am a woman, stuck indoors.
You wouldn't know me.
I've read your latest novel, *Saratbabu.*
'It's a garland of withered flowers.'
Your heroine Elokeshi was in a trance
at the age of thirty-five.
She had some sort of competition with twenty-five year olds,
no, you are generous indeed;
you made her the winner.

Let me speak about myself.
I am young in age.
The fancy of my green years
touched someone's heart.
My body used to shiver at that thought—

I forgot I was a very ordinary woman.
There are millions of women like me
with the enchantment of their youth.

I beseech you!
Please write a story about an ordinary woman.
She is very unhappy.
If there is something uncommon buried
in the depth of her nature,
how can she prove or
even how many are there who can recognise it?
The fancy of tender age is in their eyes.
Not seeking the real
we sell ourselves for the price of a mirage.
Let me tell why I am saying this.

Let us assume that his name is Naresh.
He said that he hadn't seen anyone like me.
I don't have the courage to believe such a grand statement
nor do I have the strength not to.

He went to England at some point in time.
Sometimes I get his letters.
I say to myself, for goodness sakes, so many women are there!
A crowd of them, pushing and shoving!
And how extraordinary they are,
so intelligent and so bright!
Have all of them discovered one Naresh Sen
whose particulars were buried among many in his country?
In his last mail he wrote that
he had gone with Lizzie for a swim in the ocean.
He quoted a few lines from a poem of a *Bengali poet*
where Urbashi, the heavenly nymph, rises from the ocean.
Then they sat, side by side, on the sand;
before them was the rocking of the waves of the blue sea,
the sky was flooded with bright sunshine.
Lizzie whispered into his ears,
'You came only the other day and you'll go away in a while;
two shells of an oyster
let the inside be filled with a solid drop of tear—

rare, priceless.'
What an extraordinary way of speaking!
Along with that Naresh wrote,
'It is not wrong even if the words be made up,
but beautiful—
A golden flower studded with diamonds is not real, yet isn't it so.'
Surely you can understand,
the hint of a simile in the letter jabbed me
close to my heart declaring—
I am a very ordinary woman.

I have no treasure to pay in full
the value of the invaluable.
Well, let it be so.
Let me be indebted all my life.
I humbly entreat you. Please write a story, Saratbabu,
about an utterly ordinary woman—
The unfortunate one who has to compete from a distance
with at least five or seven extraordinary women—
in other words competing with *seven goddesses*.
I know that my luck has run out
and I have been beaten.
But make the woman about whom you are going to write
victorious on my behalf.
Let my chest puff up while reading
and may all the glory come to your pen.
You may name her Malati.
That is my name.
But there is no chance of finding her identity.
There are so many Malatis like this in Bengal
and they are all ordinary women.
They don't know the French or the German.
They know only to feel sorry for themselves.

How you'll make her victorious.
Generous is your heart, all powerful is your pen.
You will probably be inclined to lead her into the path
of sacrifice,
into extreme sorrow, like *Shakuntala*.
Please have pity on me.

Come down to my level.
Lying in my bed in the darkness of night,
the unattainable boon that I seek from the gods
I'll not get that boon.
But let your heroine get it.
Why don't you keep Naresh in London for seven years,
let him flunk his exams again and again,
let his circle of admirers treat him tenderly.
Meanwhile let Malati get her M.A.,
from the Calcutta University.
Let her stand first in Mathematics with a stroke of your pen.
But if you stop there
your fame as the king of king-storytellers will be sullied.
Whatever may be my situation
don't stifle your imagination!

You are not close-fisted like God.
Send the poor woman to Europe.
All the learned, the scholars, the heroes there,
the poets, the artists and the monarchs—
let them crowd around her in droves.
Like astronomers let them discover her
not only as a scholar but also as a woman.
The world conquering magic that is in her,
let its mystery be evident, not in the *land of the ignorant*
but in the land of the connoisseurs, the appreciative
and where there are the English, the Germans and the French.
To honour Malati let meetings be arranged,
meetings of people with big name and fame.
Let us assume that flattering praises are being showered on her in
buckets,
she is moving around unaffected
like a sailboat gliding over the waves.
Gazing at her eyes they are whispering among themselves.
Everyone is saying the water laden dark cloud and bright
sunshine of India
have come together in her enchanting eyes.
(Let me say it aside,
the Creator's grace really fell on my eyes.
This had to come out from my own lips.

As my luck would have it
I haven't yet met any European connoisseur.)
Let Naresh stand in a corner
and his bevy of extraordinary admirers.
And after that?
After that my paltry crop withered in drought.
An end came to my dream. Alas ordinary woman!
Alas God's wasted power!

Translated by **Jadu Saha** [*Rabindranath Tagore: Images of women*
(New Delhi: Shipra Publications, 2004)]

Santhal girl
(*Saontal meye*)

The *santhal* girl, walks the pebbled path
Under the *shimool* tree, back and forth.
A coarse saree warps her taut, dark body.
Some strange god's design for a dark bird
Drew upon July clouds and a lightening streak
To become this woman.
Wings concealed within her, she walks and glides, unknowingly,
Her wrists encircled in red and white lacquer bangles.

On her head is a basket of mud,
Her red bordered saree like *palash* blooms stretched towards the sky.
Winter wanes, the northern wind is tempered by the west.
Himjhuri branches glow in the last light of a winter sun.
Eagles carouse in a limpid blue sky.
Amloki fruits drop from the trees

Teased by groups of playful boys.
Whirlwinds stir up dead leaves on the half lit winding pathways,
And the fat cheeked geckos lie silently in the bush.

The santhal girl, walks the pebbled path
On her head is a basket of mud.

My fanciful mud house has its foundation, its walls
Being built by the hired workers under the blazing sun.
Sometimes I hear a flute in the quiet midday
I hear temple bells when evening comes.

With shame I wonder
At this woman who is labouring for my house
With her body, her soul, her simple energy,
Her womanly strength which could be better used
In her own home caring for her loved ones.
Shamefully I have put her to work,
Stolen her valued self
With a bit of wealth.
The santhal girl, walks the pebbled path
On her head is a basket of mud.

Translated by **Malashri Lal**

The earth
(*Prithibi*)

Earth, accept my homage today,
At the end of my days, this last bow, at the altar of my Life.

Full of vigour, you are solicited by the valiant.
Ever the paradox, you are both gentle and harsh—
In your nature blends the essence of man and woman,
Baffling mankind with torturous, conflicting emotions.
    With one hand you pour the nectar,
      You shatter the vessel with the other.
You reverberate your playground with ironic laughter.
You make life unbearable for the brave who deserve a life that is noble.
You make virtue difficult to attain, forgive not the forgivable—
In your verdant landscape, you conceal the struggle of every moment.
In fruits, flowers and grains its laurel of victory becomes evident.
In this land and in this water—your theatre of merciless war—
    Death proclaims the triumph of Life.
Upon the foundation of your brutality rises civilization's portal of victory.
    Where the price of a blunder is the total destruction.

In the primordial stage of history, the might of the demon was invincible.
    He was fierce; he was savage; he was ignorant;
      His fingers were callous, devoid of skill.
With club, with mallet, he went on a rampage, destroying all—
    From the vast oceans to the mighty mountains.
Churning up a nightmare of fire and smoke, he darkened the sky.
    In the empire of the inanimate, he was the emperor.
Towards all living beings he was suspicious and blind with envy.

Then arrived God—chanted the *mantras* to tame the demon.
    The arrogance of the brute was subdued.
Spreading a green carpet the Creator seated himself.
Dawn arrived on the mountain peaks in the eastern horizon.
On the western shore, dusk descended, spreading a divine peace.

    The shackled demon was humbled.
But the primal savage still has its grip on your history.
    Suddenly he turns harmony into chaos.
From the dark hole of your primitive inclination,
    Without a warning he slithers out.
His madness still runs through your veins.
Chantings of God's *mantras*, resonating, murmuring, day and night,
    Fill up the firmament, the forests, the wind.

Still, from the deep and dark corner of your heart, ever so often,
    That half-tamed demonic serpent keeps raising its hood,
        Driving you to wound your own creatures,
           To devastate your own Creation.

At the feet of this Creation, founded on good and evil,
    In a tribute to your grace and glory,
I shall leave behind my lacerated life's last prayer.
    The grand Life, the august Death,
      That lies hidden beneath your soil,
Today I embrace it, feel it, with all of my body and soul.
    Innumerable bodies, through countless ages,
      Lie lost and scattered in its dust.
I too shall leave behind a few handfuls of dust—
The last remains of all my sorrow and happiness.
I shall leave behind my name, my form, my whole existence
In this all-devouring silent heap of dust.

      Firmly bound, the besieged Earth,
    Into the mystique cloud, the fading Earth.

In the austere silence of the mountains, the meditative Earth,
On the ceaseless waves of the blue oceans, the murmuring Earth—
In prosperity, you are glorious, in poverty you are fierce.
On the one side, your fertile land is laden with golden grains
Where the morning sun daily wipes away the dew drops
    With his scarf of shimmering rays;
And the setting sun, on the rippling corn fields,
Leaves behind an unspoken message,
        'I am pleased'.
On the other side, in your arid, barren, terror-stricken desert land,
Amidst the scattered skeletons, is the ghostly dance of the mirage.

      I have seen,
In the month of *Baishakh*, your storm, like a huge black hawk,
    Swooping down to snatch the horizon
    Pierced with its beak of lightening—
The entire sky roared like a lion heaving with anger.
Under the lashing of its tail, the spreading tree in despair,

With branches swinging in a frenzy,
Came crashing down into the dust.
Borne by the wind, flew the roof of a broken hut,
Like an imprisoned dacoit breaking free of its shackles.

I have seen,
Again in the season of spring, your feverish southern breeze,
Blending with the scent of the mango flowers
The sighing whispers of love's longings;
The heady celestial wine, bubbling over,
Filling up the golden bowl of the moon;
The gentle rustling trees, losing patience
With the daring breeze, suddenly throwing the forest in a turmoil,

You are gentle, you are fierce, ancient and yet eternally young.
From the holy primal fire of Creation you had emerged
At that first dawn, beyond countless years.
Along the elliptical path of your journey, you scattered
The meaningless remnants of many fragments of history.
Without pain, you have spread your abandoned creations
In the layered terrains of oblivion.
Cradling Life, you have reared us
In your small little compartments of measured time—
Within that is the limit of all play, end of all activities.

Today I stand before you with no alluring illusions.
Through all these years, the garland I sat down to string.
With the days and the nights,
For it, I shall not lay any claim to immortality.
On your journey around the Sun through billions of years,
The multitude of moments that keep folding and unfolding,
In a small portion of it, to any of its callings
If I have been true,
In any one of the worthy missions of Life
If I have won, through extreme suffering,
Then, with a bit of your soil, anoint my brow
With the mark of victory.
That mark will fade away at night

When all marks of distinction merge with Life's ultimate mystery.
O indifferent Earth
Before I am forgotten forever,
At your merciless feet,
I leave behind—my last bow.

Translated by **Joyasree Mukerji**

Songs

She sits by the window

(O janalar kachhe boshe)

She sits by the window
cheek resting on one hand.
Her lap is strewn with bakul flowers;
her garland lies unwoven.

Soft breezes swish and rustle past
her half reclining form.
What do they whisper in her ear?
What words unheard? What flitting thoughts?
With them she spends the live long day
her garland lying unwoven.

Clouds glide before her dewy eyes;
Birds go winging by.
All day long the falling blooms
waft gently on a sigh.

Sweet languor wraps her slender form;
a drowsy indolence...
a honeyed smile plays on her lips
that speaks of distant dreams;

of a heart in which a secret flute
plays a wondrous symphony.

Translated by **Aruna Chakravarti**
[*Songs of Tagore rendered into English* (Bombay: Vaitalik, 1984)]

Friend, dear friend
(*Olo sai*)

Friend, dear friend!
I wish I could pour out like you
The thoughts that vex my soul.
Legs stretched out in a corner;
now laughing, now weeping,
now staring at the floor.

Friend, dear friend!
Streams of words flow from your lips.
Why am I so bereft?
What can I share? With whom and when?
What pain? What joy? What inmost hopes?
I long to speak as you do, friend.
But no words come to me.

Friend, dear friend!
So much there is that you speak of.
Where lies the source I wonder!
I sit alone as dusk descends
Wallowing in my tears.

And if one asks wherefore I weep
I have no answer why.

Translated by **Aruna Chakravarti**
[*Songs of Tagore rendered into English* (Bombay: Vaitalik, 1984)]

The sky resounds to our mother's call
(*Amra milechhi aj mayer dake*)

The sky resounds to our Mother's call
'Come my children!'

From far and near, her sons, together
we come, hearts trembling in ecstasy.
Can brothers be as if they were strangers
when the voice of the Mother is heard in the land?

Scattered though we are in our own little worlds
our hearts are tied with a single cord
which pulls us together despite all striving
in mutual agony; a common bond.

We have wiped our tears away for ever,
deemed humiliation a thing of the past;
a new hope filling our swelling breasts
seeing brother stand by his brother's side.

Aeons have passed in patient striving
and today we assemble in masses.

Come let us join hands oh! sons of the land
and shout back in answer, 'We come!'.

Translated by **Aruna Chakravarti**
[*Songs of Tagore rendered into English* (Bombay: Vaitalik, 1984)]

Whosoever may abandon you
(Je tomay chaare chharuk)

Whosoever may abandon you, but I'll never abandon you, O Mother
Your feet—
O Mother, I'll ever remember your feet, I'll not care for any other,
O Mother
Who says that you have a poor house, precious gems are in your heart—
I know, I know their worth, I'll never fall for the care of others
Aspiring towards fame, let them wildly roam foreign lands—
Your tattered rug is spread out, I'll never be able to forget it O Mother!
Wealth, fame, attraction for others may try to lure me away—
O Mother, fear haunts my mind, but I'll never be defeated by others,
O Mother.

Translated by **Sanjukta Dasgupta**

Mother, will you send your own son
(*Ma, ki tui porer dware pathabi*)

Mother, will you send your own son to a stranger's land?
They neglect, hurl stones, when they see the beggar's sack
I have lowered my head, following behind the person
If in case he does carelessly give something—
But shall I roam like this giving up my own mother's largesse
That I am powerless is a grave lie
Their powerful missiles haven't yet killed me
Our own strength, our own devotion we will unfurl at your feet
I'll take and do with whatever you may have in your home
Just spread your *anchal* as always—
Our dignity lies there, our life lies there too, we pour out our hearts there
as well.

Translated by **Sanjukta Dasgupta**

O auspicious bride
(*Sumangali badhu*)

O auspicious bride, gather in your heart the nectar of love
Stay true in affection, stay steady in austerity,
In joy and sorrow keep a smile upon your lips

Overcome all hurt with infinite patience, oh.
Heed the voice of wisdom and good sense,
May your compassion and care spread peace everywhere
Bring forgiveness as a virtue in your home
May vanity of possessions never destroy your soul.
Know that destiny mocks the trickeries of wealth,
Let not your eyes be fooled by the sandstorms that come your way,
O auspicious bride.

Translated by **Malashri Lal**

Krishnakali
(*Krishnakali*)

Krishnakali I call her,
Whom others in the village call dark.
In a cloudy, cloud covered field,
I saw the dark woman's deer-dark eyes.
Her head wasn't veiled,
And her hair unplaited fanned upon her back.
Dark? However dark she may be,
Her deer-dark eyes have I seen.

Seeing the day darkened by those clouds,
Two dusky cows began calling.
The dark girl came with brisk steps
From her hut, at their bidding.
Lifting her twin brows to the sky

For a moment, she heard the rumbling of the clouds.
Dark? However dark she may be,
Her deer-dark eyes have I seen.

A sudden gust of eastern wind,
Went wavering over the paddy fields.
I stood alone by the dike,
None else there in the field.
Whether she cast a glance at me,
Only I know, or knows she.
Dark? However dark she may be,
Her deer-dark eyes have I seen.

Like this, clouds collyrium-dark
In *jaishthya*, cluster in the north-eastern sky
And, likewise, deep tender shadows,
Descend on the *tamal* forests in *ashadh*.
And in this cycle, on a *srabon* night,
A sudden shaft of joy is felt in the heart.
Dark? However dark she may be,
Her deer- dark eyes have I seen.

Krishnakali I call her,
Let others call her what they will.
In a field at *Moynapara* had I seen,
The deer-dark eyes of that dark girl.
She hid not her head beneath a veil,
And had no reason to be shy.
Dark? However dark she may be,
Her deer-dark eyes have I seen.

Translated by **Soham Pain**

I am Chitrangada
(*Ami Chitrāngada rājendro nondini*)

I am Chitrangada, I am the king's daughter
Not a goddess, nor an ordinary woman
Worshipping me and placing me on a pedestal, that is not me, not me,
Neglecting me and keeping me behind, that is not me, not me,
If you keep me by your side in crisis and in wealth
If you allow me to stand by you in all hardship and strife
You will come to know me truly
Today I merely make this submission—
I am Chitrangada, the king's daughter.

Translated by **Reba Som**
[*Rabindranath Tagore: The singer and his song* (Delhi: Viking, 2009)]

She who dwelt in secret
(*Ei sharat alo-r kamol bane*)

She who dwelt in secret, in the depths of my soul,
reveals herself in this clear autumn light
and walks abroad in the wilderness of lilies.

In the golden rays of the dawn
her bracelets make sweet tinkle,
and her veil, fluttering in the breeze,
chequers the earth with light and shadow.

Caught by the scent of her flowing hair
the languishing wind in the *shiuli* grove
lies, fainting under the trees.
Within, she makes my heart sway in my breast,
the world without is caught in her spell,
when she opens her eyes
and gazes upon the blue, blue sky.

Translated by **Aruna Chakravarti**
[*Songs of Tagore rendered into English* (Bombay: Vaitalik, 1984)]

Epics and Mythology

A vision of India's history[1]

When individual communities, who come to dwell in the same neighbour-hood, differ from each other in race and culture the first attempts at unity become too obviously mechanical in their classified compartments. Some system of adjustment is needed in all kinds of Society, but in order that a system should be successful it must completely submit itself to the principle of life and become the organ for the vital functions.

The history of India has been the history of the struggle between the constructive spirit of the machine, which seeks the cadence of order and conformity in social organization, and the creative spirit of man, which seeks freedom and love for its self-expression. We have to watch and see if the latter is still living in India; and also whether the former offers its service and hospitality to life, through which its system can be vitalized.

We know not who were the heroes of the day when the racial strife between Aryan and non-Aryan was at its height. The significant fact is that the names of such conquering heroes have not been sung in Indian epic. It may be that an episode of that race war in India lies enshrouded in the mythical version of King Janamejaya's ruthless serpent sacrifice—the attempted extermination of the entire Nāga race. There is, however, no special glorification of that king on this account. But he who strove to bring about the reconciliation between Aryan and non-Aryan is worshipped to this day as an Avatar.

[1] All the translations of the verses from the *Bhagavad-Gītā* are in the words of Annie Besant.

As the leading figures of the grand movement of that age, which sought to embrace both Aryan and non-Aryan in a larger synthesis, we find the names of three Kshatriyas standing out in the story of the Rāmāyana. There Janaka, Visvāmitra and Rāma-chandra are not merely related by bonds of kinship or affection, but through oneness of ideal. What if it be possible that Janaka, Visvāmitra and Rāma may not have been contemporaries as a matter of historical fact? That does not take away from their nearness to one another in the plane of idea. Viewed from the standpoint of intervening space, the distance between the earth and the moon may loom large, and tend to obscure the fact of their relationship. There are many double stars in the firmament of history, whose distance from each other does not affect the truth of their brotherhood. We know, from the suggestion thrown out by the poet of Rāmāyana, that Janaka, Visvāmitra and Rāma, even if actually separated by time, were nevertheless members of such a triple system.

In the history of idea, as distinguished from the history of fact, a hero often comes to mean, for his race, the *ideal;* and ceases to be an individual. In Aryan history, Janaka and Visvāmitra as well as Rāma have become historical symbols. They are composite pictures of numerous personalities having a common purpose. Just as King Arthur, from the Christendom of the Dark Ages, represents the Christian Knight, the valiant champion of the faith against all challengers, so in India we get glimpses of the Kshātra ideal gathering round its champions for a determined and prolonged crusade against its opponents. Proofs are not wanting that often these opponents were the Brahmins.

The idea, which was behind the neo-Kshatriya movement of old, cannot be known to-day in its full meaning, but still it is possible to make out the lines along which the divergence of Brahmin and Kshatriya had occurred.

The four-headed god Brahmā represents the four Vedas with all their hymns and regulations of sacrifice. The Brahmin Bhrigu, one of the most renowned priests of the ancient days, is said to have sprung from the heart of Brahmā, thereby showing that he occupied a prominent part in the cult of Vedic ceremonialism. It is said in the Bhāgavata Purāna that the Kshatriya king, Kārtavīrya, stole a sacrificial cow from Yamadagni, a priest of the same Bhrigu clan, which was the cause of the class-war led by Parasu-rāma, the son of Yamadagni, against the whole Kshatriya community. Unless the stealing of the sacrificial cow stands for an idea, such a crusade of the Brahmin against the entire Kshatriya class misses its meaning. It really indicates that among a great body of Kshatriyas there arose a spirit of resistance against sacrificial rites, and this gave rise to a fierce conflict between the two communities.

It has to be noted that the series of battles begun by Parasu-rāma, the descendant of Bhrigu, at last came to their end with his defeat at the hands of Rāma-chandra. This Kshatriya hero, as we all know, is accepted and adored as an incarnation of Vishnu, the deity of the monotheistic sect of Bhāgavatas. It certainly means that this fight was a fight of ideals, which terminated in the triumph of the religion in which, at a later date, Rāma-chandra occupied a central place.

It is well known that Rāma had an intimate relationship with the great king Janaka, which also we consider to be a relationship of ideals. Janaka has won from the people of India the tide of Rājarshi, the kingly prophet. It has been said about him in the Bhagavad-Gītā:

कर्मणैव हि संसिद्धि आस्थिता जनकादयः।

The *Bhagavad-Gītā*, 3/20

Janaka and others of his kind have attained their fulfilment through the performance of duty. This means that Janaka, and others who had the same faith as he, followed the path of moral action for attaining spiritual perfection. This was specially mentioned because it was not the path of the orthodox religion, which laid stress on ceremonials performed for the sake of averting injuries or acquiring merit or wealth. It was evidently a revolutionary movement, one of whose leaders was Janaka, and Rāma-chandra obtained his inspiration from him. Therefore when we find that it was the Kshatriya Rāma-chandra who defeated the Brahmin Parasu-rāma, we feel certain that the battle which was fought was the battle of two differing ideals.

Those institutions which are static in their nature raise their fixed walls of division. This is why, in the history of religions, priesthood has everywhere hindered the freedom of man and maintained dissensions. The moving principle of life unites. It deals with the varied, and seeks unity in order to be able to deal truly. The Brahmins, who had the static ideals of Society in their charge, spun into elaboration the different forms of ritualism and set up sectarian barriers between clans and classes. Of the two original deities of the Indo-Aryan tribe, the Sun and Fire, the latter specially represented the cult of Brahmins. Round it different forms of sacrifice gathered and grew in number, accompanied by strict rules of incantation; with it came to be intimately associated the pluralism of divinity, since fire had always been made the vehicle of oblation to numerous gods.

The Kshatriyas, on the other hand, as they sallied forth in their endeavour against all obstacles, natural and human, developed in their life the principle which was for expansion and inclusion. Born and bred amidst the clash of forces, hostile and favourable, in the field of life's strenuous conflict, the superfine complexities of the external forms of religious worship could have no special significance for them. With them the Sun-god seems to have a special connection. From him, Manu, the law giver who was a Kshatriya, and also the great kingly line of Raghu, to which belonged Rāma-chandra, are said to have sprung. This Sun-god, in course of time, developed into the personal god Vishnu, the god of the Bhāgavata sect, the god who principally belonged to the Kshatriyas.

From Brahmā's four mouths had issued the four Vedas, revealed for all time, jealously sealed against outsiders, as unchanging as the passive features of Brahmā himself rapt in meditation. This was the symbol of Brahmanism, placid and immutable, profoundly filled with the mystery of knowledge. But the four active arms of Vishnu were busy, proclaiming the sway of the Good; expanding the cycle of unity; maintaining the reign of law; supporting the spirit of beauty and plenitude. All the symbols carried by Vishnu have the different aspects of Kshatriya life for their significance.

Brahma-vidyā, the knowledge of Supreme Truth, had its origin in the seclusion of the primeval forest of India, where the human mind could intensely concentrate itself in the depth of things and the reality of spiritual existence. The world must acknowledge its debt to the contemplative Indo-Aryan for this profound vision of truth which he has revealed to man. This Brahma-vidyā in India has followed two different courses. In the one, the Supreme Soul is viewed as monistic, absolutely negating the phenomenal world; in the other as dualistic in creative imagination, yet one in essence. Unless duality is admitted there can be no worship; but, if at the same time, fundamental unity be not recognized, the worship cannot be intimate and loving.

The original gods of the Vedas were separate from man; they received worship which consisted only of external ceremony, not the homage of love. When the relationship between God and man came to be known as based on their spiritual unity, then only the worship of love became possible. That is how the mystic Brahma-vidyā brought in its train the Religion of Love, of which the god was Vishnu. There is no doubt that the religion of love had its origin, or at least its principal support, among Kshatriyas whose freedom of movement had the effect of liberating their minds from the coils of established forms of sacrifice.

That, naturally, there was a period of struggle between the cult of ritualism supported by the Brahmins, and the religion of love, is evident. The mark of the Brahmin Bhrigu's kick, which Vishnu carries on his breast, is a myth-relic of the original conflict. In the fact that Krishna, a Kshatriya, was not only at the head of the Vaishnava cult, but the object of its worship, that in his teaching, as inculcated in the Bhagavad-Gītā, there are hints of detraction against Vedic verses, we find a proof that this cult was developed by the Kshatriyas. Another proof is found in the fact that the two non-mythical human avatars of Vishnu, Krishna and Rāma-chandra, were both Kshatriyas, and the Vaishnava religion of love was spread by the teaching of the one and the life of the other.

The ideal, which was supported by the Kshatriya opponents of the priest-hood, is represented by the Bhagavad-Gītā. It was spoken to the Kshatriya hero Arjuna, by the Kshatriya prophet Krishna. The doctrine of Yoga which it advocates—the doctrine of the disinterested concentration of life, with all its thoughts and deeds, in the Supreme Being—had its tradition, according to Krishna, along the line of the Rājarshis, the kingly prophets. He says:

एवं परम्पराप्तमिमं राजर्षयो विदुः।
स कालेनेह महता योगो नष्टः परन्तप।।

The *Bhagavad-Gītā*, 4/2.

This, handed on down the line, the king-sages knew. This Yoga, by great efflux of time, decayed in the world, O Parantapa.

That this religion of Yoga, as revived by Krishna and inculcated in the Bhagavad-Gītā, was not in harmony with Vedic scriptures is directly affirmed by the Master in his teaching to his disciple Arjuna when he says:

श्रुतिविप्रतिपन्ना ते यदा स्थास्यति निश्चला।
समाधावचला बुद्धिस्तदा योगमवास्यसि।।

The *Bhagavad-Gītā*, 2/53

When thy mind, bewildered by the scriptures, shall stand immovable in contemplation, then shalt thou attain unto Yoga.

Krishna undoubtedly takes his stand against the traditional cult of sac-rificial ceremonies, which according to him distracts our minds from the unity of realization when he speaks thus:

यामिमां पुष्पितां वाचं प्रवदन्त्यविपश्चितः।
वेदवादरताः पार्थ नान्यदस्तीतिवादिनः।।
कामात्मानः स्वर्गपरा जन्मकर्मफलप्रदाम्।
क्रियाविशेषबहुलां भोगैश्वर्यगतिं प्रति।।

भोगैश्वर्यप्रसक्तानां तयानहृतचेतसाम् ।
व्यवसायात्मिका बुद्धिः समाधौ न विधीयते । ।²

The *Bhagavad-Gītā*, 2/42–44.

The flowery speech that the unwise utter, O Partha, clinging to the word of the Veda, saying there is nothing else, ensouled by desire and longing after heaven, the speech that offereth only rebirth as the ultimate fruit of action, that is full of recommendations to various rites for the sake of gaining enjoyments and sovereignty—the thoughts of those misled by that speech cleaving to pleasures and lordship, not being inspired with resolution, is not engaged in contemplation.

These words are evidently of him, who in his teachings has for his opponents the orthodox multitude, the believers in Vedic texts.

The Kurukshetra war, described in the Māhābhārata, was a war between two parties, one of which had rejected Krishna, the other consisting of his followers, guided by him in the war. The motive of this conflict, which had attracted all the great ruling powers of that age into one or other of the two opposing parties, could not have been a mere scramble for land between cousins. In this latter version of the epic the fact is suppressed that it was an unorthodox religious movement, acknowledging Krishna to be its prophet, that gave rise to the most desperate fight in the ancient ages in India. The very fact that Krishna was the charioteer of Arjuna is proof enough that it was a war of rival creeds; and for that very reason the battle ground of Kurukshetra has ever remained a sacred spot of pilgrimage.

It is significant to note that the lives of great Brahmins of the olden times, like that of Yājñavalkya, have the association of intellectual profundity and spiritual achievement, while those of great Kshatriyas represent ethical magnanimity which has love for its guiding principle. It is also significant that the people of India, though entertaining deep veneration for the Brahmin sages, instinctively ascribe divine inspiration to the Kshatriya heroes who actively realized high moral ideals in their personalities. Parasurāma, the only historical personage belonging to the Brahmin caste who has been given a place in the list of avatars, has never found a seat in the hearts of the people. This shows that, according to India, the mission of divine power in this country is to bring reconciliation, through moral influence, between races that are different—never to acquire dominance over others through physical prowess and military skill.

The most important aspect of Rāma-chandra's life, which has made the Vaishnava accept him as the incarnation of divine love, has been missed by the current version of the Rāmāyana. There he is depicted merely as an ideal son, brother and husband, a paragon of the domestic virtues, a king who holds that cultivation of popularity is a duty higher than doing justice in the teeth of clamorous disapprobation. I have no doubt that the real story of his life, which has become dim in the course of time and with the growth of conventionalism, is concerned with his sympathy for the despised races, his love for the lowly; and that this made him the ideal of the primitive people whose totem was Hanumān.

The religion represented by the third human avatar of Vishnu, who is Buddha, has in it the same moral quality which we find in the life and teaching of Rāma and Krishna. It clearly shows the tendency of the Kshātra ideal with its freedom and courage of intellect, and above all its heart, comprehensive in sympathy, generous in self-sacrifice.

Foreign critics are too often ready to misread the conservative spirit of India, putting it down as the trade artifice of an interested priestcraft. But they forget that there was no racial difference between Brahmin and Kshatriya. These merely represented two different natural functions of the body politic, which, though from the outside presenting the appearance of antagonism, have as a matter of fact co-operated in the evolution of Indian history. Sowing seed in one's own land and reaping the harvest for distant markets are apparently contradictory. The seed-sowers naturally cling to the soil which they cultivate, while the distributors of the harvest develop a different mentality, being always on the move. The Brahmins were the guardians of the seed of culture in ancient India and the Kshatriyas strove to put into wide use the harvest of wisdom. The principle of stability and the principle of movement, though they depend upon each other for their truth, are, in human affairs, apt to lose their balance and come into fierce conflict. Yet these conflicts, as meteorology tells us in the physical plane, have the effect of purifying the atmosphere and restoring its equilibrium. In fact, perfect balance in these opposing forces would lead to deadlock in creation. Life moves in the cadence of constant adjustment of opposites; it is a perpetual process of reconciliation of contradictions.

The divergence of ideals between the Brahmins, dwellers in the forest, and the Kshatriyas, founders of cities, often led to prolonged fights, a fact which is revealed by the story of the struggle between Vasishtha and Visvāmitra. The Brahmins were not all on one side, nor the Kshatriyas all on the other. Many Kshatriyas espoused the Brahmin cause. We are told how the Brahmanic *Vidyās* as personified in the form of three maidens outraged by Visvāmitra were sore distressed, and how the chivalrous Kshatriya

King, Harischandra, came to their rescue, losing his all for their sake. Then again, Krishna in the course of his endeavour to liberate the Kshatriya victims from a dread ceremonial, slew King Jarāsandha with the help of the Pāndava braves. This Jarāsandha, himself a Kshatriya, was on the other side and had defeated and imprisoned many Kshatriya kings. Krishna and the Pāndavas had to disguise themselves as Brahmins in order to gain entrance within the walls of his stronghold. Many other legends bear this out. The spiritual movement started by Krishna had something in it which went against the orthodox forms of worship. This is further hinted at by the legend, belonging to a later period, of his taking the part of the Ābhiras against their persecution by Indra, the king of the Vedic gods, and preventing the devastation of the pasture land, Govardhana, held by that tribe.

Anyhow, it is abundantly clear that the ideals represented by Krishna had divided the Aryan community into two rival camps. When King Yudhishthira, as overlord, summoned a Rājasūya Yagña in order to heal those dissensions, King Sisupāla tried to wreck the proceedings by publicly insulting Krishna, the acknowledgment of whose precedence over all assembled Brahmins and Kshatriyas was the object of that great conclave. The main motive behind the devastating Kurukshetra war was this very internal strife within the community—the party which opposed Krishna being generalled by Drona, the famous Brahmin warrior, with his kinsmen Kripa and Asvatthāmā. It is a notable fact that Drona himself was a disciple of Parasu-rāma; and Karna, one of the most important fighters who stood against Krishna's party, also had Parasu-rāma for his teacher.

There can be no doubt that the period of history covered by the main incidents related in the Rāmāyana, and that of the Kurukshetra war, are widely apart in time. Therefore, we have no other alternative but to admit that Parasu-rāma, who takes part in both the narratives, represents a long continued Brahmin movement, anti-Kshatriya in character; and Rāma and Krishna, who come out victorious in this conflict, have some common ideal, which also had a long period of struggle for its manifestation and development.

Any number of such stories show that the two epics of India were concerned with this same social revolution, that is to say, with the conflict of the new and the old within the Aryan community. We have its analogy in comparatively modern days when the Bengali epic, Kavikankan Chandī, was written. In this poem is also described the conflict of religious ideals, with the god Siva on one side and the goddess Chandī on the other. It represented the tragedy of the downfall of a higher principle of religion which had its devotees in the cultured classes, and the usurpation of its altar by the vindictive deity Chandī, patron of wild animals, who was worshipped by the aboriginal Vyādha tribes, as is described in the poem.

In the age of which the Rāmāyana tells, Rāma-chandra was the champion of the new party. Rama was born in the orthodox creed at the head of which was Vasishtha, the priest of the royal house. But from his boyhood he was won over by Visvāmitra, the implacable antagonist of Vasishtha. From this Kshatriya sage the Kshatriya prince received his initiation into a path of adventure, which evidently had behind it a mighty movement led by the great personalities of the age. It appears to me that Rama's banishment had its cause in some conflict of ideals between Vasishtha, who stood as the symbol of the Brahmanic tradition, and Visvāmitra, who had fought against it and had wrenched Rāma-chandra away from the clasp of the unwilling royal household.

When later, for sectarian reasons, the story of the great movement was retold as the Rāmāyana—a dynastic history—the absurd reason was invented about the weak old king yielding to a favourite wife, who took advantage of a vague promise which could fit itself to any demand of hers, however preposterous. This story merely reveals the later degeneracy of mind, when form assumed a greater value than spirit, and some casual words uttered in a moment of infatuation could be deemed more sacred than the truth which is based upon justice and perfect knowledge.

Janaka is considered to be an embodiment of the kingly virtues of an ideal Kshatriya. In the history of the colonization of India by the Aryans, his life must have served a great purpose. We can guess from his own position in the story of the Rāmāyana that he was the principal inspiration in an enterprise which had a large meaning, and that Rāma accepted his mission of life from Janaka. If we pierce through the mist which has gathered round the original narrative, we shall see that there is a general challenge to all Kshatriyas of that time in the story of Sītā's wedding.

Sītā is said to have been no ordinary mortal. She came out of the soil itself when King Janaka was employed in ploughing, as was his wont. 'Furrow-line' is the meaning which the name 'Sītā' bears. This daughter of the soil he promised to give in marriage to him who could break the bow of Siva. Rāma was led to this trial by Visvāmitra, and he succeeded first in bending the bow and then breaking it, thereupon being declared Worthy of receiving Sītā from the hand of Janaka. A great fact of history, which very probably occupied a large expanse of time and was borne along by several generations of heroes, appears to have been condensed in this story. Janaka was one of those sublime figures who could focus in himself all the significance of an epoch-making endeavour, scattered through time and space.

The fact that Janaka's personality comprehended in its inner realization the Brahma-vidyā, and in its outer activity the cultivation of the soil, indicates that the Kshatriya kings developed the art of agriculture, on which the civilization of the Aryans of India was established. Originally the tending of flocks had been the main occupation of the Aryan tribes. This pastoral life likewise suited the forest tracts of India, and Brahmins in their forest retreats continued to regard the cow as their principal wealth. But though tending cattle was fit for the nomad life or for that of small groups of individuals living in forests, the concentration of large bodies of men in cities required the organized production of food. Naturally, the necessity of such organization was more keenly felt by Kshatriyas, who were founders of cities, than by the others. Therefore in the life of Janaka, the ideal king of ancient India, are seen, side by side, Brahma-vidyā—the philosophy which, if truly accepted, could be the spiritual support of the unity of races—and Agriculture which could be the material support of the economic union effected by the large communities. And just as the European colonists in America, while cutting down its forests, had to contest every step with the aborigines who depended on the chase for their living, so also in India the pioneers of agriculture encountered the opposition of the non-Aryans living in its wildernesses, whose fierce onslaughts made their task far from easy.

It is interesting to note in this connection that Zarathushtra, the great spiritual master of ancient Iran, had, like Janaka himself, an ideal which combined spiritual wisdom with a faith in agricultural civilization. And it also became his mission to save agriculture from the depredation of nomadic hordes.

Let me quote from 'Zarathushtra in Gathas', translated from Dr Geiger's book on the subject, a passage which bears strong analogy to the aspect of the old Aryan history in India as revealed by the legend of Janaka. He says:

The Iranian people of the Gathic period were, in fact, subdivided into husbandmen and nomads, and in the sharp opposition which obtained between the two, the prophet Zarathushtra played a prominent part. In a number of Gathic passages we see him standing as an advocate of the settled husbandmen. He admonishes them not to be tired of their good work, to cultivate diligently the fields and to devote to their cattle that fostering care which they deserve. And far and wide spreads the dominion of husbandmen and the settlements of the pious people increase, in spite of all molestations, all persecutions and violence, which they have to suffer from the nomads who attack their settlements in order to desolate their son fields and to deprive them of their herds.

King Janaka reigned over Mithila, which shows that the Aryan colonies had extended along the North to the easternmost natural boundary of India. But the Vindhya hills were then inaccessible, and the forest regions to their South remained intact. Here the Dravidian culture had reached its height, proving a formidable rival to that of the Aryans, and here the puissant Rāvana had established the Dravidian god, Siva, defeating Indra and other Vedic deities.

The question which then arose in the Aryan community as to who should be the champion of their civilization, proving his competency to carry his standard forward by success in the preliminary trial of the breaking of *Haradhanu*, Siva's bow, is to be read in the same light. He who could break the strong resistance of the Siva-worshippers and carry into the South the civilization which had Brahma-vidyā for its spirit, and for its body Agriculture, would verily win, for his spouse, Janaka's earth-born daughter Sītā.

When Rāma-chandra set out under his master Visvāmitra on what became his life-mission he started, even at that early age, by emerging triumphant through three severe tests. First, he slew the foremost of the obstructive barbarians in the vicinity. Next, at his skilled touch, the desert soil which had lain for long years bound in the hardness of stone—becoming Ahalyā, not fit for ploughing—resumed the bloom of life. It was the self-same soil which Rishi Gautama, the foremost of the early Aryan pioneers who had striven to drive the plough southwards, had found treacherous and had abandoned in despair. Thirdly, to the prowess and wisdom of this disciple of the Kshatriya sage was due the subduing of the virulence of the anti-Kshatriya movement personified in the Brahmin Parasu-rāma.

Both in the Rāmāyana and Mahābhārata, the wedding of the principal heroes is connected with the story of a preliminary trial. This is not a mere chance coincidence. It is the crystallization, in the memory of the race, of a great fact which had an epoch-making character. In both cases, it was the acknowledgment of a difficult ideal which involved the heroic responsibility of upholding it in the teeth of desperate opposition. In both cases the bride was not a mortal woman, but a great mission. The trial described in the Mahābhārata is the piercing of a disc in the sky, difficult to discern, fixed in the centre of a revolving wheel, which has to be reached by concentrating one's attention on its shadow reflected in a vessel of water. This trial is obviously of a spiritual nature. The fixed centre of Truth in the heart of the revolving wheel of the World *(Samsāra)* is reflected in the depth of our own being, which can be reached by the one-pointed concentration of Yoga. Is not this the doctrine of the Gītā in the language of a picture? The symbolism of the piercing of the target is well known to us, as it is used in the Upanishad:

प्रणवोधनुः शरो ह्यात्माब्रह्म तत् लक्ष्यमुच्यते ।²

The *Mundakopanishad*, 2/2/36.

The bow is omkāra—the utterance of the sound Om, which helps mental concentration—the soul is the arrow, and the Infinite the target.

Though it was Arjuna who originally won the maiden whose name was Krishnā, she was accepted in marriage by all the brothers. It is ridiculous to try to establish, on the strength of this fact, that the Pāndava clan came from the Himalayan regions, where polyandry is tolerated. As a matter of fact, it was a sacred rite of ideal polyandry which came to be shared by all the brothers. Krishnā is the impersonation of the truth taught by Krishna himself, which had some association with the Sun-worship which was the original meaning of Vishnu-worship. It is related in the epic that in the vessel carried by Krishnā food would become inexhaustible when she invoked the sun to help her. This must refer to the unlimited spiritual food ready for all guests who chose to come and enjoy it.

Evidently, the Pāñchāla kingdom was one of the great centres of this unorthodox religion led by the Kshatriyas. It is to be noted that it was in Pāñchāla that the Brahmin student, Svetaketu, went to the Kshatriya King, Pravāhana Jaibāli, for instruction in the mystic philosophy consisting in the doctrine that the creative process going on in the world of stars, in sky and earth, and in man himself, is a perpetual ceremony of sacrifice, for which the sacrificial fire appears in different aspects and forms. We know the story of how the Brahmin Drona had a grudge against the King of Pāñchāla owing to the latter not recognizing the right of his Brahmin comrade to an equal share in his kingly wealth and power. It is not unlikely that in this legend lies hidden the history of the conflict between the power of the priesthood and that of the religious movement started by the Kshatriyas.

It can be surmised that it was from the province of Pāñchāla, in the close neighbourhood of Mathurā, that the Pāndava brothers received the new creed preached by Krishna. It is significant that the Brahmin Drona, who originated the quarrel, was the first general on the side of the Kurus. Krishnā was insulted by the Kuru brothers, as was Sītā by Rāvana, and she was rescued from her humiliation by Krishna. It was proved to those who tried to expose her to indignities that her veil of honour, was of unlimited length, just as the food in her vessel was inexhaustible. It was proved, in like manner, that Rāvana had not the power to defile Sītā, though, for a time, she was under his dominance, for ideal truth is inviolable ever though it may remain for a time in obscurity. That the hero of the Rāmāyana, the rescuer of Sītā, and the hero of the Mahābhārata, the friend of Krishnā, both occupied the same exalted position in the later Vaishnava religion, is not a mere accident. This fact itself gives us the clue that the original narration in the case of both the epics had for its motive the great fight for the ideal, which ushered in a new age with its new outlook upon life.

It is evident that the sun, which is the one source of light and life to us, had led the thoughts of the Indo-Aryan sages towards the monotheistic ideal of worship. The following prayer addressed to the sun, with which the Ishopanishad is concluded, is full of the mystic yearning of the soul:

हिरण्मयेन पात्रेण सत्यस्यापिहितं मुखम्।
तत्त्वं पूषन्नपावृणु सत्यधर्माय दृष्टये।।

The Ishopanishad, 15.

O Sun, nourisher of the world, Truth's face lies hidden in thy golden vessel. Take away thy cover for his eyes, who is a devotee of Truth.

According to the Chāndogya Upanishad, the teacher Ghora, after having explained to his disciple Krishna, who had become *apipāsa,* free from desire, the consecration ceremony which leads to giving oneself a new spiritual birth, and in which *austerity, almsgiving, harmlessness, truthfulness are* one's gifts for the priests, winds up his teaching with these words: 'In the final hour one should take refuge in these three thoughts: *You are the Indestructible; you are the Unshaken, you are the very Essence of Life'.* On this point there are these two Rig verses:

आदित् प्रत्नस्य रेतसो
ज्योतिष्पश्यन्ति वासरम्
परो यदिध्यते दिवि।
उदवयं तमसस्परि
ज्योतिष्पश्यन्त उत्तरम्
—स्वः पश्यन्त उत्तरम्—
देव देवत्रा सूर्यम्
आगन्म ज्योतिरुत्तममिति
—ज्योतिरुत्तममिति।।

[Quoted in the *Chhāndogya Upanishad* 3/17/7 from the *Rigveda* (8/6/30 and 1/50/10) with slight changes.]

Proceeding from primeval seed,
The early morning light they see,
That gleameth higher than the heaven,
From out of darkness all around,
We, gazing on the higher light—
Yea, gazing on the higher light—
To Surya, god among the gods,
We have attained the highest light!

—Yea, the highest light! [*The Thirteen Principal Upanishads*,
translated by R.E. Hume, 1921, pp. 212–13.]

We find a hint here of the teaching which was developed by Krishna into a great religious movement which preached freedom from desire and absolute devotion to God, and which spiritualized the meaning of ceremonies. That this religion had some association with the sun can be inferred from the legend of Krishnā finding an inexhaustible store of food in her vessel after her worship of the sun, and also the one about the piercing of the target of the disc by Arjuna, which very likely was the mystic disc of the sun, the golden vessel that holds Truth hidden in it, the Truth which has to be attained by piercing the cover.

It is interesting to see how in the history of religion the sun has also had a strong monotheistic suggestion in civilizations other than the Aryan. The great Egyptian King, Akhenaten, belonging to the 14th century BC, struggled against the congregated might of the priestly polytheistic ceremonials, substituting for them the purer form of worship of 'the radiant energy of the sun'. Here also we find the significant analogy of a religious revolution, initiated by one belonging to the kingly caste, against the opposition of the orthodox priestly sect of the land. This Egyptian King, like other prophets of his type, speaks of the truth coming to him as a personal revelation when he sings:

Thou art in my heart, there is none
Who knoweth thee excepting thy son;
Thou causest that he should have understanding,
In thy ways and in thy might.

'In ethics a great change also marks this age,' says Prof. Flinders Petrie. The motto 'Living in Truth' is constantly put forward as the keynote to the king's character, and to his changes in various lines (W.M. Flinders Petrie, *A History of Egypt*, p. 218). Thus we find that History is a plagiarist that steals its own ideals over and over again.

In connection with this we have to note that the spiritual religion which Krishna preached must have ignored the exclusiveness of priestly creeds and extended its invitation to peoples of all classes, Aryans and non-Aryans alike. The legend of his intimate relationship with the shepherd tribes supports this view, and we still find the religion, of which Krishna is the centre, to be the great refuge of the lower castes and outcastes of the present Indian population. The most significant fact of Indian history is that all the human avatars of Vishnu had, by their life and teaching, broken the barriers of priestcraft by acknowledging the relation of fellowship between the privileged classes and those that were despised.

There came the day when Rāma-chandra, the Kshatriya of royal descent, embraced as his friend and comrade the lowest of the low, the untouchable *chandāla*, Guhaka—an incident in his career which to this day is cited as proof of the largeness of his soul. During the succeeding period of conservative reaction, an attempt was made to suppress this evidence of Rāma-chandra's liberality of heart in a supplemental canto of the epic, which is an evident interpolation; and in order to fit it with the later ideal, its votaries did not hesitate to insult his memory by having it in their rendering of the episode that Rāma beheaded with his own hands an ambitious Sudra for presuming to claim equal status in the attainment of spiritual excellence. It is like the ministers of the Christian religion, in the late war, taking Christ's name for justifying the massacre of men.

However that may be, India has never forgotten that Rāma-chandra was the beloved comrade of a *chandāla;* that he appeared as divine to the primitive tribes, some of whom had the totem of monkey, some that of bear. His name is remembered with reverence because he won over his antagonists as his allies and built the bridge of love between Aryan and non-Aryan.

This is the picture we see of one swing of the pendulum in the Aryan times. We shall never know India truly unless we study the manner in which she reacted to the pull of the two opposite principles, that of self-preservation represented by the Brahmin, and that of self-expansion represented by the Kshatriya.

When the first overtures towards social union were being made, it became necessary for the Aryans to come to an understanding with the non-Aryan religion as well. In the beginning, as we have seen, there was a state of war between the followers of Siva and the worshippers of the Vedic gods. The fortune of arms favoured sometimes one side, sometimes the other. Even Krishna's valiant comrade, Arjuna, had once to acknowledge defeat at the hands of Siva of the *Kirātas,* a hunter tribe. Then there is the well known record of a refusal to give Siva place in a great Vedic sacrifice, which led to the breaking up of the ceremony by the non-Aryans. At last, by the identification of Siva with the Vedic Rudra, an attempt had to be made to bring this constant religious antagonism to an end. And yet in the Mahābhārata we find the later story of a battle between Rudra and Vishnu, which ended in the former acknowledging the latter's superiority. Even in Krishna worship we find the same struggle, and therefore in the popular recitation of Krishna legends we often hear of Brahma's attempt at ignoring Krishna, till at last the ancestor god of the Aryans is compelled to pay homage to the later divinity of the populace. These stories reveal the persisting self-consciousness of the newcomers even after they had been admitted to the privileges of the old-established pantheon.

The advent of the two great Kshatriya founders of religion, Buddha and Mahāvīra, in the same eastern part of India where once Janaka had his seat, brought into being a spirit of simplification. They exercised all their force against the confusing maze of religions and doctrines, which had beset the bewildered country and through which it could not find its goal. Amidst the ceremonial intricacies on the one hand, and the subtleties of metaphysical speculation on the other, the simple truth was overlooked that creeds and rites have no value in themselves; that human welfare is the one object towards which religious enthusiasm has to be directed. These two Kshatriya *sannyāsins* refused to admit that any distinctions between man and man were inherent and perpetual; according to their teaching, man could only be saved by realizing truth, and not by social conformity or non-ethical practice. It was wonderful how the triumph of these Kshatriya teachers rapidly overcame all obstacles of tradition and habit, and swept over the whole country.

Long before the full flood of the Buddhistic influence had subsided, most of the protecting walls had been broken down, and the banks of the discipline through which the forces of unification had been flowing in a regulated stream had been obliterated. In fact, in departing, Buddhism left all the numerous aboriginal diversities of India to rear their heads unchecked, because one of the two guiding forces of Indian history had been enfeebled, which with its spirit of resistance had been helping the process of assimilation.

In the midst of the Buddhistic revolution only the Brahmins were able to keep themselves intact, because the maintaining of exclusiveness had all along been their function. But the Kshatriyas had become merged into the rest of the people, and so in the succeeding age we find that most of the kings had ceased to belong to Kshatriya dynasties. Then there were the Sakas and the Hunas whose repeated hordes flowed into India and got mixed with the elder inhabitants. The Aryan civilization, thus stricken to the quick, put forth all its life force in a supreme attempt at recovery, and its first effort was directed to regaining its race consciousness, which had been overwhelmed.

During the long period of this social and religious revolution, which had the effect of rubbing out the individual features of the traditional Aryan culture, the question 'What am I?' came to the forefront. The rescue of the racial personality from beneath the prevailing chaos became the chief endeavour. Aroused by the powerful shock of a destructive opposition, it was then, for the first time, that India sought to define her individuality. When she now tried to know and name herself, she called to mind the empire of Bhārata, a legendary suzerain of by-gone days, and defining her boundaries accordingly, she called herself Bhāratavarsha. She tried to pick up the lost threads of her earlier achievements in order to restore the fabric of her original civilization. Thus collection and compilation, not new creation, were characteristics of this age. The great sage of this epoch, Vyāsa, who is reported to have performed this function, may not have been one real person, but he was, at any rate, the personification of the spirit of the times.

The movement began with the compilation of the Vedas. Now that it had become necessary to have some common unifying agent, the Vedas, as the oldest part of Aryan lore, had to be put on a pedestal for the purpose, in order to serve as a fixed centre of reference round which the distracted community could rally.

Another task undertaken by this age was the gathering and arranging of historical material. In this process, spread over a long period of time, all the scattered myths and legends were brought together, and not only these but also the beliefs and discussions of every kind which still lingered in the racial memory. And thus a great literacy image of the Aryan India of old was formed which was called the Mahābhārata—the great Bhārata. The very name shows the awakened consciousness of the unity of the people struggling to find its expression and permanent record.

The eager effort to gather all the drifting fragments from the wreck resulted in the overloading with indiscriminate miscellanies of the central narrative of the epic. The natural desire of the artist to impart an aesthetic relevancy to the story was swamped by the exigency of the time. The most important need of the age was for an immortal epic, a majestic ship fit to cross the sea of time, to serve the purpose of carrying various materials for the building of a permanent shelter for the race mind.

Therefore, though the Mahābhārata may not be history in the modern western definition of the term, it is, nevertheless, a receptacle of the historical records which had left their impress upon the living memory of the people for ages. Had any competent person attempted to sift and sort and analyse this material into an ordered array of facts, we should have lost the changing picture of Aryan society which they present, a picture in which the lines are vivid or dim, connected or confusedly conflicting, according to the lapses of memory, changes of ideal, and variations of light and shade incident to time's perspective. Self-recording annals of history, as they are imprinted on the living tablet of ages, are bared before our sight in this great work.

The genius of that extraordinary age did not stop short at the discovery of the thread of unity on which were strung the variegated materials scattered through its history; it also searched out the unity of a spiritual philosophy running through all contradictions that are to be found in the metaphysical speculations of the Vedas. The outline presentation of this philosophy was made by the same Vyāsa, who had not only the industry to gather and piece together details, but also the power to visualize the whole in its completeness. His compilation is a creative synthesis.

One thing which remains significant is the fact that this age of compilation has insisted upon the sacredness of the Brahmins and Brahminic lore by constant reiteration in exaggerated language. It proves that there was a militant spirit fighting against odds, and that a complete loss of faith in the freedom of intellect and conscience of the people had come about. Its analogy can be found in the occasional distrust of democracy which we observe among some modern intellectuals of Europe.

The main reason for this was that, during the period of alternating ascendancy of Brahmin and Kshatriya, the resulting synthesis had its unity of Aryan character, but when during the Buddhist period not only non-Aryans but also non-Indians from outside gained free access, it became difficult to maintain organic coherence. A strong undercurrent of race-mingling and religious compromise had set in, and as the mixed races and beliefs began to make themselves felt, the Aryan forces of self-preservation struggled to put up wall beyond wall in order to prevent successive further encroachments. Only those intrusions which could not be resisted found a place within extended barriers.

Let no one imagine, however, that the non-Aryan contributions were taken in by sheer force of circumstance only, and that they had no value of their own. As a matter of fact, the old Dravidian culture was by no means to be despised, and the result of its combination with the Aryan, which formed the Hindu civilization, was that the latter acquired both richness and depth under the influence of its Dravidian component. Dravidians might not be introspective or metaphysical, but they were artists, and they could sing, design and construct. The transcendental thought of the Aryan by its marriage with the emotional and creative art of the Dravidian gave birth to an offspring which was neither fully Aryan, nor Dravidian, but Hindu.

With its Hindu civilization, India attained the gift of being able to realize in the commonplaceness of life, the infinity of the Universal. But on the other hand, by reason of the mixed strain in its blood, whenever Hinduism has failed to take its stand on the reconciliation of opposites which is of its essence, it has fallen a prey to incongruous folly and blind superstition. This is the predicament in which Hindu India has been placed by its birthright. Where the harmony between the component differences has been organically effected, there beauty has blossomed; so long as it remains wanting, there is no end to deformities. Moreover, we must remember that not only the Dravidian civilization, but things appertaining to primitive non-Aryan tribes also, found entrance into the Aryan polity; and the torment of these unassimilable intrusions has been a darkly cruel legacy left to the succeeding Hindu society.

When the non-Aryan gods found place in the Aryan pantheon, their inclusion was symbolized by the Trinity, Brahmā, Vishnu and Siva— Brahmā standing for the ancient tradition, exclusive externalism; Vishnu for the transition when the original Vedic Sun-god became humanized and emerged from the rigid enclosure of scriptural texts into the world of the living human heart; and Siva for the period when the non-Aryan found entrance into the social organization of the Aryan. But though the Aryan and non-Aryan thus met, they did not merge completely. Like the Ganges and the Jumna at their confluence, they flowed on together in two separately distinguishable streams.

In spite of Siva's entry amongst the Aryan gods, his Aryan and non-Aryan aspects remained different. In the former, he is the lord of ascetics, who, having conquered desire, is rapt in the bliss of *nirvāna,* as bare of raiment as of worldly ties. In the latter, he is terrible, clad in raw, bleeding elephant hide, intoxicated by the hemp decoction. In the former, he is the replica of Buddha, and as such has captured many a Buddhist shrine; in the latter, he is the overlord of demons, spirits and other dreadful beings, who haunt the places of the dead, and as such has appropriated to himself the worshippers of the phallus, and of snakes, trees and other totems. In the former, he is worshipped in the quietude of meditation; in the latter, in frenzied orgies of self-torture.

Similarly in the Vaishnava cult, Krishna, who became the mythological god of the non-Aryan religious legends, was not the same in character as the brave and sagacious ruler of Dvārakā who acted as the guide, philosopher and friend of the valiant Arjuna. Alongside the heights of the Song Celestial are ranged the popular religious stories of the cowherd tribes.

But in spite of all that was achieved, it was quite impossible, even for the Aryan genius, to bring into harmony with itself and assimilate each and every one of the practices, beliefs and myths of innumerable non-Aryan tribes. More and more of what was non-Aryan came to be not merely tolerated, but welcomed in spite of incongruities, as the non-Aryan element became increasingly predominant in the race mixture. This led to the formulation of the principle that any religion which should satisfy the capacity of a particular sect was enough for its salvation. But in consequence, the organizing force was reduced to the mere compulsion of some common customs, some repetition of external practices, which barely served loosely to hold together these heterogeneous elements. For the mind which has lost its vigour, all external habits become tyrannical. The result for India is that the tie of custom which is extraneous has become severely tight, hardly leaving any freedom of movement even in insignificant details of life. This has developed in the people an excessively strong sense of responsibility to the claims of the class tradition which divides, but not the conviction of that inner moral responsibility which unites.

We have seen how, after the decline of Buddhism, a path had to be cleared through the jungle of rank undergrowth which had been allowed to run wild during the prolonged inaction of the Brahmanic hierarchy. At the latter end of its career in India the mighty stream of Buddhism grew sluggish and lost itself in morasses of primitive superstitions and promiscuous creeds and practices, which had their root in non-Aryan crudities. It had lost its depth of philosophy and breadth of humanity, which had their origin in the Aryan mind.

Therefore the time came for the Brahmins to assert themselves and bring back into the heart of all this incongruity some unity of ideal, which it had always been their function to maintain. It was now a difficult task for them because of the varied racial strains which had become part of the constitution of the Indian people. And so, in order to save their ideals from the attack of this wild exuberance of heterogeneous life, they fixed them in a permanent rigidity. This had the reactionary effect of making their own ideals inert, and unfit for adaptation to changes of time; while it left to all the living elements of the different races included in the people their freedom of growth, unguided by any dictates of reason. The result has been our huge medley of customs, ceremonials and creeds, some of which are the ruins of the old, and some merely the anomalies of the living outgrowths which continue clinging to them and smothering them in the process.

And yet the genius of India went on working, albeit through the tremendous obstacle of the shackled mind of the people. In the Vedic times, as we have seen, it was mainly the Kshatriyas who repeatedly brought storms of fresh thought into the atmosphere of the people's life whenever it showed signs of stagnation. In later ages, when the Kshatriyas had lost their individuality, the message of the spiritual freedom and unity of man mainly sprang from the obscure strata of the community, where belonged the castes that were despised. Though it has to be admitted that in the medieval age the Brahmin Rāmānanda was the first to give voice to the cry of unity, which is India's own, and in consequence lost his honoured privileges as a Brahmin guru, yet it is none the less true that most of our great saints of that time, who took up this cry in their life and teaching and songs, came from the lower classes, one of them being a Muhammadan weaver, one a cobbler, and several coming from ranks of society whose touch would pollute the drinking water of the respectable section of Hindus. And thus the living voice of India ever found its medium even in the darkest days of our downfall, the voice which proclaimed that he only knows Truth who knows the unity of all beings in the spirit.

The age in which we now live, we cannot see clearly in its true features, as from without. Yet we feel that the India of to-day has roused herself once more to search out her truth, her harmony, her oneness, not only among her own constituent elements, but with the great world. The current of her life, which had been dammed up in stagnation, has found some breach in the wall and can feel the pulse of the tidal waves of humanity outside. We shall learn that we can reach the great world of man, not through the effacement but through the expansion of our own individuality. We shall know for certain that just as it is futile mendicancy to covet the wealth of others in place of our own, so also to keep ourselves segregated and starved by refusing the gift which is the common heritage of man because it is brought to us by a foreign messenger, only makes for utter destitution.

Our western critics, whose own people, whenever confronted with non-western races in a close contact, never know any other solution of the problem but extermination or expulsion by physical force, and whose caste feeling against darker races is brutally aggressive and contemptuous, are ready to judge us with a sneering sense of superiority when comparing India's history with their own. They never take into consideration the enormous burden of difficulty which Indian civilization has taken upon itself from its commencement. India is the one country in the world where the Aryan colonizers had to make constant social adjustments with peoples who vastly outnumbered them, who were physically and mentally alien to their own race, and who were for the most part distinctly inferior to the invaders. Europe, on the other hand, is one in mind; her dress, custom, culture, and with small variations her habits, are one. Yet her inhabitants, although only politically divided, the perpetually making preparations for deadly combats, wherein entire populations indulge in orgies of wholesale destruction unparalleled in ferocity in the history of the barbarian. It is not merely such periodic irruptions of bloody feuds that are the worst characteristic of the relationship between the countries of Europe, even after centuries of close contact and intellectual co-operation, but there is also the intense feeling of mutual suspicion generating diplomatic deceitfulness and shameless moral obliquities.

India's problem has been far more complex than that of the West, and I admit that our rigid system of social regulation has not solved it. For, to bring order and peace at the cost of life is terribly wasteful, whether in the policy of government or of society. But all the same, I believe that we have cause to be proud of the fact that for a long series of centuries beset with vicissitudes of stupendous proportions, crowded with things that are incongruous and facts that are irrelevant, India still keeps alive the inner principle of her own civilization against the cyclonic fury of contradictions and the gravitational pull of the dust.

This has been the great function of the Brahmins of this land, to keep the lamp lighted when the storm has been raging on all sides. It has been their endeavour gradually to permeate the tremendous mass of obstructive material with some quickening ideal of their own that would transmute it into the life-stuff of a composite civilization; to discover some ultimate meaning in the inarticulate primitive forms struggling for expression, and to give it a voice. In a word, it was the mission of the Brahmin to comprehend by the light of his own mature understanding the undeveloped minds of the people.

It would be wrong for us, when we judge the historical career of India, to put all the stress upon the accumulated heap of refuse, gross and grotesque, that has not yet been assimilated in one consistent cultural body. Our great hope lies there, where we realize that something positively precious in our achievements still persists in spite of circumstances that are inclement. The best of us still have our aspiration for the supreme end of life, which is so often mocked at by the prosperous people who hold their sway over the present-day world. We still believe that the world has a deeper meaning than what is apparent, and that therein the human soul finds its ultimate harmony and peace. We still know that only in this spiritual wealth and welfare does civilization attain its end, and not in a prolific production of materials, not in the competition of intemperate power with power.

It has certainly been unfortunate for us that we have neglected the cult of *Anna Brahma*, the infinite as manifested in the material world of utility, and we are dearly paying for it. We have set our mind upon realizing the eternal in the intensity of spiritual consciousness so long, that we have overlooked the importance of realizing the infinite in the world of extension by ever pursuing a path which is endless. And in this great field of adventure the West has attained its success, for which humanity has to be immensely grateful to it.

But the true happiness and peace are awaiting the children of the West in the *tapasyā*, which is for realizing Brahma in spirit, for acquiring the luminous inner vision before which the sphere of immortality reveals itself. If ever that time comes, if the western world does not meet its catastrophic end under the trampling tread of contending commerce and politics, of monstrous greed and hatred, then the world will owe its gratitude to the Brahmins for the faith in the infinitude of the human spirit which they have upheld in the face of forces that spurned it, exultingly counting the skulls of their victims.

I love India, not because I cultivate the idolatry of geography, not because I have had the chance to be born in her soil, but because she has saved through tumultuous ages the living words that have issued from the illuminated consciousness of her great sons: *Satyam, Jñānam, Anantam Brahma,* Brahma is truth, Brahma is wisdom, Brahma is infinite; *Sāntam, Sivam, Advaitam,* peace is in Brahma, goodness is in Brahma, and the unity of all beings.

ब्रह्मनिष्ठोगृहस्थः स्यात् तत्त्वज्ञानपरायणः ।
यादयंत् कर्म प्रकुर्वीत तद्ब्रह्मणि समर्पयत् ।।

The *Mahānirvān Tantra,* 8/23.

The householder shall have his life established in Brahma, shall pursue the deeper truth of all things and in all activities of life dedicate his works to the Eternal Being.

Thus we have come to know that what India truly seeks is not a peace which is in negation or in some mechanical adjustment, but that which is in *Sivam,* in goodness, which is in *Advaitam,* in the truth of perfect union; that India does not enjoin her children to cease from *karma,* but to perform their *karma* in the presence of the Eternal, with the pure knowledge of the spiritual meaning of existence; that this is the true prayer of Mother India:

य एकोऽवर्णोबहुधा शक्तियोगाद्
वर्णाननेकान्निहितार्थोदधाति।
विचैति चान्ते विश्वमादौ सदेवः
सनोबुद्ध्या शुभया संयुनक्तु।।

The *Svetāsvataropanishad,* 4/1

He who is one, who is above all colour distinctions, who dispenses the inherent needs of men of all colours, who comprehends all things from their beginning to the end, let Him unite us to one another with the wisdom which is the wisdom of goodness.

1923

Transcreated by **Rabindranath Tagore** [Sisir Das, ed., *English writings of Tagore,* vol. III (New Delhi: Sahitya Akademi, 2008 reprint)]

Urbashi
(*Urbashi,* from *Balaka*)

Not a mother, not a daughter, not a bride
You are, beautiful and fair,
O Urbashi, denizen of heaven!
When evening descends on the pastures—
Her tired body wrapped in a golden scarf,
You do not in the corner of any home
Kindle your evening light
You do not in the still middle of night
With hesitant steps and a trembling heart,
With soft downcast eyes,
And a smile on your lips,
Go forth bedecked
Bashfully to meet your lover.
You are unveiled as the coming of the dawn
And no embarrassment you suffer.

When did you blossom out of yourself,
Urbashi,

Like a stemless flower?
You arose out of the foam of the sea
In the earliest dawn of Spring
With a pot of nectar in your right hand
And a pot of poison in your left.

The surging sea fell at your feet
Like a serpent charmed
Lowering myriad of its spread-out hoods.
As white as a lily, in naked beauty, and
Admired of the gods
Blameless you are.

Weren't you ever a budding teenage girl?
O Urbashi, eternally young?
In whose home under the dark sea
You played with gems and pearls
Your childhood's games all alone?
In whose arms did you sleep
Lulled by the murmur of the sea
With an innocent smile
On a bed of corals in a room lighted up
By lamps of gems?
You woke up in the world a woman,
Full-grown and young.

From ages and ages
Only you are the world's heart's desire
O resplendent Urbashi!
Ascetics leave their meditation
And lay their spiritual gains at your feet.
At your sidelong glance
All the world becomes restless
With the longing of youth.
The unseeing wind carries
Your maddening aroma all around
And the charmed poet with his wild songs
Wanders about tempted like a honey-drunk
bee.
Your anklets tinkle
As you move in dishabille robes
Quick as a lightning flash.

When you dance before the assembly of gods
O Urbashi, in a delectable swing,

With the rhythm of your dance
Waves come up dancing on the sea,
Draperies of earth shiver in the stalks of corn
And from the necklace on your breasts
Stars shoot out in the sky.
On a sudden, the heart of man loses itself
Within his breast
And in a twinkling on the horizon

Your girdle comes undone,
O loosely robed one.

You are the dawn herself at sunrise in paradise
O Urbashi, Temptress of the World!
The glow of your body is washed
In tears of the world,
And the tint of your toes
Is painted in the blood of its heart.
With your braid hanging loose, O Naked One,
You have put your feather-light foot
Within the full-blown lotus of the world's
desire.
In the paradise of the world's heart
You exude infinite charm
O Companion of Dreams.

Listen, there is wailing for you everywhere
O Urbashi, cruel and deaf,
Will you come back again
To this old and primeval world?
Will you arise again with dripping hair
From the boundless and bottomless abyss?
When your body will first emerge
On the first dawn of that day
All your limbs struck by the gaze of the world
Will weep in dripping drops of water.
And all of a sudden
The vast ocean will swell in waves
In a burst of wonderful song.

No, no, she will not come back again
That glorious moon is set forever
And Urbashi's sun is set.
And so on this earth a sigh of eternal
Separation
Mingles and blows with the cheer of spring.
When on a full moon night
All around is full of laughter
A distant memory brings from somewhere
The song of a wistful flute
And tears in abundance flow.
Yet hope lives within the sorrows of life,
You are free from all ties.

Translated by **Charu Chowdhury**
[*Purabi: The east in its feminine gender* (London: Seagull Books, 2007)]

Dialogue between Karna and Kunti
(*Karna–Kunti sambad*)

Karna:
On sacred Jahnavi's shore I say my prayers
to the evening sun. Karna is my name,
son of Adhirath the charioteer, and Radha is my
mother.
That's who I am. Lady, who are you?

Kunti:
Child, in the first dawn of your life
it was I who introduced you to this wide world.
That's me, and today I've cast aside
all embarrassment, to tell you who I am.

Karna:
Respected lady, the light of your lowered eyes
melts my heart, as the sun's rays melt
mountain snows. Your voice
pierces my ears as a voice from a previous birth
and stirs strange pain. Tell me then,
by what mystery's chain is my birth linked
to you, unknown woman?

Kunti:
Oh, be patient,
child, for a moment! Let the sun-god first
slide to his rest, and let evening's darkness

thicken round us.—Now let me tell you, warrior,
I am Kunti.

Karna:

You are Kunti! The mother of Arjun!

Kunti:

Arjun's mother indeed! But son,
don't hate me for that. How I still recall
the day of the tournament when you, a young
bachelor,
slowly entered the arena in Hastina-city
as the newly rising sun enters the margin
of the eastern sky, still pricked out with stars!
Of all the women watching from behind a screen
who was she, bereft of speech, of luck,
who felt within her tortured breast the pangs
of hungering love, a thousand she-snake fangs?
Whose eyes covered your limbs with blessing's
kisses?
It was Arjun's mother! When Kripa advanced
and smiling, asked you to announce your father's
name,
saying, 'He who is not of a royal family born
has no right to challenge Arjun at all,'—
then you, speechless, red with shame, face lowered,
just stood there, and she whose bosom your gleam
of embarrassment burnt like fire: who was that
unlucky woman? Arjun's mother it was!
Blessed is that lad Durjodhan, who thereupon
at once crowned you prince of Anga. Yes, I praise
him!
And as you were crowned, the tears streamed from
my eyes
to rush towards you, to overflow your head,
when, making his way into the arena,
in entered Adhirath the charioteer, beside himself
with joy, and you, too, in your royal gear
in the midst of the curious crowds milling around
bowed your only-just-anointed head, and saluted
the feet of the old charioteer, calling him Father.
Cruelly, contemptuously they smiled—

the friends of the Pandavs; and right at that instant
she who blessed you as a hero, O you jewel
amongst heroes,
I am that woman, the mother of Arjun.

Karna:

I salute you, noble lady. A royal mother you are:
so why are you here alone? This is a field of battle,
and I am the commander of the Kaurav army.

Kunti:

Son, I've come to beg a favour of you—
Don't turn me away empty-handed.

Karna:

A favour? From me!
Barring my manhood, and what dharma requires,
the rest will be at your feet if you so desire.

Kunti:

I have come to take you away.

Karna:

And where will you take me?

Kunti:

To my thirsty bosom—to my maternal lap.

Karna:

A lucky woman you are, blessed with five sons,
and I am just a petty princeling, without pedigree—
where would you find room for me?

Kunti:

Right at the top!
I would place you above all my other sons,
for you are the eldest.

Karna:

By what right
would I enter that sanctum? Tell me how
from those already cheated of empire
I could possibly take a portion of that wealth,
a mother's love, which is fully theirs.
A mother's heart cannot be gambled away
nor be defeated by force. It's a divine gift.

Kunti:

O my son,
with a divine right indeed you had one day

come to this lap—and by that same right
return again, with glory; don't worry at all—
take your own place amongst all your brothers,
on my maternal lap.

Karna:
As if in a dream
I hear your voice, honoured lady. Look, darkness
has
engulfed the entire horizon, swallowed the four
quarters,
and the river has fallen silent. You have whisked
me off
to some enchanted world, some forgotten home,
to the very dawn of awareness. Your words
like age-old truths touch my fascinated heart.
It's as if my own inchoate infancy,
the very obscurity of my mother's womb
was encircling me today. O royal mother,
loving woman,—be this real, or a dream,—
come place your right hand on my brow, my chin
for just a moment. Indeed I had heard
that I had been abandoned by my natural mother.
How often in the depth of night I've had this dream:
that slowly, softly my mother had come to see me,
and I've felt so bleak, and beseeched her in tears,
'Mother, remove your veil, let me see your face,'—
and at once the figure has vanished, tearing apart
my greedy thirsty dream. That very dream—
has it come today in the guise of the Pandav mother
this evening, on the battlefield, by the Bhagirathi?
Behold, lady, on the other bank, in the Pandav camp
the lights come on, and on this bank, not far,
in the Kaurav stables a hundred thousand horses
stamp their hooves. Tomorrow morning
the great battle begins. Why tonight
did I have to hear from Arjun's mother's throat
my own mother's voice? Why did my name
ring in her mouth with such exquisite music—

so much so that suddenly my heart
rushes towards the five Pandavs, calling them
'brothers'?
Kunti:
Then come on, son, come along with me.
Karna:
Yes, Mother, I'll go with you. I won't ask
questions—
without a doubt, without a worry, I'll go.
Lady, you are my mother! And your call
has awakened my soul—no longer can I hear
the drums of battle, victory's conch-shells.
The violence of war, a hero's fame, triumph and
defeat—
all seem false. Take me. Where should I go?
Kunti:
There, on the other bank,
where the lamps burn in the still tents
on the pale sands.
Karna:
And there a motherless son
shall find his mother for ever! There the pole star
shall wake all night in your lovely generous
eyes. Lady, one more time
say I am your son.
Kunti:
My son!
Karna:
Then why
did you discard me so ingloriously—
no family honour, no mother's eyes to watch me—
to the mercy of this blind, unknown world? Why
did you
let me float away on the current of contempt
so irreversibly, banishing me from my brothers?
You put a distance between Arjun and me,
whence from childhood a subtle invisible bond
of bitter enmity pulls us to each other
in an irresistible attraction.—

Mother, you have no answer?
I sense your embarrassment piercing these dark
layers
and touching all my limbs without any words,
closing my eyes. Let it be then—
you don't have to explain why you cast me aside.
A mother's love is God's first gift on this earth;
why that sacred jewel you had to snatch
from your own child is a question you may choose
not to answer! But tell me then:
why have you come to take me back again?

Kunti:

Child, let your reprimands
like a hundred thunderclaps rend this heart of mine
into a hundred pieces. That I'd cast you aside
is a curse that hounds me, which is why
my heart is childless even with five dear sons,
why it is *you* that my arms go seeking in this world,
flapping and flailing. It is for that deprived child
that my heart lights a lamp, and by burning itself
pays its homage to the Maker of this universe.
Today I count myself fortunate
that I have managed to see you. When your mouth
hadn't yet uttered a word, I did commit
a horrendous crime. Son, with that same mouth
forgive your bad mother. Let that forgiveness burn
fiercer than any rebukes within my breast,
reduce my sins to ashes and make me pure!

Karna:

O Mother, give—give me the dust of your feet,
and take my tears!

Kunti:

Son, I did not come
simply in the happy hope of clutching you to my
breast,
but to take you back where you by right belong.
You are not a charioteer's son, but of royal birth—
so cast aside the insults that have been your lot
and come where they all are—your five brothers.

Karna:
But Mother, I *am* a charioteer's son,
and Radha's my mother—glory greater than that
I have none. Let the Pandavs be Pandavs, the
Kauravs
Kauravs—I envy nobody.
Kunti:
With the puissance of your arms
recover the kingdom that's your own, my son.
Judhisthir will cool you, moving a white fan;
Bhim will hold up your umbrella; Arjun the hero
will drive your chariot; Dhaumya the priest
will chant Vedic mantras; and you, vanquisher of
foes,
will live with your kinsmen, sole ruler in your
kingdom,
sitting on your jewelled throne, sharing power with
none.
Karna:
Throne, indeed! To one who's just refused the
maternal bond
are you offering, Mother, assurances of a kingdom?
The riches from which you once disinherited me
cannot be returned—it's beyond your powers.
When I was born, Mother, from me you tore
mother, brothers, royal family—all at one go.
If today I cheat my foster-mother, her of charioteer
caste,
and boldly address as my own mother a royal
materfamilias,
if I snap the ties that bind me to the lord
of the Kuru clan, and lust after a royal throne,
then fie on me!
Kunti:
Blessed are you, my son, for you are
truly heroic. Alas, Dharma, how stern your justice
is!
Who knew, alas, that day
when I forsook a tiny, helpless child,

that from somewhere he would gain a hero's
powers,
return one day along a darkened path,
and with his own cruel hands hurl weapons at those
who are his brothers, born of the same mother!
What a curse this is!

Karna:

Mother, don't be afraid.
Let me predict: it's the Pandavs who will win.
On the panel of this night's gloom I can clearly read
before my eyes the dire results of war:
legible in starlight. This quiet, unruffled hour
from the infinite sky a music drifts to my ears:
of effort without victory, sweat of work without
hope—
I can see the end, full of peace and emptiness.
The side that is going to lose—
please don't ask me to desert that side.
Let Pandu's children win, and become kings,
let me stay with the losers, those whose hopes will
be dashed.
The night of my birth you left me upon the earth:
nameless, homeless. In the same way today
be ruthless, Mother, and just abandon me:
leave me to my defeat, infamous, lusterless.
Only this blessing grant me before you leave:
may greed for victory, for fame, or for a kingdom
never deflect me from a hero's path and salvation.

15 Phalgun 1306
[Spring 1900]

Translated by **Ketaki Kushari Dyson**
[*I won't let you go: Selected poems of Rabindranath Tagore*
(Penguin India, 2010)]

Kacha and Devayani
(*Bidaay abhishaap*)

[*Young Kacha came from Paradise to learn the secret of immortality from a Sage who taught the Titans, and whose daughter Devayani fell in love with him.*]

Kacha: The time has come for me to take leave, Devayani; I have long sat at your father's feet, but to-day he completed his teaching. Graciously allow me to go back to the land of the Gods whence I came.

Devayani: You have, as you desired, won that rare knowledge coveted by the Gods:—but think, do you aspire after nothing further?

Kacha: Nothing.

Devayani: Nothing at all! Dive into the bottom of your heart; does no timid wish lurk there, fearful lest it be blighted?

Kacha: For me the sun of fulfilment has risen, and the stars have faded in its light. I have mastered the knowledge which gives life.

Devayani: Then you must be the one happy being in creation. Alas! now for the first time I feel what torture these days spent in an alien land have been to you, though we offered you our best

Kacha: Not so much bitterness! Smile, and give me leave to go.

Devayani: Smile! But, my friend, this is not your native Paradise. Smiles are not so cheap in this world, where thirst, like a worm in the flower, gnaws at the heart's core; where baffled desire hovers round the desired, and memory never ceases to sigh foolishly after vanished joy.

Kacha: Devayani, tell me how I have offended?

Devayani: Is it so easy for you to leave this forest, which through long years has lavished on you shade and song? Do you not feel how the wind wails through these glimmering shadows, and dry leaves whirl in the air, like ghosts of lost hope;—while you alone, who part from us, have a smile on your lips?

Kacha: This forest has been a second mother to me, for here I have been born again. My love for it shall never dwindle.

Devayani: When you had driven the cattle to graze on the lawn, yonder banyan tree spread a hospitable shade for your tired limbs against the mid-day heat.

Kacha: I bow to thee. Lord of the Forest! Remember me, when under thy shade other students chant their lessons to an accompaniment of bees humming and leaves rustling.

Devayani: And do not forget our Venumati, whose swift water is one stream of singing love.

Kacha: I shall ever remember her, the dear companion of my exile, who, like a busy village girl, smiles on her errand of ceaseless service and croons a simple song.

Devayani: But, friend, let me also remind you that you had another companion whose thoughts were vainly busy to make you forget an exile's cares.

Kacha: The memory of her has become a part of my life.

Devayani: I recall the day when, little more than a boy, you first arrived. You stood there, near the hedge of the garden, a smile in your eyes.

Kacha: And I saw you gathering flowers—clad in white, like the dawn bathed in radiance. And I said, 'Make me proud by allowing me to help you!'

Devayani: I asked in surprise who you were, and you meekly answered that you were the son of Vrihaspati, a divine sage at the court of the God Indra, and desired to learn from my father that secret spell which can revive the dead.

Kacha: I feared lest the Master, the teacher of the Titans, those rivals of the Gods, should refuse to accept me for a disciple.

Devayani: But he could not refuse me when I pleaded your cause, so greatly he loves his daughter.

Kacha: Thrice had the jealous Titans slain me, and thrice you prevailed on your father to bring me back to life; therefore my gratitude can never die.

Devayani: Gratitude! Forget all—I shall not grieve. Do you only remember benefits? Let them perish! If after the day's lessons, in the evening solitude, some strange tremor of joy shook your heart, remember that—but not gratitude. If, as some one passed, a snatch of song got tangled among your texts or the swing of a robe fluttered your studies with delight, remember that when at leisure in your Paradise. What, benefits only!—and neither beauty nor love nor...?

Kacha: Some things are beyond the power of words.

Devayani: Yes, yes, I know. My love has sounded your heart's deepest, and makes me bold to speak in defiance of your reserve. Never leave me! remain here! fame gives no happiness. Friend, you cannot now escape, for your secret is mine!

Kacha: No, no, Devayani.

Devayani: How 'No'? Do not lie to me! Love's insight is divine. Day after day, in raising your head, in a glance, in the motion of your hands, your love spoke as the sea speaks through its waves. On a sudden my voice would send your heart quivering through your limbs—have I never witnessed it? I know you, and therefore you are my captive for ever. The very king of your Gods shall not sever this bond.

Kacha: Was it for this, Devayani, that I toiled, away from home and kindred, all these years?

Devayani: Why not? Is only knowledge precious? Is love cheap? Lay hold on this moment. Have the courage to own that a woman's heart is worth all as much penance as men undergo for the sake of power, knowledge, or reputation.

Kacha: I gave my solemn promise to the Gods that I would bring them this lore of deathless life.

Devayani: But is it true you had eyes for nothing save your books? That you never broke off your studies to pay me homage with flowers, never lay in wait for a chance, of an evening, to help me water my flower-beds? What made you sit by me on the grass and sing songs you brought hither from the assembly of the stars, while darkness stooped over the river bank as love droops over its own sad silence? Were these parts of a cruel conspiracy plotted in your Paradises? Was all for the sake of access to my father's heart?—and after success, were you, departing, to throw some cheap gratitude, like small coins, to the deluded door-keeper?

Kacha: What profit were there, proud woman, in knowing the truth? If I did wrong to serve you with a passionate devotion cherished in secret, I have had ample punishment. This is no time to question whether my love be true or not; my life's work awaits me. Though my heart must henceforth enclose a red flame vainly striving to devour emptiness, still I must go back to that Paradise which will nevermore be Paradise to me. I owe the Gods a new divinity, hard won by my studies, before I may think of happiness. Forgive me, Devayani, and know that my suffering is doubled by the pain I unwillingly inflict on you.

Devayani: Forgiveness! You have angered my heart till it is hard and burning like a thunderbolt! You can go back to your work and your glory, but what is left for me? Memory is a bed of thorns, and secret shame will gnaw at the roots of my life. You came like a wayfarer, sat through the sunny hours in the shade of my garden, and to while time away you plucked all its flowers and wove them into a chain. And now, parting, you snap the thread and let the flowers drop on the dust! Accursed be that great knowledge you have earned!—a burden that, though others share equally with you, will never be lightened. For lack of love may it ever remain as foreign to your life as the cold stars are to the unespoused darkness of virgin Night!

Transcreated by **Rabindranath Tagore**
[*The English writings of Rabindranath Tagore*
(New Delhi: Sahitya Akademi, 2004)]

The mother's prayer
(*Gandharir abedan*)

Dhritarashtra: You have compassed your end.

Duryodhana: Success is mine!

Dhritarashtra: Are you happy?

Duryodhana: I am victorious.

Dhritarashtra: I ask you again, what happiness have you in winning the undivided kingdom?

Duryodhana: Sire, a Kshatriya thirsts not after happiness but victory, that fiery wine pressed from seething jealousy. Wretchedly happy we were, like those inglorious stains that lie idly on the breast of the moon, when we lived in peace under the friendly dominance of our cousins. Then these Pandavas milked the world of its wealth, and allowed us a share, in brotherly tolerance.

Now that they own defeat and expect banishment, I am no longer happy but exultant.

Dhritarashtra: Wretch, you forget that both Pandavas and Kauravas have the same forefathers.

Duryodhana: It was difficult to forget that, and therefore our inequalities rankled in my heart. At midnight the moon is never jealous of the noonday sun. But the struggle to share one horizon between both orbs cannot last forever. Thank heaven, that struggle is over, and we have at last won solitude in glory.

Dhritarashtra: The mean jealousy!

Duryodhana: Jealousy is never mean—it is in the essence of greatness. Grass can grow in crowded amity, not giant trees. Stars live in clusters, but the sun and moon are lonely in their splendour. The pale moon of the Pandavas sets behind the forest shadows, leaving the new-risen sun of the Kauravas to rejoice.

Dhritarashtra: But right has been defeated.

Duryodhana: Right for rulers is not what is right in the eyes of the people. The people thrive by comradeship: but for a king, equals are enemies. They are obstacles ahead, they are terrors from behind. There is no place for brothers or friends in a king's polity; its one solid foundation is conquest.

Dhritarashtra: I refuse to call a conquest what was won by fraud in gambling.

Duryodhana: A man is not shamed by refusing to challenge a tiger on equal terms with teeth and nails. Our weapons are those proper for success, not for suicide. Father, I am proud of the result and disdain regret for the means.

Dhritarashtra: But justice—

Duryodhana: Fools alone dream of justice—success is not yet theirs: but those born to rule rely on power, merciless and unhampered with scruples.

Dhritarashtra: Your success will bring down on you a loud and angry flood of detraction.

Duryodhana: The people will take amazingly little time to learn that Duryodhana is king and has power to crush calumny under foot.

Dhritarashtra: Calumny dies of weariness dancing on tongue-tips. Do not drive it into the heart to gather strength.

Duryodhana: Unuttered defamation does not touch a king's dignity. I care not if love is refused us, but insolence shall not be borne. Love depends upon the will of the giver, and the poorest of the poor can indulge in such generosity. Let them squander it on their pet cats, tame dogs, and our good cousins the Pandavas. I shall never envy them. Fear is the tribute I claim for my royal throne. Father, only too leniently you lent your ear to those who slandered your sons: but if you intend still to allow those pious friends of yours to revel in shrill denunciation at the expense of your children, let us exchange our kingdom for the exile of our cousins, and go to the wilderness, where happily friends are never cheap!

Dhritarashtra: Could the pious warnings of my friends lessen my love for my sons, then we might be saved. But I have dipped my hands in the mire of your infamy and lost my sense of goodness. For your sakes I have heedlessly set fire to that ancient forest of our royal lineage—so dire is my love. Clasped breast to breast, we, like a double meteor, are blindly plunging into ruin. Therefore doubt not my love; relax not your embrace till the brink of annihilation be reached. Beat your drums of victory, lift your banner of triumph. In this mad riot of exultant evil, brothers and friends will disperse till nothing remain save the doomed father, the doomed son and God's curse.

Enter an Attendant.
Sire, Queen Gandhari asks for audience.
Dhritarashtra: I await her.
Duryodhana: Let me take my leave.
Dhritarashtra: Fly! For you cannot bear the fire of your mother's presence.
Gandhari: At your feet I crave a boon.
Dhritarashtra: Speak, your wish is fulfilled.
Gandhari: The time has come to renounce him.
Dhritarashtra: Whom, my queen!
Gandhari: Duryodhana!
Dhritarashtra: Our own son, Duryodhana?
Gandhari: Yes!
Dhritarashtra: This is a terrible boon for you, his mother, to crave!
Gandhari: The fathers of the Kauravas, who are in Paradise, join me in beseeching you.
Dhritarashtra: The divine Judge will punish him who has broken His laws. But I am his father.
Gandhari: Am I not his mother? Have I not carried him under my throbbing heart? Yes, I ask you to renounce Duryodhana the unrighteous.
Dhritarashtra: What will remain to us after that?
Gandhari: God's blessing.
Dhritarashtra: And what will that bring us?
Gandhari: New afflictions. Pleasure in our son's presence, pride in a new kingdom, and shame at knowing both purchased by wrong done or connived at, like thorns dragged two ways, would lacerate our bosoms. The Pandavas are too proud ever to accept back from us the lands which they have relinquished; therefore it is only meet that we draw some great sorrow down on our heads so as to deprive that unmerited reward of its sting.
Dhritarashtra: Queen, you inflict fresh pain on a heart already rent.
Gandhari: Sire, the punishment imposed on our son will be more ours than his. A judge callous to the pain that he inflicts loses the right to judge. And if you spare your son to save yourself pain, then all the culprits ever punished by your hands will cry before God's throne for vengeance,—had they not also their fathers?
Dhritarashtra: No more of this, Queen, I pray you. Our son is abandoned of God: that is why I cannot give him up. To save him is no longer in my power, and therefore my consolation is to share his guilt and tread the path

of destruction, his solitary companion. What is done is done; let follow what must follow!

(*Exit*)

Gandhari: Be calm, my heart, and patiently await God's judgment Oblivious night wears on, the morning of reckoning nears, I hear the thundering roar of its chariot. Woman, bow your head down to the dust! and as a sacrifice fling your heart under those wheels! Darkness will shroud the sky, earth will tremble, wailing will rend the air and then comes the silent and cruel end,—that terrible peace, that great forgetting, and awful extinction of hatred—the supreme deliverance rising fire the fire of death.

Transcreated by **Rabindranath Tagore**
[*The English writings of Rabindranath Tagore*
(New Delhi: Sahitya Akademi, 2004)]

Play

Chitra
(*Chitra*)

Preface

This lyrical drama was written about twenty-five years ago. It is based on the following story from the Mahabharata.

In the course of his wanderings, in fulfilment of a vow of penance, Arjuna came to Manipur. There he saw Chitrangada, the beautiful daughter of Chitravahana, the king of the country. Smitten with her charms, he asked the king for the hand of his daughter in marriage. Chitravahana asked him who he was, and learning that he was Arjuna the Pandava, told him that Prabhanjana, one of his ancestors in the kingly line of Manipur, had long been childless. In order to obtain an heir, he performed severe penances. Pleased with these austerities, the god Shiva gave him this boon, that he and his successors should each have one child. It so happened that the promised child had invariably been a son. He, Chitravahana, was the first to have only a daughter Chitrangada to perpetuate the race. He had, therefore, always treated her as a son and had made her his heir. Continuing, the king said:

'The one son that will be born to her must be the perpetuator of my race. That son will be the price that I shall demand for this marriage. You can take her, if you like, on this condition.'

Arjuna promised and took Chitrangada to wife, and lived in her father's capital for three years. When a son was born to them, he embraced her with affection, and taking leave of her and her father, set out again on his travels.

The characters

Gods:

Madana (Eros)
Vasanta (Lycoris)

Mortals:

Chitra, daughter of the King of Manipur.

Arjuna, a prince of the house of the Kurus. He is of the Kshatriya or 'Warrior' caste, and during the action is living as a hermit retired in the forest.

Villagers from an outlying district of Manipur.

[Note: The dramatic poem *Chitra* has been performed in India without scenery—the actors being surrounded by the audience. Proposals for its production here having been made to the author, he went through this translation and provided stage directions, but wished these omitted if it were printed as a book.]

SCENE I

Chitra: Art thou the god with the five darts, the Lord of Love?
Madana: I am he who was the first born in the heart of the Creator. I bind in bonds of pain and bliss the lives of men and women!
Chitra: I know, I know what that pain is and those bonds.—And who art thou, my lord?
Vasanta: I am his friend—Vasanta—the King of the Seasons. Death and decrepitude would wear the world to the bone but that I follow them and constantly attack them. I am Eternal Youth.
Chitra: I bow to thee, Lord Vasanta.
Madana: But what stern vow is thine, fair stranger? Why dost thou wither thy fresh youth with penance and mortification? Such a sacrifice is not fit for the worship of love. Who art thou and what is thy prayer?

Chitra: I am Chitra, the daughter of the kingly house of Manipur. With godlike grace Lord Shiva promised to my royal grandsire an unbroken line of male descent. Nevertheless, the divine word proved powerless to change the spark of life in my mother's womb—so invincible was my nature, woman though I be.

Madana: I know, that is why thy father brings thee up as his son. He has taught thee the use of the bow and all the duties of a king.

Chitra: Yes, that is why I am dressed in man's attire and have left the seclusion of a woman's chamber. I know no feminine wiles for winning hearts. My hands are strong to bend the bow, but I have never learnt Cupid's archery, the play of eyes.

Madana: That requires no schooling, fair one. The eye does its work untaught, and he knows how well, who is struck in the heart.

Chitra: One day in search of game I roved alone to the forest on the bank of the Purna river. Tying my horse to a tree trunk I entered a dense thicket on the track of a deer. I found a narrow sinuous path meandering through the dusk of the entangled boughs, the foliage vibrated with the chirping of crickets, when of sudden I came upon a man lying on a bed of dried leaves, across my path. I asked him haughtily to move aside, but he heeded not. Then with the sharp end of my bow I pricked him in contempt. Instantly he leapt up with straight, tall limbs, like a sudden tongue of fire from a heap of ashes. An amused smile flickered round the corners of his mouth, perhaps at the sight of my boyish countenance. Then for the first time in my life I felt myself a woman, and knew that a man was before me.

Madana: At the auspicious hour I teach the man and the woman this supreme lesson to know themselves. What happened after that?

Chitra: With fear and wonder I asked him, 'Who are you?' 'I am Arjuna', he said, 'of the great Kuru Clan'. I stood petrified like a statue, and forgot to do him obeisance. Was this indeed Arjuna, the one great idol of my dreams? Yes, I had long ago heard how he had vowed a twelve-years' celibacy. Many a day my young ambition had spurred me on to break my lance with him, to challenge him in disguise to single combat, and prove my skill in arms against him. Ah, foolish heart, whither fled thy presumption? Could I but exchange my youth with all its aspirations for the clod of earth under his feet, I should deem it a most precious grace. I know not in what whirlpool of thought I was lost, when suddenly I saw him vanish through the trees. O foolish woman, neither didst thou greet him, nor speak a word, nor beg forgiveness, but stoodest like a barbarian boor while he contemptuously walked away! … Next morning I laid aside my man's clothing. I donned bracelets, anklets, waist-chain, and a gown of purple-red silk. The unaccustomed dress clung about my shrinking shame; but I hastened on my quest, and found Arjuna in the forest temple of Shiva.

Madana: Tell me the story to the end. I am the heart-born god, and I understand the mystery of these impulses.

Chitra: Only vaguely can I remember what things I said, and what answer I got. Do not ask me to tell you all. Shame fell on me like a thunderbolt, yet could not break me to pieces, so utterly hard, so like a man am I. His last words as I walked home pricked my ears like red-hot needles. 'I have taken the vow of celibacy. I am not fit to be thy husband!' Oh, the vow of a man! Surely thou knowest, thou god of love, that unnumbered saints and sages have surrendered the merits of their lifelong penance at the feet of a woman. I broke my bow in two and burnt my arrows in the fire. I hated my strong, lithe arm, scored by drawing the bow-string. O Love, god Love, thou hast laid low in the dust the vain pride of my manlike strength; and all my man's training lies crushed under thy feet. Now teach me thy lessons; give me the power of the weak and the weapon of the unarmed hand.

Madana: I will be thy friend. I will bring the world-conquering Arjuna a captive before thee, to accept his rebellion's sentence at thy hand.

Chitra: Had I but the time needed, I could win his heart by slow degrees, and ask no help of the gods. I would stand by his side as a comrade, drive the fierce horses of his war-chariot, attend him in the pleasures of the chase, keep guard at night at the entrance of his tent, and help him in all the great duties of a Kshatriya, rescuing the weak, and meting out justice where it is due. Surely at last the day would have come for him to look at me and wonder, 'What boy is this? Has one of my slaves in a former life followed me like my good deeds into this?' I am not the woman who nourishes her despair in lonely silence, feeding it with nightly tears and covering it with the daily patient smile, a widow from her birth. The flower of my desire shall never drop into the dust before it has ripened to fruit. But it is the labour of lifetime to make one's true self known and honoured. Therefore I have come to thy door, thou world-vanquishing Love, and thou, Vasanta, youthful Lord of the Seasons, take from my young body this primal injustice, an unattractive plainness. For a single day make me superbly beautiful, even as beautiful as was the sudden blooming of love in my heart. Give me but one brief day of perfect beauty, and I will answer for the days that follow.

Madana: Lady, I grant thy prayer.

Vasanta: Not for the short span of a day, but for one whole year the charm of spring blossoms shall nestle round thy limbs.

SCENE II

Arjuna: Was I dreaming or was what I saw by the lake truly there? Sitting on the mossy turf, I mused over bygone years in the sloping shadows of the evening when slowly there came out from the folding darkness of foliage an apparition of beauty in the perfect form of a woman, and stood on a white slab of stone at the water's brink. It seemed that the heart of the earth must heave in joy under her bare white feet. Methought the vague veilings of her body should melt in ecstasy into air as the golden mist of dawn melts from off the snowy peak of the eastern hill. She bowed herself above the shining mirror of the lake and saw the reflection of her face. She started up in awe and stood still; then smiled, and with a careless sweep of her left arm unloosed her hair and let it trail on the earth at her feet. She bared her bosom and looked at her arms, so flawlessly modelled, and instinct with an exquisite caress. Bending her head she saw the sweet blossoming of her youth and the tender bloom and blush of her skin; she beamed with a glad surprise. So, if the white lotus-bud on opening her eyes in the morning were to arch her neck and see her shadow in the water, would she wonder at herself the livelong day. But a moment after the smile passed from her face and a shade of sadness crept into her eyes. She bound up her tresses, drew her veil over her arms, and sighing slowly, walked away like a beauteous evening fading into the night. To me the supreme fulfilment of desire seemed to have been revealed in a flush and then to have vanished.... But who is it that pushes the door?

(Enter Chitra, dressed as a woman)

Ah! It is she. Quiet, my heart!
Fear me not, lady! I am a Kshatriya.

Chitra: Honoured Sir, you are my guest. I live in this temple. I know not in what way I can show you hospitality.
Arjuna: Fair lady, the very sight of you is indeed the highest hospitality. If you will not take it amiss I would ask you a question.
Chitra: You have permission.
Arjuna: What stern vow keeps you immured in this solitary temple, depriving all mortals of a vision of so much loveliness?
Chitra: I harbour a secret desire in my heart, for the fulfilment of which I offer daily prayers to Lord Shiva.

Arjuna: Alas, what can you desire, you who are the desire of the whole world? From the easternmost hill on whose summit the morning sun first prints his fiery foot to the end of the sunset land have I travelled. I have seen whatever is most precious, beautiful and great on the earth. My knowledge shall be yours, only say for what or for whom you seek.

Chitra: He whom I seek is known to all.

Arjuna: Indeed! Who may this favourite of the gods be, whose fame has captured your heart?

Chitra: Sprung from the highest of all royal houses, the greatest of all heroes is he.

Arjuna: Lady, offer not such wealth of beauty as is yours on the altar of false reputation. Spurious fame spreads from tongue to tongue like the fog of the early dawn before the sun rises. Tell me who in the highest of kingly lines is the supreme hero?

Chitra: Hermit, you are jealous of other men's fame. Do you not know that all over the world the royal house of the Kurus is the most famous?

Arjuna: The house of the Kurus!

Chitra: And have you never heard of the greatest name of that far-famed house?

Arjuna: From your own lips let me hear it.

Chitra: Arjuna, the conqueror of the world. I have culled from the mouths of the multitude that imperishable name and hidden it with care in my maiden heart. Hermit, why do you look perturbed? Has that name only a deceitful glitter? Say so, and I will not hesitate to break this casket of my heart and throw the false gem to the dust.

Arjuna: Be his name and fame, his bravery and prowess false or true, for mercy's sake do not banish him from your heart—for he kneels at your feet even now.

Chitra: You, Arjuna!

Arjuna: Yes, I am he, the love-hungered guest at your door.

Chitra: Then it is not true that Arjuna has taken a vow of chastity for twelve long years?

Arjuna: But you have dissolved my vow even as the moon dissolves the night's vow of obscurity.

Chitra: Oh, shame upon you! What have you seen in me that makes you false to yourself? Whom do you seek in these dark eyes, in these milk-white arms, if you are ready to pay for her the price of your probity? Not my true self, I know. Surely this cannot be love, this is not man's highest homage to woman. Alas, that this frail disguise, the body, should make one blind to the light of the deathless spirit! Yes, now indeed I know, Arjuna, the fame of your heroic manhood is false.

Arjuna: Ah, I feel how vain is fame, the pride of prowess! Everything seems to me a dream. You alone are perfect; you are the wealth of the world, the end of all poverty, the goal of all efforts, the one woman! Others there are who can be but slowly known, while to see you for a moment is to see perfect completeness once and for ever.

Chitra: Alas, it is not I, not I, Arjuna! It is the deceit of a god. Go, go my hero, go! Woo not falsehood, offer not your great heart to an illusion. Go!

SCENE III

Chitra: No, impossible! To face that fervent gaze that almost grasps you like clutching hands of the hungry spirit within; to feel his heart struggling to break its bounds, urging its passionate cry through the entire body—and then to send him away like a beggar—no, impossible!

(Enter Madana and Vasanta)

Ah, god of love, what fearful flame is this with which thou hast enveloped me? I burn, and I burn whatever I touch.

Madana: I desire to know what happened last night.

Chitra: At evening I lay down on a grassy bed strewn with the petals of spring flowers, and recollected the wonderful praise of my beauty I had heard from Arjuna; drinking drop by drop the honey that I had stored during the long day. The history of my past life like that of my former existences was forgotten. I felt like a flower, which has, but a few fleeting hours to listen to all the humming flatteries and whispered murmurs of the wood-lands and then must lower its eyes from the sky, bend its head and at a breath give itself up to the dust without a cry, thus ending the short story of a perfect moment that has neither past nor future.

Vasanta: A limitless life of glory can bloom and spend itself in a morning.

Madana: Like an endless meaning in the narrow span of a song.

Chitra: The southern breeze caressed me to sleep. From the flowering Malati bower overhead silent kisses dropped over my body. On my hair, my breast my feet, each flower chose a bed to die on. I slept. And, suddenly in the depth of my sleep, I felt as if some intense eager look, like tapering fingers of flame, touched my slumbering body. I started up and saw the Hermit standing before me. The moon had moved to the west, peering through the leaves to espy this wonder of divine art wrought in a fragile human frame. The air was heavy with perfume; the silence of the night was vocal with the chirping of crickets; the reflections of the trees hung motionless in the lake; and with his staff in his hand he stood, tall and straight and still, like a forest tree. It seemed to me that I had, on opening my eyes, died to all realities of life and undergone a dream, birth into a shadow land. Shame slipped to my feet like loosened clothes. I heard his call—'Beloved, my most beloved!' And all my forgotten lives united as one and responded to it. I said, 'Take me, take all I am!' And I stretched out my arms to him. The moon set behind the trees. One curtain of darkness covered all. Heaven and earth, time and space, pleasure and pain, death and life merged together in an unbearable ecstasy... With the first gleam of light, the first twitter of birds, I rose up and sat leaning on my left arm. He lay asleep with a vague smile about his lips like the crescent moon in the morning. The rosy red glow of the dawn fell upon his noble forehead. I sighed and stood up. I drew together the leafy lianas to screen the streaming sun from his face. I looked about me and saw the same old earth. I remembered what I used to be, and ran and ran like a deer afraid of her own shadow, through the forest path strewn with *Shephali* flowers. I found a lonely nook, and sitting down covered my face with both hands, and tried to weep and cry. But no tears came to my eyes.

Madana: Alas, thou daughter of mortals! I stole from the divine storehouse the fragrant wine of heaven, filled with it one earthly night to the brim, and placed it in thy hand to drink—yet still I hear this cry of anguish!

Chitra (bitterly): Who drank it? The rarest completion of life's desire, the first union of love was proffered to me, but was wrested from my grasp! This borrowed beauty, this falsehood that enwraps me, will slip from me taking with it the only monument of that sweet union, as the petals fall from an overblown flower; and the woman ashamed of her naked poverty will sit weeping day and night. Lord Love, this cursed appearance companions me like a demon robbing me of all the prizes of love—all the kisses for which my heart is athirst.

Madana: Alas, how vain thy single night had been! The barque of joy came in sight, but the waves would not let it touch the shore.

Chitra: Heaven came so close to my hand that I forgot for a moment that it had not reached me. But when I woke in the morning from my dream I found that my body had become my own rival. It is my hateful task to deck her every day, to send her to my beloved and see her caressed by him. O god, take back thy boon!

Madana: But if I take it from you how can you stand before your lover? To snatch away the cup from his lips when he has scarcely drained his first draught of pleasure, would not that be cruel? With what resentful anger he must regard thee then!

Chitra: That would be better far than this. I will reveal my true self to him, a nobler thing than this disguise. If he rejects it, if he spurns me and breaks my heart, I will bear even that in silence.

Vasanta: Listen to my advice. When with the advent of autumn the flowering season is over, then comes the triumph of fruitage. A time will come of itself when the heat-cloyed bloom of the body will droop and Arjuna will gladly accept the abiding fruitful truth in thee. O child, go back to thy mad festival.

SCENE IV

Chitra: Why do you watch me like that, my warrior?

Arjuna: I watch how you weave that garland. Skill and grace, the twin brother and sister, are dancing playfully on your fingertips. I am watching and thinking.

Chitra: What are you thinking, sir?

Arjuna: I am thinking that you, with this same lightness of touch and sweetness, are weaving my days of exile into an immortal wreath, to crown me when I return home.

Chitra: Home! But this love is not for a home!

Arjuna: Not for a home?

Chitra: No. Never talk of that. Take to your home what is abiding and strong. Leave the little wild flower where it was born; leave it beautifully to die at the day's end among all fading blossoms and decaying leaves. Do not take it to your palace hall to fling it on the stony floor which knows no pity for things that fade and are forgotten.

Arjuna: Is ours that kind of love?

Chitra: Yes, no other! Why regret it? That which was meant for idle days should never outlive them. Joy turns into pain when the door by which it should depart is shut against it. Take it and keep it as long as it lasts. Let not the satiety of your evening claim more than the desire of your morning could earn... The day is done. Put this garland on. I am tired. Take me in your arms, my love. Let all vain bickering of discontent die away at the sweet meeting of our lips.

Arjuna: Hush! Listen, my beloved, the sound of prayer-bells from the distant village temple steals upon the evening air across the silent trees!

SCENE V

Vasanta: I cannot keep pace with thee, my friend! I am tired. It is a hard task to keep alive the fire thou hast kindled. Sleep overtakes me, and the fan drops from my hand, and cold ashes cover the glow of the fire. I start up again from my slumber and with all my might rescue the weary flame. But this can go on no longer.

Madana: I know, thou art as fickle as a child. Ever restless is thy play in heaven and on earth. Things that thou for days buildest up with endless detail thou dost shatter in a moment without regret. But this work of ours is nearly finished. Pleasure-winged days fly fast, and the year, almost at its end, swoons in rapturous bliss.

SCENE VI

Arjuna: I woke in the morning and found that my dreams had distilled a gem. I have no casket to inclose it, no king's crown whereon to fix it, no chain from which to hang it, and yet have not the heart to throw it away. My Kshatriya's right arm, idly occupied in holding it, forgets its duties.

(*Enter Chitra*)

Chitra: Tell me your thoughts, sir!

Arjuna: My mind is busy with thoughts of hunting to-day. See, how the rain pours in torrents and fiercely beats upon the hillside. The dark shadow of the clouds hangs heavily over the forest, and the swollen stream, like reckless youth, overleaps all barriers with mocking laughter. On such rainy days we five brothers would go to the Chitraka forest to chase wild beasts. Those were glad times. Our hearts danced to the drumbeat of rumbling clouds. The woods resounded with the screams of peacocks. Timid deer could not hear our approaching steps for the patter of rain and the noise of waterfalls; the leopards would leave their tracks on the wet earth, betraying their lairs.

Our sport over, we dared each other to swim across turbulent streams on our way back home. The restless spirit is on me. I long to go hunting.

Chitra: First run down the quarry you are now following. Are you quite certain that the enchanted deer you pursue must needs be caught? No, not yet. Like a dream the wild creature eludes you when it seems most nearly yours. Look how the wind is chased by the mad rain that discharges a thousand arrows after it. Yet it goes free and unconquered. Our sport is like that, my love! You give chase to the fleet-footed spirit of beauty, aiming at her every dart you have in your hands. Yet this magic deer runs ever free and untouched.

Arjuna: My love, have you no home where kind hearts are waiting for your return? A home which you once made sweet with your gentle service and whose light went out when you left it for this wilderness?

Chitra: Why these questions? Are the hours of unthinking pleasure over? Do you not know that I am no more than what you see before you? For me there is no vista beyond. The dew that hangs on the tip of a *Kinsuka* petal has neither name nor destination. If offers no answer to any question. She whom you love is like that perfect bead of dew.

Arjuna: Has she no tie with the world? Can she be merely like a fragment of heaven dropped on the earth through the carelessness of wanton god?

Chitra: Yes.

Arjuna: Ah, that is why I always seem about to lose you. My heart is unsatisfied, my mind knows no peace. Come closer to me, unattainable one! Surrender yourself to the bonds of name and home and parentage. Let my heart feel you on all sides and live with you in the peaceful security of love.

Chitra: Why this vain effort to catch and keep the tints of the clouds, the dance of the waves, the smell of the flowers?

Arjuna: Mistress mine, do not hope to pacify love with airy nothings. Give me something to clasp, something that can last longer than pleasure, that can endure even through suffering.

Chitra: Hero mine, the year is not yet full, and you are tired already! Now I know that it is Heaven's blessing that has made the flower's term of life short. Could this body of mine have drooped and died with the flowers of last spring it surely would have died with honour. Yet, its days are numbered, my love. Spare it not, press it dry of honey, for fear your beggar's heart come back to it again and again with unsated desire, like a thirsty bee when summer blossoms lie dead in the dust.

SCENE VII

Madana: To-night is thy last night.

Vasanta: The loveliness of your body will return tomorrow to the inexhaustible stores of the spring. The ruddy tint of thy lips freed from the memory of Arjuna's kisses, will bud anew as a pair of fresh *asoka* leaves, and the soft, white glow of thy skin will be born again in a hundred fragrant jasmine flowers.

Chitra: O gods, grant me this prayer! To-night, in its last hour, let my beauty flash its brightest, like the final flicker of a dying flame.

Madana: Thou shalt have thy wish.

SCENE VIII

Villagers: Who will protect us now?

Arjuna: Why, by what danger are you threatened?

Villagers: The robbers are pouring from the northern hills like a mountain flood to devastate our village.

Arjuna: Have you in this kingdom no warden?

Villagers: Princess Chitra was the terror of all evildoers. While she was in this happy land we feared natural deaths, but had no other fears. Now she has gone on a pilgrimage, and none knows where to find her.

Arjuna: Is the warden of this country a woman?

Villagers: Yes, she is our father and mother in one.

[Exeunt]
(Enter Chitra)

Chitra: Why are you sitting all alone?

Arjuna: I am trying to imagine what kind of woman Princess Chitra may be. I hear so many stories of her from all sorts of men.

Chitra: Ah, but she is not beautiful. She has no such lovely eyes as mine, dark as death. She can pierce any target she will, but not our hero's heart.

Arjuna: They say that in valour she is a man, and a woman in tenderness.

Chitra: That, indeed, is her greatest misfortune. When a woman is merely a woman; when she winds herself round and round men's hearts with her smiles and sobs and services and caressing endearments; then she is happy. Of what use to her are learning and great achievements? Could you have seen her only yesterday in the court of the Lord Shiva's temple by the forest path, you would have passed by without deigning to look at her. But have you grown so weary of woman's beauty that you seek in her for a man's strength?

With green leaves wet from the spray of the foaming waterfall, I have made our noonday bed in a cavern dark as night. There the cool of the soft green mosses thick on the black and dripping stone kisses your eyes to sleep. Let me guide you thither.

Arjuna: Not to-day, beloved.

Chitra: Why not to-day?

Arjuna: I have heard that a horde of robbers has neared the plains. Needs must I go and prepare my weapons to protect the frightened villagers.

Chitra: You need have no fear for them. Before she started on her pilgrimage, Princess Chitra had set strong guards at all the frontier passes.

Arjuna: Yet permit me for a short while to set about a Kshatriya's work. With new glory will I ennoble this idle arm, and make of it a pillow more worthy of your head.

Chitra: What if I refuse to let you go, if I keep you entwined in my arms? Would you rudely snatch yourself free and leave me? Go then! But you must know that the liana, once broken in two, never joins again. Go, if your thirst is quenched. But, if not, then remember that the goddess of pleasure is fickle, and waits for no man. Sit for a while, my lord! Tell me what uneasy thoughts tease you. Who occupied your mind to-day? Is it Chitra?

Arjuna: Yes, it is Chitra. I wonder in fulfilment of what vow she has gone on her pilgrimage. Of what could she stand in need?

Chitra: Her needs? Why, what has she ever had, the unfortunate creature? Her very qualities are as prison walls, shutting her woman's heart in a bare cell. She is obscured, she is unfulfilled. Her womanly love must content itself dressed in rags; beauty is denied her. She is like the spirit of a cheerless morning, sitting upon the stony mountain peak, all her light blotted out by dark clouds. Do not ask me of her life. It will never sound sweet to man's ear.

Arjuna: I am eager to learn all about her. I am like a traveller come to strange city at midnight. Domes and towers and garden-trees look vague and shadowy, and the dull moan of the sea comes fitfully through the silence of sleep. Wistfully he waits for the morning to reveal to him all the strange wonders. Oh, tell me her story.

Chitra: What more is there to tell?

Arjuna: I seem to see her, in my mind's eye, riding on a white horse, proudly holding the reins in her left hand, and in her right a bow, and like the goddess of Victory dispensing glad hope all round her. Like a watchful lioness she protects the litter at her dugs with a fierce love. Woman's arms, though adorned with aught but unfettered strength, are beautiful! My heart is restless, fair one, like a serpent reviving from his long winter's sleep. Come, let us both race on swift horses side by side like twin orbs of light sweeping through space. Out from this slumbrous prison of green gloom, this dank, dense cover of perfumed intoxication, choking breath.

Chitra: Arjuna, tell me true, if, now at once, by some magic I could shake myself free from this voluptuous softness, this timid bloom of beauty shrinking from the rude and healthy touch of the world, and fling it from my body like borrowed clothes, would you be able to bear it? If I stand up straight and strong with the strength of a daring heart spurning the wiles and arts of twining weakness, if I hold my head high like a tall young mountain fir, no longer trailing in the dust like a liana, shall I then appeal to man's eye? No, no, you could not endure it. It is better that I should keep spread about me all the dainty playthings of fugitive youth, and wait for you in patience. When it pleases you to return, I will smilingly pour out for you the wine of pleasure in the cup of this beauteous body. When you are tired and satiated with this wine, you can go to work or play; and when I grow old I will accept humbly and gratefully whatever corner is left for me. Would it please your heroic soul if the playmate of the night aspired to be the helpmate of the day, if the left arm learnt to share the burden of the proud right arm?

Arjuna: I never seem to know you aright. You seem to me like a goddess hidden within a golden image. I cannot touch you, I cannot pay you my dues in return for your priceless gifts. Thus my love is incomplete. Sometimes in the enigmatic depth of your sad look, in your playful words mocking at their own meaning, I gain glimpses of a being trying to rend asunder the languorous grace of her body, to emerge in a chaste fire of pain through a vaporous veil of smiles. Illusion is the first appearance of Truth. She advances towards her lover in disguise. But a time comes when she throws off her ornaments and veils and stands clothed in naked dignity. I grope for that ultimate *you*, that bare simplicity of truth.

Why these tears, my love? Why cover your face with your hands? Have I pained you, my darling? Forget what I said. I will be content with the present. Let each separate moment of beauty come to me like a bird of mystery from its unseen nest in the dark bearing a message of music. Let me for ever sit with my hope on the brink of its realization, and thus end my days.

SCENE IX

(Chitra and Arjuna)

Chitra (cloaked): My lord, has the cup been drained to the last drop? Is this, indeed, the end? No, when all is done something still remains, and that is my last sacrifice at your feet.

I brought from the garden of heaven flowers of incomparable beauty with which to worship you, god of my heart. If the rites are over, if the flowers have faded, let me throw them out of the temple (*unveiling in her original male attire*). Now, look at your worshipper with gracious eyes.

I am not beautifully perfect as the flowers with which I worshipped. I have many flaws and blemishes. I am a traveller in the great world-path, my garments are dirty, and my feet are bleeding with thorns. Where should I achieve flower-beauty, the unsullied loveliness of a moment's life? The gift that I proudly bring you is the heart of a woman. Here have all pains and joys gathered, the hopes and fears and shames of a daughter of the dust; here love springs up struggling toward immortal life. Herein lies an imperfection which yet is noble and grand. If the flower-service is finished, my master, accept *this* as your servant for the days to come!

I am Chitra, the king's daughter. Perhaps you will remember the day when a woman came to you in the temple of Shiva, her body loaded with ornaments and finery. That shameless woman came to court you as though she were a man. You rejected her; you did well. My lord, I am that woman. She was my disguise. Then by the boon of gods I obtained for a year the most radiant form that a mortal ever wore, and wearied my hero's heart with the burden of that deceit. Most surely I am not that woman.

I am Chitra. No goddess to be worshipped, nor yet the object of common pity to be brushed aside like a moth with indifference. If you deign to keep me by your side in a path of danger and daring, if you allow me to share the great duties of your life, then you will know my true self. If your babe, whom I am nourishing in my womb, be born a son, I shall myself teach him to be a second Arjuna, and send him to you when the time comes, and then at last you will truly know me. To-day I can only offer you Chitra, the daughter of a king.

Arjuna: Beloved, my life is full!

Transcreated by **Rabindranath Tagore** [*The English writings of Rabindranath Tagore* (New Delhi: Sahitya Akademi, 2004)]

Short Stories

Profit and loss[1]
(*Denapaona*)

When a daughter was born, after five sons, her parents dotingly named her Nirupama.[2] Such a high-flown name had never been heard in the family before. Usually names of gods and goddesses were used—Ganesh, Kartik, Parvati and so on.

The question of Nirupama's marriage now arose. Her father Ramsundar Mitra searched and searched without finding a groom he really liked, but in the end he procured the only son of a grand Raybahadur. The ancestral wealth of this Raybahadur had diminished considerably, but the family was certainly noble. They asked for a dowry of 10,000 rupees, and many additional gifts. Ramsundar agreed without a thought—such a groom should not be allowed to slip through one's fingers. But no way could he raise all the money. Even after pawning, selling, and using every method he could, he still owed 6,000 or 7,000 rupees; and the day of the wedding was drawing near.

The wedding day came. Someone had agreed to lend the rest of the money at an extortionate rate of interest, but he failed to turn up on the day. A furious scene broke out in the marriage room. Ramsundar fell on his knees before the Raybahadur, implored him not to bring bad luck by breaking off the ceremony, insisted he would pay him in full. 'If you can't

---

[1] *Denāpāonā* in Bengali, meaning 'debit and credit' or 'investment and return' but also a deal, claim, transaction etc.

[2] 'Peerless one'.

hand the money to me, now,' replied the Raybahadur, 'the bridegroom will not be brought here.'

The women of the house wept and wailed at this disastrous upset. The root cause of it sat mutely in her silk wedding-dress and ornaments, her forehead decorated with sandal-paste. It cannot be said that she felt much love or respect for her prospective husband's family.

Suddenly the impasse was resolved. The groom rebelled against his father, saying firmly, 'This haggling and bartering means nothing to me. I came here to marry, and marry I shall.'

'You see, sir, how young men behave these days,' said his father to everyone he turned to.

'It's because they have no training in morality or the Shastras,' said some of the oldest there. The Raybahadur sat despondent at seeing the poisonous fruits of modern education in his own son. The marriage was completed in a gloomy, joyless sort of way.

As Nirupama left for her in-laws' house her father clasped her to his breast and could not hold back his tears. 'Won't they let me come and visit you, father?' she asked. 'Why shouldn't they, my love?' said Ramsundar. 'I'll come and fetch you.'

Ramsundar often went to see his daughter, but he had no honour in his son-in-law's house. Even the servants looked down on him. Sometimes he saw his daughter for five minutes in a separate outer room of the house; sometimes he was not allowed to see her at all. To be disgraced so in a kinsman's house was unbearable. He decided that somehow or other the money would have to be paid, but the burden of debt on his shoulders was already hard to control. Expenses dragged at him terribly; he had to resort to all sorts of petty subterfuges to avoid running into his creditors.

Meanwhile his daughter was treated spitefully at every turn. She shut herself into her room and wept—a daily penance for the insults heaped on her family. Her mother-in-law's assaults were especially vicious. If anyone said, 'How pretty the girl is—it's a pleasure to look at her', she would burst out, 'Pretty indeed! Pretty as the family she came from!' Even her food and clothing were neglected. If a kind neighbour expressed concern, her mother-in-law would say, 'She has more than enough'—implying that if the girl's father had paid full price she would have received full care. Everyone treated her as if she had no rights in the household, and had entered it by deceit.

Naturally news of the contempt and shame his daughter was suffering reached Ramsundar. He decided to sell his house. He did not, however, tell his sons that he was making them houseless: he intended to rent the house back after selling it. By this ploy, his sons would not know the true situation till after his death. But his sons found out. They came and protested vigorously. The three elder boys, particularly, were married and probably had children: their objections were so forceful that the sale was stopped. Ramsundar then started to raise money by taking out small loans from various quarters at high interest—so much so, that he could no longer meet household expenses.

Nirupama understood everything from her father's expression. The old man's grey hair, pallid face and permanently cowering manner all indicated poverty and worry. When a father lets down his own daughter, he cannot disguise the guilt he feels. Whenever Ramsundar managed to get permission to speak to his daughter for a few moments, it was clear at once even from his smile how heartbroken he was.

She longed to return to her father's house for a few days to console him. To see his sad face made it awful to be away. One day she said to Ramsundar, 'Father, take me home for a while.'

'Very well,' he replied—but he had no power to do so, the natural claims that a father has to his daughter had been pawned in place of a dowry. Even a glimpse of his daughter had to be begged for meekly, and if on any occasion it was not granted he was not in a position to ask a second time. But if his daughter herself wished to come home, how could he not bring her?

It is better not to tell the story of the indignity, shame and hurt that Ramsundar had to endure in order to raise the 3,000 rupees that he needed for an approach to his daughter's father-in-law. Wrapping the banknotes in a handkerchief tied into a corner of his chadar, he went to see him. He began breezily with local news, describing at length a daring theft in Harekrishna's house. Comparing the abilities and characters of Nabinmadhab and Radhamadhab, he praised Radhamadhab and criticized Nabinmadhab. He gave a hair-raising account of a new illness in town. Finally, putting down the hookah, he said as if in passing, 'Yes, yes, brother, there's still some money owing, I know. Every day I remember, and mean to come along with some of it, but then it slips my mind. I'm getting old, my friend.' At the end of this long preamble, he casually produced the three notes, which were really like three of his ribs. The Raybahadur burst into coarse laughter at the sight of them. 'Those are no use to me,' he said, making it plain by using a current proverb that he did not want to make his hands stink for no reason.

After that, to ask to bring Nirupama home seemed out of the question, though Ramsundar wondered what good he was doing to himself by observing polite forms. After sitting in heart-stricken silence for a long time, he did at last softly raise the matter. 'Not now,' said the Raybahadur, giving no reason; then he left, to go about his work.

Unable to face his daughter, hands trembling, Ramsundar tied the three banknotes back into the end of his chadar and set off home. He resolved never to return to the Raybahadur's house until he had paid the money in full; only then could he lay claim to Nirupama confidently.

Many months passed. Nirupama sent messenger after messenger, but her father never appeared. In the end she took offence, and stopped sending. This grieved Ramsundar sorely, but he still would not go to her. The month of Āśvin came. 'This year I shall bring Nirupama home for the *pūjā* or *else!*' he said to himself, making a fierce vow.

On the fifth or sixth day of the *pūjā*-fortnight, Ramsundar once again tied a few notes into the end of his chadar and got ready to go out. A five-year-old grandson came and said, 'Grandpa, are you going to buy a cart for me?' For weeks he had set his heart on a push-cart to ride in, but there had been no way of meeting his wish. Then a six-year-old grand-daughter came and said tearfully that she had no nice dress to wear for the *pūjā*. Ramsundar knew that well, and had brooded over it for a long time as he smoked. He had sighed to think of the women of his house-hold attending the *pūjā* celebrations at the Raybahadur's house like paupers receiving charity, wearing whatever miserable ornaments they had; but his thoughts had no result other than making the old man's lines on his fore-head even deeper.

With the cries of his poverty-stricken household ringing in his ears, Ramsundar arrived at the Raybahadur's house. Today there was no hesi-tation in his manner, no trace of the nervous glances with which he had formerly approached the gatekeeper and servants: it was if he was enter-ing his own house. He was told that the Raybahadur was out—he would have to wait a while. But he could not hold back his longing to meet his daughter. Tears of joy rolled down his cheeks when he saw her. Father and daughter wept together; neither of them could speak for some moments. Then Ramsundar said 'This time I shall take you, my dear. Nothing can stop me now.'

Suddenly Ramsundar's eldest son Haramohan burst into the room with his two small sons. 'Father,' he cried, 'have you really decided to turn us out on the streets?'

Ramsundar flared up. 'Should I condemn myself to hell for your sakes? Won't you let me do what is right?' He had sold the house: he had gone to great lengths to conceal the sale from his sons, but to his anger and dismay it appeared that they had found out all the same. His grandson clasped him round his knees looked up, saying, 'Grandpa, haven't you bought me that cart?' When he got no answer from the now crestfallen Ramsundar, the little boy went up to Nirupama and said, 'Auntie, will you buy me a cart?'

Nirupama had no difficulty in understanding the whole situation. 'Father,' she said, 'if you give a single paisa more to my father-in-law, I swear solemnly you will never see me again.'

'What are you saying, child?' said Ramsundar, 'if I don't give the money, the shame will be forever on my head—and it will be your shame too.'

'The shame will be greater if you pay the money,' said Nirupama. 'Do you think I have no honour? Do you think I am just a money-bag, the more money in it the higher my value? Father, don't shame me by paying this money. My husband doesn't want it anyway.'

'But then they won't let you come and see me,' said Ramsundar 'That can't be helped,' said Nirupama. 'Please don't try to fool me anymore.'

Ramsundar tremblingly pulled his chadar—with the money tied into it—back round his shoulders, and left the house thief again, avoiding everyone's stare.

It did not, however, remain a secret that Ramsundar had come with the money and that his daughter had forbidden him to hand it over. An inquisitive servant, a listener at keyholes, passed the information on to Nirupama's mother-in-law, whose menace towards her daughter-in-law now went beyond all limits. The household became a bed of nails for her. Her husband had set off a few days after their wedding to be Deputy Magistrate in another part of the country. Claiming that Nirupama would be corrupted by contact with her relatives, her in-laws now consciously forbade her from seeing them.

She now fell seriously ill. But this was not wholly her mother-in-law's fault. She herself had neglected her health dreadfully. On chilly autumn nights she lay with her head near the open door, and she wore no extra clothes during the winter. She ate irregularly. The servants would sometimes forget to bring her any food: she would not then say anything to remind them. She was forming a fixed belief that she was herself a servant in the household, dependent on the favours of her master and mistress. But her mother-in-law could not stand even this attitude. If Nirupama showed lack of interest in food, she would say, 'What a princess she is! A poor household's fare is not to her liking!' Or else she would say, 'Look at her. What a beauty! She's more and more like a piece of burnt wood.'

When her illness got worse, her mother-in-law said, 'It's all put on.' Finally one day Nirupama said humbly, 'Let me see my father and brothers just once, Mother.'

'Nothing but a trick to get to her father's house,' said her mother-in-law.

It may seem unbelievable, but the evening when Nirupama's breath began to fail was when the doctor was first called, and it was the last visit that he made too.

The eldest daughter-in-law in the household had died, and the funeral rites were performed with appropriate pomp. The Raychaudhuris were renowned in the district for the lavishness with which they performed the immersion of the deity at the end of *Durgā-pūjā,* but the Raybahadur's family became famous for the way Nirupama was cremated: such a huge sandalwood pyre had never been seen. Only they could have managed such elaborate rites, and it was rumoured that they got rather into debt as a result.

Everyone gave Ramsundar long descriptions of the magnificence of his daughter's death, when they came to condole with him. Meanwhile a letter from the Deputy Magistrate arrived: 'I have made all necessary arrangements here, so please send my wife to me quickly.' The Raybahadur's wife replied, 'Dear son, we have secured another girl for you, so please take leave soon and come home.'

This time the dowry was 20,000 rupees, cash down.

Translated by **William Radice**
[Rabindranath Tagore: Selected short stories
(London: Penguin Books, 2005, ed.)]

The housewife
(*Ginni*)

Pandit Shibnath used to teach us two or three classes below the scholarship level. He was clean-shaven, and had trimmed hair and a short tuft. A mere glimpse of him was enough for the hearts of the children to shrink in fear.

It is generally seen in the animal world that the creatures with stings lack tusks. Our teacher was simultaneously gifted with both. On the one hand, blows and slaps used to rain on us like hail on a sapling, and on the other hand, his poisoned tongue seemed to squeeze our lives out.

He used to lament that the ancient *guru–sishya* (preceptor–disciple) relationship is lost, that students no more revere their teacher as though he is a deity; saying this, he would hurl his neglected glory with all his might on our heads, and his occasional shouts were so blended with raw vocabulary that nobody would mistake them for thunderous roars from heaven. If Abuse disguises itself as Thunder, does it not reveal its pettiness?

Be that as it may, nobody would mistake this deity in charge of the second division of the third grade of our school for Indra, Chandra, Varuna or Kartika; the only god with whom some resemblance could be drawn was Yama, the god of death, and after so many years, there is no harm, and certainly no fear on my part, in confessing that we used to long inwardly that he should not delay setting out for the abode of the deity last mentioned.

But it was firmly felt that there was no greater danger than a human god. The celestial gods do not trouble you. They are content if you offer a flower plucked from a tree, and they do not pester you if you don't. Our human gods demand a lot more, and when they run after us with reddened eyes at our slightest transgressions, by no means do they appear godlike.

Our Pandit Shibnath had a typical weapon for chastising children, which seems trivial to hear about but was actually quite severe. He used to rename the boys. Though a name is nothing more than a mere word, people generally love it more than themselves; what troubles don't people undertake in order to make their names known, so much so that they don't even fear dying in order to save their name.

Distorting the name of such a name-loving creature amounts to inflicting wounds on spots dearer than life. Even one whose name is Bhutnath (lord of ghosts) would feel it insufferable if you call him Nalinikanta (lover of the lily).

The conclusion that one may deduce from all these observations is that man values the unreal more than the concrete; for him, the making charge for gold work is more important than the gold, honour is dearer than life and his name dearer than himself.

Driven by this inherent intricate law of human nature, Sasisekhar was depressed when the pandit named him *Bhetki*, a flat fish. Especially, the realisation that his physical appearance was the target of the new name doubled his suffering, but he had to bear it calmly, and keep sitting silently in the class.

Ashu was named 'The Housewife' (*Ginni*), and this name had its own history.

He was a typical, poor, good boy in the class. He never talked to anybody and was very shy; he was possibly the youngest in the class, and he would smile gently at every word. He prepared his lessons well. Many of the boys in school were eager to befriend him, but he would not play with any, and would not delay a moment to set off for his home as soon as the classes were over.

At one o'clock in the afternoon, a maid would come carrying a few sweets in a stack and water in a brass tumbler. Ashu would feel awkward at this, as though he would be relieved if the maid left. He was very unwilling to reveal before the boys that he was something more than a student of the school; as though his being somebody in a household, or being a child to his parents, or a sibling to his brother and sister were top secrets to be maintained, not to be told by any means to his peers; such was his ardent effort.

He had no deficiencies in learning, barring occasional delays in arrival, for which he had no convincing replies when charged by Shibnath pandit. This sometimes made him face unbearable harassment. The pandit would make him stand by the staircase near the corridor, stooping and placing his arms on his knees. The pupils of all the four classes could witness this abashed, wretched fellow in this condition.

It was a holiday on the occasion of an eclipse. The next day, the teacher was sitting on his stool, and as he glanced at the door, he noticed Ashu entering the classroom with his slate and books packed in a cloth bag blotted with ink, a little more hesitant than he was on other days.

Shibnath pandit laughed wryly and said, 'Here comes the housewife.'

Then, after the lessons were over, he called the students and said, 'Listen, all of you.'

The boy felt a downward pull exerted by all the gravitational force of the earth. But he remained seated with the plaited end of his dhoti and his legs dangling from the bench, all eyes on him. Ashu might have grown quite adult now, and he must have faced many incidents of extreme joy, sorrow and shame, but the chronicle of the child's heart that day remains unparalleled.

But the issue is trivial and can be wound up in just a few words.

Ashu had a younger sister; she had no other companion or sister of her age, and therefore, Ashu was her only playmate.

The garage of Ashu's household was within a gated, iron railing. It was a cloudy day, and raining heavily. The few pedestrians who were treading the streets with their shoes in their hands, and umbrellas over their heads, had no time to spare. Amid that cloudy darkness, and the pattering showers, Ashu and his sister were playing throughout the holiday, seated on the staircase of the garage.

It was the wedding of their dolls. Ashu was busy with the arrangements and advising his sister solemnly.

Now the debate arose as to who should play the priest. The little girl ran out quickly and asked a person, 'O, will you be our priest?'

Ashu turned back to see a half-drenched Shibnath pandit with folded umbrella standing at their garage. He was passing by, and had to take shelter in the garage to avoid the rain. The little girl was offering him the position of priesthood.

The moment he saw Shibnath pandit, Ashu left his sister and the game and instantly disappeared inside the house. His holiday was ruined completely.

Next day, when Shibnath pandit narrated the incident with dry humour as a prologue to Ashu's public renaming as 'The Housewife', initially, he tried to participate in the banter around him with his usual mild smile; at this point, the bell rang, and all other classes were dissolved, and the maid came and stood at the door with two pats of sweets in a *sal*-leaf platter and water in a shining brass vessel.

Then he laughed and laughed until his ears and face blushed rosy red, the veins of his aching forehead swelled and his gushing tears knew no bounds.

Shibnath pandit, having had his meal, sat down relaxed to smoke his share of tobacco in the resting room. The boys surrounded Ashu and began to shout, 'Housewife! Housewife!' in sheer derision. Playing with his little sister on that holiday appeared to Ashu as a most shameful mistake, and he could not get himself to believe that a time would come when people on earth would forget the incident.

Translated by **Soham Pain**

Kabuliwala
(*Kabuliwallah*)

My five-year-old daughter Mini cannot stop talking—even for a second. She spent about a year after her birth learning the art of speaking. Ever since then, she does not waste any precious moment of her waking hours in silence. Her mother has many a time soundly scolded her and thus shut her up. But this is an impossibility for me. A silent Mini is something so unnatural that it becomes impossible for me to tolerate this situation for a very long time. It is for this exact reason that all conversations between us are conducted with a great deal of enthusiasm.

In the morning I was about to begin the seventeenth chapter of my novel, when Mini put in an appearance and began with, 'Father, Ramdayal the guard called a crow *koua*—he doesn't know a thing, does he?'

Before I could enlighten her on the intricacies of the various languages of the world, she had already started on another topic, 'Father, Bhola was saying the other day that because elephants spray the sky with water from their trunks, it rains. Imagine! Bhola can really talk such a lot of nonsense! He can only talk and talk all day long'.

Not waiting for a moment for my response, all of a sudden she suddenly asked, 'Father, how is mother related to you?'

Muttering an inane response I replied, 'Mini, why not go and play with Bhola now, I have a lot of work in hand'.

She then placed herself firmly at my feet on the ground and in no time at all became engrossed in a childish game of her making. At the time, in the 17th chapter of my novel, the hero and the heroine were preparing, under the shelter of the dark night, to escape from the dungeon by plunging into the waters of the river.

My room overlooks the road. All of a sudden Mini discarded her game and running up to the window started calling out vigorously, 'Kabuliwallah, O Kabuliwallah!'

Clad in filthy loose clothes, a turban around his head, a massive sack on his back and holding on firmly to a couple of boxes, a tall Kabuliwallah was walking slowly by. I am not quite sure what kind of emotions he evoked in my daughter, but she frenetically began to call out to him. I thought, a nuisance carrying a load on his back would definitely be turning up in a short while—finishing the seventeenth chapter of my book would be an impossibility.

But no sooner had the Kabuliwallah smilingly turned around and started walking towards our house, Mini desperately ran inside and not a trace of her could be found. She had the unwavering conviction that if that huge sack could be investigated, undoubtedly, a few young children like her would definitely be unearthed.

The Kabuliwallah came up to me and smilingly greeted me. I thought to myself—though my protagonists were in a desperate situation, it certainly would not do to call the man and then not purchase anything from him.

Some purchases were made and then the conversation continued. Finally, just before he took his leave the man asked, 'Babu, where is your daughter?'

Intending to get rid of her false apprehensions, I sent for Mini. She clung to my side and cast suspicious glances—once at the Kabuliwallah and once at the huge bag he carried. He delved into the sack and taking out dry fruits tried to hand them to her—Mini steadfastly refused to accept. Even more warily she sidled closer. The first introduction followed this pattern.

One evening, I had to leave the house on some urgent work. I observed that seated on a bench near the door my daughter was chattering away nineteen to the dozen; smilingly the Kabuliwallah was sitting at her feet and listening and even commenting in half-broken Bengali. In the five years of Mini's life, besides her father, never had she had such a patient and uncomplaining listener. I also noticed that she had her lap full of cashew and raisins. I said to the Kabuliwallah, 'Why did you do that? Please refrain in the future'. I handed him a coin, which he accepted unhesitatingly and put in his pocket.

On returning I found that that coin was at the root of a storm of trouble.

Holding a shining round coin in her hand Mini's mother was scolding her, 'Where did you get hold of this coin?'

Mini answered, 'The Kabuliwallah gave it to me'.

'Just because he gave it to you—did you have to accept?'

On the verge of tears Mini reiterated, 'But I did not ask for it—he gave it...'

Rescuing Mini from imminent troubles, I brought her away.

I learnt that this was far from their second meeting. The Kabuliwallah had taken to visiting practically every day; by a judicious bribe of dry fruits, he had almost won over my little daughter's covetous little heart.

There were some standard jokes and jocular remarks that were exchanged between the two friends. On seeing Rehmat, my daughter would start laughing and ask, 'Kabuliwallah, O Kabuliwallah, what is in that sack of yours?'

Responding in absolutely unnecessary nasal tones, Rehmat would answer, 'An elephant'. There was no subtlety in the joke, but it amused them both no end. Observing this simple friendship between the old man and the little child in the background of this festive season also brought me a strange kind of joy.

Another remark was quite frequently to be heard between them both, Rehmat would tell Mini, 'Khoki, little one—you must never go away to your in-law's house'.

In an average Bengali household, girls are quite conversant with the concept of in-law's house from a very young age. However, having brought up our daughter on somewhat modern lines, she was not very familiar with the term. So, though not very sure about the nature of this request, it was totally contrary to her nature not to immediately come up with an answer. She would proceed to turn the table and ask, 'Will you then go to your in-law's?'

Rehmat would shake his fist at an imaginary father-in-law and affirm, 'I will beat my father-in-law'.

Hearing this Mini would be highly amused at the discomfiture and the sorry plight of this unknown person named 'father-in-law'.

It was the beautiful festive season—in ancient times, the period when royalty set out to conquer. I had never left Kolkata to travel—which is probably why my mind travelled the whole world. In the little corner of my room, I was an inveterate traveller; my mind always yearned to see the sprawling vistas of the universe. The name of a foreign country evoked in me a wanderlust; similarly the sight of someone from foreign climes—I could clearly visualise in the midst of rivers, mountains and forests a small cottage... Thoughts of a joyous independent life-style created a picture with magnetic appeal.

But I was so tied to my room that even the thought of emerging outside felt as though a thunderbolt had struck me. This is why talking to the Kabuliwallah sitting at my desk quenched my thirst for travel to some extent.

Remote roads on both sides rocky, isolated, reddish hued towering mountain peaks; in their midst narrow mountain path along which slowly moved lengthy lines of camels. They were accompanied by businessmen and travellers—some on foot and some on camel-back. Some travelled armed, while others remained bare-handed. The Kabuliwallah, in deep soft tones, would narrate tales of all of these and the scenes would flash before my eyes.

Mini's mother was inherently wary by nature; the slightest sound on the roads would convince her that all the drunken louts that could be found were making their way to our house. The nightmare that the entire world was over-populated with dacoits, drunkards, tigers, snakes and militant white-soldiers had never quite vanished from her mind.

She was still not completely sanguine about Rehmat Kabuliwallah. Repeated requests were made to me to keep an eye on him. When, jesting, I tried to laugh away her fears, she asked me a couple of questions consecutively, 'Has nobody's child ever been kidnapped; Does slavery not exist in Kabul; Was it entirely impossible for a towering Kabuli to steal a small child'.

I was forced to accept that, while not impossible, the matter was unlikely. The same degree of belief or disbelief was not in everybody—so my wife continued to nurture her doubts. But just based on these suspicions, I could not forbid Rehmat to come to our house for no fault of his own.

Rehmat would travel to his own country once annually. During this period he would remain extremely busy collecting all his pending dues. He would have to visit many houses, but in the midst of it all, Rehmat would always find time to visit Mini. Observing them both, it would truly seem that there was some sort of a conspiracy going on. If sometime he couldn't come in the morning, he would surely turn up in the evening. Seeing that gigantic Kabuliwallah clad in loose clothes, in one corner of the dark room, was definitely a little unnerving. But seeing Mini run up to him joyously and the jocular friendship between two people with such a vast age difference truly gladdened my heart.

One morning I sat in my tiny room, going through the proof of my books. Before final departing of winter, the past couple of days had been particularly chilly. Some sunlight penetrated the window and lightly warmed my feet, leaving behind a very pleasant sensation. It was getting on to be eight; almost all the warmly clad people all around had finished their morning walk and returned. All of a sudden a loud clamour was heard on the roads.

I looked out to find that Rehmat, firmly bound, was being taken along by two guards and a line of curious boys were trailing behind them. Rehmat's clothes were blood-spattered and one of the guards carried a bloody knife. Stepping out I stopped the guards and asked what the matter was.

Gleaning some information from him and some from the guards, I came to understand that a man owed Rehmat some money, having purchased some goods from him. Lying, he denied the debt and, in the ensuing controversy, Rehmat had knifed him.

Rehmat was addressing a volley of abuses towards the barefaced liar when all of a sudden Mini appeared crying out 'Kabuliwallah, O Kabuliwallah'. In a flash Rehmat's face overflowed with a gentle joviality. Today, there was no sack across his back, hence the usual jocular remark could not be made. Mini took the plunge straightaway and asked, 'Are you going to your in-laws?'

Rehmat laughed, 'That's exactly where I am going'.

When he saw that the answer did not amuse Mini he extended his hand to Mini and said, 'I would have beaten my father-in-law, but what to do, my hands are tied'.

Rehmat was sentenced to a few years' imprisonment for having caused grievous injuries.

I all but forgot about him. When, within the boundaries of our home, we went about our daily chores, it did not even occur to us how a man—an independent traveller—spent all these years in the close confines of prison.

Even a doting father must confess that, indeed, the light-hearted Mini's behaviour was shameful. Very easily she forgot her old friend and established new bonds with the coachman. As she grew up these friends were replaced by female mates. As a matter of fact, these days she can barely be seen even in her father's study. You could say that in a way I have even stopped being friends with her.

The years rolled by and it was time for yet another festive season. My Mini's marriage had been fixed—she would be getting married within the holidays. Just as the divine Goddess left bereft her father and journeyed back to her husband, Lord Shiva, my darling who brought such joy would turn her father's home into darkness and leave to be with her husband.

It was a beautiful morning. After the rains, this fresh sunlight of the season appeared to be wrapped in the golden embrace of love. As a matter of fact, even the skeletal worn out concrete houses of the city took on an indescribable charm. Since the previous night the strains of the *shehnai* had been resounding in my house and with it the very bones of my heart cried out in anguished pain. The notes of the music mingled and merged with the impending sorrow of parting and permeated the surroundings around along with the warmth of the sunlight. It was my daughter's wedding day.

Ever since the morning there was chaos, with people milling all around. Temporary decorative structures were being put up all around and there was no dearth of noise and people crying out.

I was checking the accounts in my room, when suddenly Rehmat entered and greeting me stood aside.

At first it was impossible to recognise him—neither did he sport the beard nor was there any sack on his back. He did not have the same robust appearance either. Ultimately it was his unforgettable smile that jolted my memory.

'Is that you Rehmat, when did you return?'

'They released me from jail yesterday evening'.

The very mention of jail cast a jarring note. Never before had I seen a murderous criminal—seeing Rehmat at such close quarters my entire being cringed. On this auspicious day all that I wanted was that he would go away.

I told him, 'There are certain celebrations in my house today and I am somewhat busy. It is better that you leave now'.

Immediately he turned around; on reaching the door, hesitantly, he said, 'Can I not meet the little one?'

It seemed that he still retained the picture of Mini as she had been all those years ago. Probably he nurtured the impression that Mini would still run up to him crying out, 'Kabuliwallah, O Kabuliwallah'. None would cry halt to their pleasant banter. As a matter of fact, in honour of past memories, he even now carried with him a box of grapes and a few raisins wrapped in paper—probably borrowed from a fellow country man, he himself not having the means any longer.

I answered, 'We are all busy at home today—it is not possible to meet anybody'.

The remark seemed to upset him a little. For a while he gazed steadily at me and then with a quiet, 'Babu Salaam', he left.

My heart filled with a kind of pain. I thought of calling him back, when I looked up to find that he himself had returned.

Rehmat drew close and said, 'These few dry fruits are for the little one, please give them to her'.

As I tried to hand him some money, all of a sudden he firmly clasped my hands, 'Babu, all your kindness I will never forget—please do not pay me. Just like your little one, I too have a daughter back home. She constantly remains with me and it is in memory of that that I bring these little gifts—trading was not my intention in coming here'.

Saying this Rehmat drew from inside his loose garb a worn out and shabby bit of paper. With great tenderness he opened the folds and put it on the table.

There was the palm-imprint of a small child—it was not a photograph or any studio-picture; some soot had been smeared on a bit of paper and the touch of a beloved daughter had thus been captured. Clinging on to that memory of his loved child Rehmat would wander about the streets of Kolkata every year to sell dry fruits. It was as though that tender loving touch rejuvenated that towering gigantic rough and ready Kabuliwallah.

My eyes brimmed with tears. I no longer remembered that I was a noble Bengali with a lineage to be proud of; he and I were the same—both of us were fathers. The palm-print of his little daughter born and brought up in the rocky mountains were a reflection of my little Mini. Immediately I sent for Mini; there were a lot of protests from the inner sanctum, but I overrode all objections. A shy awkward Mini in all her bridal finery shyly appeared before me.

The Kabuliwallah was so taken aback that he lost the words of their former jokes. Finally he smiled and asked, 'So, little one, you go to your in-laws?'

Mini now understood the meaning of the term; there was no ready response, embarrassed, she turned away. The memory of Mini's first meeting with him suddenly came to mind. A strange kind of ache filled my entire being.

As Mini left, a deep sigh rent Rehmat and he collapsed onto the ground. All of a sudden he clearly felt that his daughter too must have grown up and new ties would have to be forged with her. Never would it be possible to re-establish the same kind of relationship again. Who knows what had happened in the course of these eight years. That morning, in the soothing sunlight of a day in Kolkata, Rehmat could only visualise a mountain scene in far away Afghanistan.

Handing him some large notes I said, 'Rehmat, return to your daughter; may the joy of your reunion shower all blessings on my Mini'.

Having given away the money, some of the festivities had to be curtailed somewhat. The sparkling lights could not be afforded and neither was it possible to get the music band. The women in the inner sanctum expressed great resentment. But the lights of the wedding glowed even brighter on this auspicious occasion.

Translated by **Malobika Chaudhuri** [*Tagore's best short stories*
(London, Kolkata: Frontpage Publications Ltd, 2011)]

Mahamaya

(*Mahamaya*)

Mahamaya and Rajiblochan met at a dilapidated shrine by the river.

Mahamaya didn't say a word but looked at Rajiblochan with a grave glance that was natural to her. The meaning behind the gesture was—'How dare you summon me today at such a wrong hour at this place? Just because I have obeyed you so far and done all you said, how could you have grown so audacious?'

In the first place, Rajiblochan had always been slightly afraid of Mahamaya; on top of that, this look left him dumb. He had planned to say a few words in a well-knit form; that intent had to be instantly given up. But that wouldn't work if he failed to produce a reason for this meeting immediately. So, he rapidly said, 'Let me suggest something. Let's elope from here and get married.' Rajib definitely said what he had meant to say, but there was in it nothing of the prologue he had prepared in his mind. The suggestion sounded very gross and plain, and, more so, even absurd. Rajib himself felt awkward at the line he had spoken, and lost the presence of mind to add a few more words to soften it. Having invited Mahamaya at the dilapidated shrine by the river in the noon, this foolish man only said, 'Come, let's get married!'

Mahamaya was a maiden from a *kulin* family. She was twenty-four—full in age and beauty. It appeared as though she was an image made of melted gold, very much like the autumnal sunshine; like that very sunshine, she was bright and silent, and her gaze was open and unafraid like daylight.

She had no father, but an elder brother, who was named Bhabanicharan Chattopadhyay. The siblings were of an almost similar character—they were largely mute, but they possessed a certain heat which silently burns like the midday. People unnecessarily feared Bhabanicharan.

Rajib was not a native to this place. The head of the silk factory had brought him along. Rajib's father was an employee under the sahib. After his death, the outsider took upon himself the responsibility of his little son's upbringing, and brought him to the head office here at Bamanhati. The child had only his affectionate aunt by his side. The two were neighbours of Bhabanicharan. Mahamaya and Rajib were childhood playmates and Mahamaya developed a firm bond of affection with Rajib's aunt.

Rajib gradually crossed sixteen, seventeen, eighteen and even nineteen, but he would not marry despite repeated requests from his aunt. The sahib was very happy to learn about such good sense on the part of a Bengali boy. He surmised that the boy had accepted him only as the ideal in life. The sahib was a bachelor. In the meantime, the aunt passed away as well.

On the other hand, a suitable groom from an equal lineage could not be found for Mahamaya without expenses beyond capability. Her maiden years also kept increasing.

It goes without saying that although the deity who presides over matrimonial bonds had displayed indifference to this human pair, the one who presides over romantic love had not wasted much time. When the old Prajapati, the god of marriage, was dozing, the young Kandarpa, the angel of love, was wide awake.

Lord Kandarpa's grace manifests differently with respect to different people. Rajib, induced by him, looked for moments to say a few words; Mahamaya did not give him the opportunity. Her silent, reserved gaze put Rajib's impatient heart in fear.

Today, after much hesitation, Rajib had finally succeeded in bringing Mahamaya to this dilapidated shrine. Therefore, he thought that today he would say whatever he wanted to; then, either a lifelong happiness or a lifelong death may follow. On such a precarious day in his life, Rajib could only say, 'Come, let's get married then.' And after that, being dumbfounded, he kept silent like a student who had forgotten his lesson. Mahamaya had not expected such a proposal from Rajib. So, she remained silent for a long time.

There are quite a few vague and plaintive sounds characteristic of the midday; they began to ring in this silence. The broken, half-attached door-panel of the shrine kept opening and closing with a gentle moaning. Doves sitting on the window of the shrine keep cooing, the woodpecker seated on the branch of the kapok tree outside continued with its monotonous rapping, the lizard darted through the heap of dry leaves making a rustling sound, a sudden gust of wind rose from the field and blew through the trees with a hissing sound, and the waters of the river suddenly woke up and began to stroke the stairs of the broken ghat. A rustic note emerging from a cowherd's flute from beneath a distant tree, was heard through all these sudden, lazy sounds. Rajib, not being brave enough to look Mahamaya straight in her eyes, stood leaning against the base of the shrine, in a stiff, spellbound manner, looking at the river.

After a while, Rajib turned away and once again looked at Mahamaya's face in a begging manner. Mahamaya shook her head and said, 'No, that's not possible.'

The moment Mahamaya shook her head, Rajib's hopes were shattered. Because Rajib knew very well that Mahamaya's head shook at her own will; nobody else had the power to control its movement. A tremendous pride of lineage had flowed through Mahamaya's family for ages; could she ever concede to marrying a non-*kulin* brahmin like Rajib? Love is one thing and marriage is another. Be that as it may, Mahamaya could realise that it was due to *her* indiscreet behaviour that Rajib's audacity had this height. She immediately made up her mind to leave the shrine.

Rajib sensed the situation and hurriedly uttered, 'I am leaving this place tomorrow.'

Mahamaya had initially thought to show an indifferent response which would imply—'How does it matter to me?' But she could not. As she tried to take a step, her feet remained tethered. She asked placidly, 'Why?'

Rajib said, 'My sahib is being transferred to the head office at Sonapur; he is taking me along.'

Mahamaya once again remained silent for a long time. She thought—their lives were taking two different courses. A person cannot be kept under observation forever. Therefore, she slightly parted her pressed lips and said, 'Alright.' That sounded like a deep sigh. Having uttered only this brief phase, Mahamaya was once again about to leave. Just at this moment, Rajib was startled and uttered, 'Mr Chatterjee!'

Mahamaya saw that Bhabanicharan was coming towards the shrine, and understood that he had learnt about the two of them. Rajib saw the possibility of threat to Mahamaya and tried to leap out through the shrine's ruined base. Mahamaya forcefully grasped his arm and held him back. Bhabanicharan entered the temple, and gave a silent look at the pair.

Mahamaya turned to Rajib and said in an unwavering voice, 'Rajib, I shall go only to *your* home. Please wait for me.'

Bhabanicharan silently walked out of the temple, and Mahamaya followed him silently, while Rajib stood petrified as though he had heard the verdict of death.

II

That very night, Bhabanicharan brought a scarlet silk and commanded Mahamaya, 'Drape yourself in this and come.'

Mahamaya donned the scarlet silk and came. Then he said, 'Come with me.'

Nobody had ever violated Bhabanicharan's order, or even a signal. Not even Mahamaya.

The two headed towards the cremation ground by the river in the night. The cremation ground was not far from the house. There at the shelter for dying men brought to the Ganges, an old Brahmin was awaiting his death. The two went and stood by his bed. A Brahmin priest was in a corner of the room; Bhabanicharan signalled to him. He stood prepared with the arrangements for the auspicious occasion without delay. Mahamaya understood that her wedding was to be arranged with this dying man. She did not display an iota of objection. Mahamaya's marriage was conducted in the near-dark hut situated between two not-so-distant funeral pyres, where the groans of the dying mingled with indistinct chants.

Mahamaya was widowed the day after her wedding. The widow did not feel much sorrow at this mishap, and Rajib, too, was not as broken at the news of her widowhood as he had been about her marriage. Actually, he was somewhat happy. But the emotion did not sustain. A second blow almost shattered Rajib. He learnt that there was great pomp at the cremation ground. Mahamaya was to die on her husband's funeral pyre. The first thought that occurred to him was to send a word to the sahib and get this cruel ceremony stopped by force. But then, he remembered that just today the sahib had left for Sonapur, where he had been transferred. Rajib was asked to accompany him, but Rajib had asked for a month's leave and stayed back.

Mahamaya had said to him, 'Wait for me.' He could never ignore those words. For now, he had a month's leave; if required, he could extend it to two or three months, and finally he might leave the sahib's job and beg from door to door, but he wouldn't give up waiting throughout his life.

While Rajib was going mad with thoughts of either suicide or something worse, a devastating storm with torrential rain came in the evening.

The storm was so violent that it appeared to Rajib as though the house would collapse over his head. When he saw that a tumult like the one going on in his inner world had also appeared in the sky, he felt somewhat calm. The power he had intended to exert but failed had been unleashed by nature across the heavens.

At this point, somebody pushed the door from outside with tremendous might. Rajib hurriedly opened the door. A woman in drenched clothing entered with her entire face veiled. Rajib instantly recognised her—it was Mahamaya.

Excited, he asked, 'Mahamaya, have you risen from the pyre?'

Mahamaya answered, 'Yes. I had made a commitment that I shall come to your home. I have come to keep that word. But Rajib, I am no more what I was; everything is changed. It's only in my mind that I am the same Mahamaya. You can tell me your decision even now; there is still time to go back to the pyre. But if you promise that you will never remove my veil, never try to view my face, then I can stay in your house.

It seems sufficient to have pulled back something from the mouth of death; everything else appears to be trivial. Rajib quickly said, 'You stay here in whatever way you want. I won't live if you abandon me.'

Mahamaya said, 'Then let's immediately set out for the place where your sahib has been transferred.'

Rajib left everything that was in his house and set out with Mahamaya in that stormy night. The storm was so violent that it was difficult to stand. Pebbles blown by the gust of the storm were piercing the body along with the sharp rain drops. Afraid of trees being uprooted and squashing their heads, the two abandoned the path and began to walk through the open field. The wind pushed them from behind. It seemed as though two humans had been uprooted from their habitat and were being funnelled towards annihilation.

III

The readers should not think that the story is trivial or supernatural. When the custom of widow burning was prevalent, such incidents were occasionally heard.

Mahamaya, her limbs tied up, had been consigned to the flames, and the pyre was lit at the usual hour. When the flames flared up, the tremendous storm and torrential rain started. Those who had come for the cremation hurriedly took shelter in the hut reserved for the dying men and closed the door. In no time, the funeral fire was put out by the downpour. In the meantime, Mahamaya's knots had burnt out and her hands were free. Despite insufferable pain due to the burns, she remained silent; she sat up and freed her legs. Then, somehow draping herself in largely burnt pieces of clothing, an almost nude Mahamaya rose from the pyre and at first returned to her own house. Nobody was there; everybody was at the burning ghat. She lit a lamp, donned herself in a piece of cloth and had a look at her face in the mirror. Then she dashed the mirror to the floor and mused for a moment. Then she pulled a long veil over her face and went to Rajib's place which was not far. What followed next is not unknown to the readers.

Mahamaya was now in Rajib's house, but there was no happiness in Rajib's life. The gulf between the two was not massive, but only that of a veil. But that veil was eternal like death, and more tormenting than death itself. Because, despair dims the pang of separation cast by death, but the separation created by this veil was tormenting a living need every moment every single day.

To begin with, Mahamaya always had a reserved, silent attitude, and added to this, the silence behind this veil seemed doubly painful. It seemed as though she was living cocooned in a sphere of death. This silent death entangled Rajib's life and began shrinking it every day. Rajib lost the Mahamaya whom he knew in the past; on the other hand, this veiled figure constantly by his side began to silently destroy the memory he had preserved of consecrating this household with her presence. Rajib thought natural distances exist between people—especially, Mahamaya seemed to sport an armour like the mythical Karna—she was born with a veil around her nature, and then she seemed to have taken a second birth and once again donned yet another veil. In spite of remaining by his side every moment, she had become so distant that Rajib couldn't reach out to her. Standing outside a dark circle with an insatiate, thirsty heart, he was trying to penetrate this sharp mystery.

In this manner, two unmatched, solitary individuals lived together for a long time.

On the tenth night of a bright fortnight of a rainy season, the clouds dispersed and the moon appeared. A still moonlit night stood awake by the head of a sleeping earth. That night, Rajib too was sitting by the window, having abandoned his sleep. A fragrance from the summer-stricken woods along with the tired drone of the crickets was wafting into his room. Rajib could see the motionless lake at the margin of the range of trees was shining like a silver foil. It is difficult to say whether men think about any one particular thing at such an hour. It is as though his entire inner being keeps pushing in one direction—it emits fragrance like the forest, and drones like the night crickets. I can't say what Rajib thought, but it seemed as though all old rules had broken today. Today, the rainy night had taken off her cloudy veil, and in this night, she was looking silent, beautiful and reserved like the Mahamaya of yore. His entire self surged towards Mahamaya.

Rajib entered Mahamaya's sleeping chamber as though driven by a dream. Mahamaya was asleep at that time.

Rajib stood near. He stooped and saw—the moonlight had fallen on Mahamaya's face. But, a shock! What was this! Where was that face that he had known? The cruel tongue of the pyre had scoured away a part of Mahamaya's left cheek and left a trace of its hunger.

Rajib was startled, and an inarticulate sound might also have escaped from him. Mahamaya woke up in a jolt, and saw Rajib. Immediately, she pulled her veil on and stood up, leaving the bed. Rajib realised that now the bolt was about to smite. He fell to the ground, clutched her feet and said, 'Forgive me.'

Mahamaya did not utter a word in response, and without looking back for a moment, made her way out of the room. She never again returned to Rajib's house. Since then, she could not be found anywhere. The silent, wrathful flames of that unforgiving adieu left a prolonged scar on Rajib's entire life.

Translated by **Malashri Lal**

The girl between
(*Madhyabartini*)

Nibaran's world was matter-of-fact in the extreme, without even a whiff of romance in it. Indeed the notion that anyone might need such a spice in his life had yet to occur to him. He took his place in society as if sliding his feet into comfortable old slippers. Not once did he think of, debate or speculate on romance—even unwittingly.

He rose early and began his day by sitting bare-chested at the door of his house facing the lane, placidly smoking the tobacco in his hookah. People came and went in the road, horses and carriages trundled by, Vaishnava beggars sang emotionally, and a peddler hawked old bottles: this ever-changing scene kept him superficially distracted. On those days when the vendors of green mangoes or mango-fish came, he bought some after a protracted haggle, in anticipation of special delicacies for his evening meal. Then, at a settled time, he oiled his body thoroughly and bathed, took his midday meal, fetched his *chapkan* from its rope hanger, put it on, took another puff or two at the hookah, popped another *pan* into his mouth, and set out for the office. As for his evenings, they were spent in somnolence at the house of his neighbour, Ramlochan Ghosh, followed by a late meal at home, and thence to his bedroom to meet his wife Hara Shundari.

The subjects they touched on there—what to send the Mitra boy as a wedding present, the audacity of the new servant girl, which spice to use for which curry—are not the stuff of poems; and this naturally caused Nibaran no regrets.

Then, during the month of *Phalgun,* Hara Shundari fell critically ill. Her fever would not abate. The more the doctor administered quinine, the higher her temperature rose, like a powerful stream when dammed. Day after day, for forty days, the danger continued.

Nibaran did not go to the office. He avoided Ramlochan's evening sessions too. He felt at his wits' end, divided between visits to the bedroom to hear his wife's latest condition, and a chair on the verandah, where he sat smoking and looking worried. He changed physicians twice daily and experimented with every remedy others suggested. On the fortieth day, in spite of such lovingly muddled treatment, the patient began to recover. But her body was so frail that she seemed like a ghost calling faintly from a remote distance, 'Here I am.'

Then came spring, a south wind blew, and on balmy nights moonlight crept through the now-open doors of conjugal and nuptial bedrooms.

Beneath the windows of the bedroom where Hara Shundari lay was the neighbours' back garden. One could not say that it was a particularly enchanting view. Someone had once decided to plant a few croton bushes there and then had forgotten all about them. Pumpkin vines had climbed on top of a heap of dead branches. Below some ageing jujube trees grew a veritable jungle. And a wall near the neighbours' kitchen had half collapsed into a pile of bricks to which cinders and ashes were added daily.

Even so, as she gazed out, Hara Shundari all at once experienced a delight she had never before tasted in her insignificant life. She felt like a village stream in summer, when the current dwindles to a trickle over its sandy bed and the water becomes crystal clear, when the rays of the morning sun quiver in its depths, breezes caress its scintillating surface, and at night its dark waters mirror the stars as if they were pleasant memories in the mind. Unseen fingers seemed to touch slender strings within her, and an unknown music was heard, whose mood Hara Shundari did not fully comprehend.

When, at such moments, the husband sitting beside her asked, 'How are you feeling?', tears welled up in her eyes. In her wasted face they appeared over-whelming, an outpouring of love and gratitude as she looked at her husband, holding his hand wordlessly in her own withered one; and in him they induced a kind of glow he had not felt before.

This state of mind persisted for some time. One night, when an enormous moon came up behind the branches of the stunted fig tree growing from the broken-down wall and a roaming breeze suddenly stirred the sultriness of the night making the branches sigh, Hara Shundari ran her fingers lightly through her husband's hair and said, 'We won't have any children. You should marry again.'

For some time she had been mulling this over. When the mind fills with immense joy and vast love, one feels: I can do anything. A tremendous urge towards self-sacrifice gathers momentum. Like a wave flinging itself down on an unyielding shore, tenderness, exuberant delight and the desire for some great self-denial combine in readiness to be dedicated to a noble, anguished cause.

In this ecstatic condition she decided: I shall offer something to my husband worthy of my worship of him. But alas, what a gulf there was between desire and deed! What had she to give? She had no riches, no brilliance, no influence, only her life—and if she could somehow give that, what was it worth?

She thought: if only I could give him a child of doll-like perfection, fresh as milk-froth, soft as cream, lovely as the infant Cupid. But it cannot be, even if I sacrifice my life. Then the truth struck her: he must marry again. She wondered why wives so dreaded the idea. Where was the difficulty? If she loved her husband, was it so impossible to love a co-wife? Her heart swelled at the prospect.

The first time he heard the proposal, Nibaran laughed it off. The second and third times he ignored it. The more she saw of his reluctance and indifference, the greater became her confidence and the firmer her resolution. As for Nibaran, the more often he heard the idea, the less impossible it seemed. As he sat at his door puffing a hookah, a pleasant picture of a home filled with children began to glow brightly in his mind.

In due course he introduced the subject himself. 'At this advanced age I can hardly take on a young thing and bring her up.'

Hara Shundari reassured him. 'Don't worry. Bringing her up is my responsibility.' The childless woman could visualise an adolescent bride, shy and barely out of her mother's arms, and the picture made her heart melt with affection. Nibaran said, 'What about the office? And my other work? I haven't time to listen to the whims of some little girl.'

'They won't cost you any time at all, you'll see,' Hara Shundari persisted. In the end she joked, 'Well now, I'm going to make sure I survive to see what happens to everything—your work, your world, and mine.' Rather than reply, Nibaran tapped her on the cheek with his finger, as if reprimanding her.

2

He did get married—to a dainty little girl with tears on her cheeks and a ring in her nose, named Shailabala. The name charmed him, and so did the freshness of her features. He longed to take a good look at them, the expressions playing upon them, and the way she moved, but he did not have the chance. Instead he had to pretend that this slip of a girl had got him into deep water, from which it would be a relief to escape and turn his attention to matters more appropriate to his age.

Hara Shundari observed Nibaran's predicament and secretly enjoyed it. Sometimes she seized his hand and said, 'Where are you running off to? She's only a little girl; she won't eat you up.' Nibaran would become doubly flustered: 'What do you mean? What are you talking about? I have urgent work to do.' He sounded trapped. His wife would laugh, close the door firmly, and say, 'Now you can't escape.' The helpless Nibaran had no choice but to surrender and sit down. Hara Shundari would whisper in his ear, 'You really mustn't disregard the daughter of your father-in-law, now that you have brought her into the house.' Then she would get hold of Shailabala, seat her on Nibaran's left, insist on lifting her veil and raising her chin, and say to Nibaran, 'Ah! see her face! It's like the moon.' Or she might get up and leave the two of them sitting there, saying she had work to do, closing the door ostentatiously as she went. Nibaran felt certain a pair of eyes was glued to some chink or other, and so with studied indifference he would turn aside and doze off. Shailabala would pull down her veil, cower, and vanish into a corner.

At last Hara Shundari, getting nowhere, relinquished the helm without any great regrets. That was the signal for Nibaran to seize it himself. A great curiosity, a deep mystery drove him on. Like a man holding a diamond in his hand, who feels compelled to admire it from various angles, he beheld the heart of this wondrous small person. He wanted to touch it, caress it, and gaze upon it in secret. A quick flick of her earrings, a backward tweak of her veil, a lightning glance at the face beneath, or perhaps a stare as steadfast as the stars, were just some of the ways he liked to enter this new land of enchantment.

Mr Nibaran Chandra, Head Clerk of the McMoran Company, had never in his life experienced anything quite like it. When first married he had been a mere boy. By the time he was a young man, his wife was long familiar to him, marriage a routine affair. He knew he loved Hara Shundari, but it was love of which he had never become conscious at any time.

An insect born inside a ripe mango will never lack for juice but will also never know any other taste. Let loose among the blossoming flowers of spring, how frantically it will dash from one half-opened rose to another! The slightest fragrance, the least hint of nectar, will make it dizzy with delight.

Nibaran began to buy Shailabala pretty things in secret: a china doll in a frock, a small bottle of perfume, some sweetmeats. They encouraged a little intimacy. In due course Hara Shundari, between household chores one day, peeped through the chink in the door and discovered Nibaran and Shailabala playing a childish game with cowrie shells.

What a pastime for a mature man! After his meal that morning he had acted as if he were going to the office, but instead he had gone to Shailabala's room. Why this deception? She felt as if her eyes had been opened with a hot poker and the searing heat had evaporated all her tears. She thought to herself: I brought her into this house, I pushed them together, so why do they treat me like this, as if I were a thorn in their happiness?

Recently she had been instructing Shailabala in household matters. At one point Nibaran had burst out, 'She's just a child! You're making her work too hard, she's not all that strong.' A sharp retort had occurred to Hara Shundari, but she had held her tongue and said nothing.

After that, the co-wife was given no more chores; Hara Shundari herself looked after all the cooking and household management. Shailabala did not need to lift a finger, waited upon by Hara Shundari as if by a slave, and entertained by her husband as if he were a court jester. Ideas about sharing the running of a house and caring for others as important duties in life were lessons Shailabala never learned. Hara Shundari quietly carried out every task and took solemn pride in it. She did not feel inferior or wretched. She liked to say, 'You two go and play. I'm in charge of everything at home.'

3

Where now had that strength vanished that had once impelled her calmly and unconditionally to surrender forever half her claim on her husband's love? When a tide sweeps through one like the tide at full moon, flooding both banks, one can believe oneself capable of achieving anything. Tremendous resolutions are made, which must then be kept in the long hours of the ebb-tide as they drag at one's whole life. Suddenly the pledge made at the stroke of a pen in prosperity must be repaid bit by tedious bit in the years of adversity. Only then does it become obvious how humble we are, how fragile are our hearts, and how severely limited are our powers.

Following her long convalescence Hara Shundari had been feeble, anaemic, jaundiced in colour, as insubstantial as the crescent moon floating freely above the earth. She had imagined that she no longer needed anything. But as she grew stronger and began to feel more vigorous in body, her mind was invaded from nowhere by a crowd of thoughts that shouted, 'You may have signed the decree *nisi,* but we won't give up our rights.'

The day she finally realised her quandary, she handed over to Nibaran and Shailabala her bedroom and went to a strange room to sleep alone. She had first slept in her bedroom at the age of eight, on her wedding night; twenty-seven years later she gave up her claim. As she blew out the lamp and lay down with an unbearably heavy heart, a popular song in raga Behag came floating across the street: the voice of a refined young man, accompanied by a tabla and the appreciative cries of his friends at the end of each rhythmic cycle. In that still moonlight it sounded rather soothing to the occupants of the room next to Hara Shundari's. There the little Shailabala's eyes drooped heavily with sleep, while Nibaran, lips close to her ear, cooed 'Sweetheart'.

By now he had caught up with Bankim Chandra's novel *Chandrashekhar* and had read to Shailabala the work of several modern poets. A fountain of youth that had always been neglected was tapped and suddenly shot up at a highly unlikely time in his life. No one was prepared for this, and it played havoc with Nibaran's wits and domestic arrangements. The poor fellow had never even suspected the existence of so many disruptive elements within human beings—elements so wild and untameable they could throw a well-organised, nicely-calculated life into total disarray.

Not only Nibaran but Hara Shundari too encountered a new anguish. Why this yearning, why this unbearable agony? she asked herself. What she was now dying for she had earlier never cried for or received. In the days when Nibaran had gone regularly to his office, as men in his position do, and, prior to falling asleep, had discussed with her the milkman's bills, the rising cost of living, and social obligations, there had been no hint of this inner turmoil. They had been in love, yes, but not with fire or flame. Their love had been more like a pile of unlit kindling.

Hara Shundari felt as if someone had come and cheated her of her crown in life. Her heart felt as if it had been permanently starved, her womanhood grossly impoverished. She had spent twenty-seven priceless years as a servant with all the bother of managing groceries, *pan* and kitchen spices; and now today, at the midpoint of her life, in the very next bedroom, a chit of a girl was unlocking a secret storehouse of genuine treasures and becoming maharani of the house. Of course a woman was meant to serve—but she was also meant to reign. Here, however, one woman had become servant, the other maharani, and in the process the servant had lost her pride and the maharani her happiness.

For the fact was, Shailabala too was dissatisfied. She received such unremitting attention that she had not a moment left over for love. When a river flows its course and merges with the ocean, it fulfils the purpose for which it was created. But if the ocean, borne by the tide, continually washes into the river, the river swells up unnaturally. That was the condition of this house; it had concentrated all its affection on Shailabala, day and night, and her self-importance was highly inflated. She had come to believe that the world existed for her, and that she owed nothing to anyone. There is plenty of vanity in such a view, but little contentment.

4

One day the sky became black with clouds, and it was so dark indoors that work was impossible. Rain fell in sheets. The jungle of weeds and creepers beneath the jujube tree was practically submerged, and along the broken wall turbid water gurgled in a torrent. Hara Shundari sat silent and solitary in the darkness beside the window of her new bedroom.

Nibaran came to the door stealthily, like a thief, and paused, wondering whether to go or enter. His wife was aware of his presence but did not say a word. Quite suddenly he seemed to shoot across the room and blurted out in one breath, 'I must have a few pieces of your jewellery. You know I have lots of debts, creditors are hounding me, and I must pawn something. I'll get it back quickly.' There was no reply from his wife. He stood there like a criminal. After a long pause, he mumbled, 'Then you won't oblige me now?'

'No.'

Exiting from the room was as difficult for Nibaran as entering. He looked this way and that, muttered 'Then I'll try somewhere else', and fled.

Hara Shundari knew all about his tale of debts and the need to pawn jewellery. She knew that the previous night her co-wife had nagged her tame and bewitched husband and had said, 'Elder Sister has a safe full of jewellery. Can't I wear even one piece of it?'

She slowly got up, opened the iron safe, and took out all the pieces, one by one. She called Shailabala, wrapped her in the Benares sari first worn at her own wedding, and then draped her from head to toe with the entire collection of jewellery. Carefully she dressed her hair, lit a lamp, and looked at the girl's face. She saw how sweet and round it was, as luscious and immaculate as a ripe and fragrant fruit. When Shailabala walked away, the jingle of the jewellery rang in Hara Shundari's blood for hours afterwards. She thought: today you and I may not have much in common. But once I too was young. I too was filled to the brim with youth. Why didn't someone explain it to me then? My hour of glory came and went, and I never even knew. Just look at the pride Shailabala takes in herself. She's like a wave when she moves.

While Hara Shundari had known only household chores, how much this jewellery had meant to her! Could she have let it go then, like a fool, at a moment's notice? Now that she had an inkling of something greater than housework, such trinkets and provisions for the future were utterly trivial.

As for Shailabala, flashing and glittering with valuables on her way to her bedroom, she did not dwell for one second on their worth. All she knew was that in the normal course of things, all gold, all glory, and all good fortune eventually gravitated to her, for she was Shailabala, darling of the house.

5

In dreams people can walk fearlessly along the most perilous of paths without a moment's hesitation. And there are many who behave in the same way when fully awake, who show no judgement at all, keep blithely on, and finally awaken to catastrophe.

Our head clerk of the McMoran Company was just such a case. Shailabala was like a whirlpool at the centre of his life, sucking in costly items that had nothing to do with her. They included not only Nibaran's sense of dignity and monthly wages but also Hara Shundari's welfare and possessions. Cash in hand belonging to the McMoran Company was surreptitiously drawn in, and in due course bundles of notes, either singly or severally. Nibaran would resolve to replace the money a little at a time from his next month's wages. But when these were received, they too were sucked into the vortex, down to the last two-anna piece twinkling for a jiffy before it vanished like a streak of lightning.

In the end he was caught. His post was a hereditary one. The sahib in charge was fond of him and allowed him two days to replace the cash.

The amount involved—two and a half thousand rupees—surprised Nibaran himself: he could not understand how so much had been spent. Like a madman he turned to Hara Shundari and confessed, 'I'm ruined.'

She listened to the whole story and turned ashen.

He cried, 'Quickly, get out the jewellery.'

'I've given it to Shailabala,' said his wife.

Nibaran became completely childish: 'Why did you give it to her? Why did you give it? Who told you to give it?'

She withheld the real reason. 'What harm has been done? It's not sunk for good.'

The cowardly Nibaran replied hesitantly, 'Then maybe, if you can make some excuse, you can get it back? But don't, for heaven's sake, go and say I'm the one who wants it or why.'

Disdain and disgust cut Hara Shundari to the quick. She replied, 'Is this the time for excuses or for sweet shows of affection? Come on.' She led him to the younger wife's room.

Shailabala refused to grasp a thing. To whatever was said, she responded 'What do I know about it?'

Had she ever agreed that she might have to think about the rest of the family? Wasn't everyone supposed to look after their own affairs and then join in thinking how to make Shailabala as happy as possible? The sudden exception to this golden rule struck her as dreadfully unfair.

Nibaran fell weeping at Shailabala's feet. She merely said, 'I know nothing about this. Why should I give up what is mine?'

Nibaran realised that this delicate and tender-looking girl would prove stronger than the iron safe. Hara Shundari observed her husband's weakness in the crisis and was overcome with revulsion. She tried to wrest Shailabala's key from her. The girl promptly flung it over the wall into a pond.

The elder wife urged her bewildered husband, 'Why not break the lock?'

Quite serenely, Shailabala said, 'Then I'll hang myself.'

'I'll go and try another source,' stammered Nibaran and rushed out of the house in confusion. Within two hours he had sold his ancestral home for two thousand five hundred rupees.

Thus he narrowly escaped handcuffs, but he lost his job. Of his entire goods and chattels, moveable and immoveable, only the two wives remained. Of them, the distraught girl-wife became still more immoveable by becoming pregnant. The tiny family took refuge in a decrepit little house in an alley.

6

Shailabala's vexation and misery were unending. She adamantly refused to accept that her husband could do nothing about them. If he could do nothing, why had he married her?

The house had only two rooms upstairs. One was the bedroom she occupied with Nibaran. The other was left to Hara Shundari. Shailabala would grumble, 'I can't spend day and night in a bedroom.' Nibaran, giving her false hope, would say, 'I'm looking for a better house. We'll move soon.'

'Why move when there's another room next door?'

She wanted nothing to do with their former neighbours. Distressed at hearing of Nibaran's difficulties, they came to see him. She bolted herself in and refused to come out. When they had gone she flew into a rage, wept, starved herself, and let the entire neighbourhood know she was having hysterics. Such disturbances became routine.

Eventually, Shailabala contracted such a serious illness that there was a real possibility of miscarriage. Nibaran seized his elder wife's hands and begged, 'You must save her.'

Hara Shundari devoted herself day and night to the task. Though Shailabala cursed her for the slightest slip, she did not retort. The girl refused to drink barley-water and flung it about along with the cup, and when her temperature ran high she demanded rice and green-mango chutney. If she did not get it she had a tantrum. But Hara Shundari merely tried to comfort her as if she were a child, calling her 'My Lakshmi', 'My good girl', and 'My darling sister'.

Shailabala did not live. Having garnered a world of devotion and affection, the girl ended her short, futile existence as an utterly wretched malcontent.

7

At first Nibaran was devastated, but soon he sensed that a shackle had been broken. Though grieving, he felt a marvellous liberation. A nightmare had been vanquished, and he was animated and incredibly light at heart. But had not a fond tie that had embraced his life like the tendrils of a creeper— his precious Shailabala—just been torn away? He took a deep breath and the truth came to him: no, she had been his hangman's noose.

And what of his life-long companion, Hara Shundari? He realised that she, and she alone, occupied the seat of honour in his shrine of memories, she who had shared all his joys and sorrows. But still he felt a rift between them. A bright, cruel little blade had partitioned his heart and had left an aching gap in its centre.

Several weeks later, in the dead of night, when the whole city slept, Nibaran stole into his wife's lonely bedroom. Silently he lay down on the right-hand side of the bed, just as he used to do. But now he felt like an intruder in what once had been his sole domain.

Neither of them said one word. Side by side they lay there, just as they had lain before; but immediately between them there lay a dead girl, and neither of them was able to violate her shade.

Translated by **Krishna Dutta and Mary Lago**
[*Selected short stories of Rabindranath Tagore*
(Calcutta: Rupa and Co., 1992)]

Giribala
(*Manbhanjan*)

Giribala is overflowing with exuberance of youth that seems spilling over in spray all around her,—in the folds of her soft dress, the turning of her neck, the motion of her hands, in the rhythm of her steps, now quick now languid, in her tinkling anklets and ringing laughter, in her voice and glances. She would often be seen, wrapped in a blue silk, walking on her terrace, in an impulse of unaccountable restlessness. Her limbs seem eager to dance to the time of an inner music unceasing and unheard. She takes pleasure in merely moving her body, causing ripples to break out in the flood of her young life. She would suddenly pluck a leaf from a plant in the flower-pot and throw it up in the sky, and her bangles would give a sudden tinkle, and the careless grace of her hand, like a bird freed from its cage, would fly unseen in the air. With her swift fingers she would brush away from her dress a mere nothing; standing on tiptoe she would peep over her terrace walls for no cause whatever, and then with a rapid motion turn round to go to another direction, swinging her bunch of keys tied to a corner of her garment. She would loosen her hair in an untimely caprice, sitting before her mirror to do it up again, and then in a fit of laziness would fling herself upon her bed, like a line of stray moonlight slipping through some opening of the leaves, idling in the shadow.

She has no children and, having been married in a wealthy family, has very little work to do. Thus she seems to be daily accumulating her own self without expenditure, till the vessel is brimming over with the seething surplus. She has her husband, but not under her control. She has grown up from a girl into a woman, yet escaping, through familiarity, her husband's notice.

When she was newly married and her husband, Gopinath, was attending his college, he would often play the truant and under cover of the midday siesta of his elders secretly come to make love to Giribala. Though they lived under the same roof, he would create occasions to send her letters on tinted paper perfumed with rosewater, and would even gloat upon some exaggerated grievances of imaginary neglect of love.

Just then his father died and he became the sole owner of his property. Like an unseasoned piece of timber, the immature youth of Gopinath attracted parasites which began to bore into his substance. From now his movements took the course that led him in a contrary direction from his wife.

There is a dangerous fascination to be leaders of men, to which many strong minds have succumbed. To be accepted as the leader of a small circle of sycophants, in his own parlour, has the same fearful attraction for a man who suffers from a scarcity of brains and character. Gopinath assumed the part of a hero among his friends and acquaintances, and tried daily to invent new wonders in all manner of extravagance. He won a reputation among his followers for his audacity of excesses, which goaded him not only to keep up his fame, but to surpass himself at all costs.

In the meanwhile, Giribala, in the seclusion of her lonely youth, felt like a queen who had her throne, but no subjects. She knew she had the power in her hand which could make the world of men her captive; only that world itself was wanting.

Giribala has a maidservant whose name is Sudha. She can sing and dance and improvise verses, and she freely gives expression to her regret that such a beauty as that of her mistress should be dedicated to a fool who forgets to enjoy what he owns. Giribala is never tired of hearing from her the details of her charms, while at the same time contradicting her, calling her a liar and a flatterer, exciting her to swear by all that is sacred that she is earnest in her admiration, which statement, even without the accompaniment of a solemn oath, is not difficult for Giribala to believe.

Sudha used to sing to her a song beginning with the line, 'Let me write myself a slave upon the soles of thy feet', and Giribala in her imagination could feel that her beautiful feet were fully worthy of bearing inscriptions of everlasting slavery from conquered hearts, if only they could be free in their career of conquest.

But the woman to whom her husband Gopinath has surrendered himself as a slave is Lavanga, the actress, who has the reputation of playing to perfection the part of a maiden languishing in hopeless love and swooning on the stage with an exquisite naturalness. When her husband had not altogether vanished from her sphere of influence, Giribala had often heard from him about the wonderful histrionic powers of this woman and in her jealous curiosity had greatly desired to see Lavanga on the stage. But she could not secure her husband's consent, because Gopinath was firm in his opinion that the theatre was a place not fit for any decent woman to visit.

At last she paid for a seat and sent Sudha to see this famous actress in one of her best parts. The account that she received from her on her return was far from flattering to Lavanga, both as to her personal appearance and her stage accomplishments. As, for obvious reasons, she had great faith in Sudha's power of appreciation, where it was due, Giribala did not hesitate to believe her in her description of Lavanga, which was accompanied by a mimicry of a ludicrous mannerism.

When at last her husband deserted her in his infatuation for this woman, she began to feel qualms of doubt. But as Sudha repeatedly asserted her former opinion with ever greater vehemence, comparing Lavanga to a piece of burnt log dressed up in a woman's clothes, Giribala determined secretly to go to the theatre herself and settle this question for good.

And she did go there one night with all the excitement of a forbidden entry. Her very trepidation of heart lent a special charm to what she saw. She gazed at the faces of the spectators, lit up with an unnatural shine of lamplight; and, with the magic of its music and the painted canvas of its scenery, the theatre seemed to her like a world where society was suddenly freed from its law of gravitation.

Coining from her walled up terrace and joyless home, she had entered a region where dreams and reality had clasped their hands in friendship, over the wine cup of art.

The bell rang, the orchestra music stopped, the audience sat still in their seats, the stage-lights shone brighter, and the curtain was drawn up. Suddenly appeared in the light, from the mystery of the unseen, the shepherd girls of the Vrinda forest, and with the accompaniment of songs commenced their dance, punctuated with the uproarious applause of the audience. The blood began to throb all over Giribala's body, and she forgot for the moment that her life was limited to the circumstances and that she was not free in a world where all laws had melted in music.

Sudha came occasionally to interrupt her with her anxious whispers urging her to hasten back home for the fear of being detected. But she paid no heed to her warning, for her sense of fear had gone.

The play goes on. Krishna has given offence to his beloved Radha and she in her wounded pride refuses to recognize him. He is entreating her, abasing himself at her feet, but in vain. Giribala's heart seems to swell. She imagines herself as offended Radha; and feels that she also has in her this woman's power to vindicate her pride. She had heard what a force was woman's beauty in the world but to-night it became to her palpable.

At last the curtain dropped, the light grew dim, the audience got ready to leave the theatre, but Giribala sat still like one in a dream. The thought that she would have to go home had vanished from her mind. She waited for the curtain to rise again and the eternal theme of Krishna's humiliation at the feet of Radha to continue. But Sudha came to remind her that the play had ended and the lamps would soon be put out.

It was late when Giribala came back home. A kerosene lamp was dimly burning in the melancholy solitude and silence of her room. Near the window upon her lonely bed a mosquito curtain was gently moving in the breeze. Her world seemed to her distasteful and mean like a rotten fruit swept into the dustbin.

From now she regularly visited the theatre every Saturday. The fascination of her first sight of it lost much of its glamour. The painted vulgarity of the actresses and the falseness of their affectation became more and more evident, yet the habit grew upon her. Every time the curtain rose the window of her life's prison-house seemed to open before her and the stage, bordered off from the world of reality by its gilded frame and scenic display, by its array of lights and even its flimsiness of conventionalism, appeared to her like a fairyland where it was not impossible for herself to occupy the throne of the fairy queen.

When for the first time she saw her husband among the audience shouting his drunken admiration for a certain actress she felt an intense disgust and prayed in her mind that a day might come when she might have an opportunity to spurn him away with her contempt. But the opportunity became rarer every day, for Gopinath was hardly ever to be seen at his home now, being carried away, one knew not where, in the centre of a dust-storm of dissipation.

One evening in the month of March, in the light of the full moon, Giribala was sitting on her terrace dressed in her cream-coloured robe. It was her habit daily to deck herself with jewellery as if for some festive occasion. For these cosily gems were like wine to her—they sent heightened consciousness of beauty to her limbs; she felt like a plant in spring tingling with the impulse of flowers in all its branches. She wore a pair of diamond bracelets on her arms, a necklace of rubies and pearls on her neck, and a ring with a big sapphire on the little finger of her left hand. Sudha was sitting near her bare feet admiringly touching them with her hand and expressing her wish that she were a man privileged to offer her life as homage to such a pair of feet.

Sudha gently hummed a lovesong to her and the evening wore on to night. Every body in the household had finished their evening meal, and gone to sleep. When suddenly Gopinath appeared reeking with scent and liquor, and Sudha drawing for cloth-end over her face, hastily ran away from the terrace.

Giribala thought for a moment that her day had come at last. She turned away her face and sat silent.

But the curtain in her stage did not rise and no song of entreaty came from her hero, with the words—'Listen to the pleading of the moon-light, my love, and hide not thy face.'

In his dry unmusical voice Gopinath said, 'Give me your keys.'

A gust of south wind like a sigh of the insulted romance of the poetic world scattered all over the terrace the smell of the night-blooming jasmines and loosened some wisp of hair on Giribala's cheek. She let go her pride, and got up and said, 'You shall have your keys if you listen to what I have to say.' Gopinath said, 'I cannot delay. Give me your keys.'

Giribala said, 'I will give you the keys and everything that is in the safe, but you must not leave me.'

Gopinath said, 'That cannot be. I have urgent business.'

'Then you shan't have the keys,' said Giribala.

Gopinath began to search for them. He opened the drawers of the dressing table, broke open the lid of the box that contained Giribala's toilet requisites, smashed the glass panes of her almirah, groped under the pillows and mattress of the bed, but the keys he could not find. Giribala stood near the door stiff and silent like a marble image gazing at vacancy. Trembling with rage Gopinath came to her and said with an angry growl, 'Give me your keys or you will repent.' Giribala did not answer and Gopinath, pinning her to the wall, snatched away by force her bracelets, necklace and ring, and, giving her a parting kick, went away.

Nobody in the house woke up from his sleep, none in the neighborhood knew of this outrage, the moonlight remained placid and the peace of the night undisturbed. Hearts can be rent never to heal again amidst such serene silence.

The next morning Giribala said she was going to see her father and left home. As Gopinath's present destination was not known and she was not responsible to anybody else in the house her absence was not noticed.

The new play of 'Manorama' was on rehearsal in the theatre where Gopinath was a constant visitor. Lavanga was practising for the part of the heroine Manorama, and Gopinath, sitting in the front seat with his rabble of followers, would vociferously encourage his favourite actress with his approbation. This greatly disturbed the rehearsal but the proprietors of the theatre did not dare to annoy their patron of whose vindictiveness they were afraid. But one day he went so far as to molest an actress in the greenroom and he had to be turned away by the aid of the police.

Gopinath determined to take his revenge,—and when, after a great deal of preparation and shrieking advertisements, the new play 'Manorama' was about to be produced, Gopinath took away the principal actress Lavanga with him and disappeared. It was a great shock to the manager, who had to postpone the opening night, and, getting hold of a new actress, taught her the part, and brought out the play before the public with considerable misgivings in his mind.

But the success was as unexpected as it was unprecedented. When its news reached Gopinath he could not resist his curiosity to come and see the performance.

The play opens with Manorama living in her husband's house neglected and hardly noticed. Near the end of the drama her husband deserts her and concealing his first marriage manages to marry a millionaire's daughter. When the wedding ceremony is over and the bridal veil is raised from her face she is discovered to be the same Manorama, only no longer the former drudge, but queenly in her beauty and splendour of dress and ornaments. In her infancy she had been brought up in a poor home being kidnapped from the house of her rich father, who having traced her to her husband's home, has brought her back to him and celebrates her marriage once again in a fitting manner.

In the concluding scene, when the husband is going through his period of penitence and humiliation, as is fit in a play which has its moral, a sudden disturbance arose among the audience. So long as Manorama appeared obscured in her position of drudgery Gopinath showed no sign of perturbation. But when after the wedding ceremony she came out dressed in her red bridal robe and took her veil off, when with a majestic pride of her overwhelming beauty she turned her face towards the audience and, slightly bending her neck, shot a fiery glance of exultation at Gopinath, applause broke out in wave after wave and the enthusiasm of the spectators became unbounded.

Suddenly Gopinath cried out in a thick voice, 'Giribala', and like a madman tried to rush upon the stage. The audience shouted, 'Turn him out,' the police came to drag him away and he struggled and screamed, 'I will kill her,' while the curtain dropped.

Transcreated by **Rabindranath Tagore**
[*The English writings of Rabindranath Tagore*
(New Delhi: Sahitya Akademi, 2004)]

The visitor
(*Atithi*)

Chapter 1

Motilal Babu, the zamindar of Kanthaley, was travelling accompanied by his family. At noon, anchoring near the banks of the river, preparations were underway for the midday meal when all of a sudden a Brahmin lad, of about fifteen–sixteen, came up and asked, 'Babu, where are all of you going?'

Mori Babu answered, 'To Kanthaley'.

'On the way, could you put me down at Nandigaon?'

Assenting, the babu asked, 'What's your name?'

'Tarapada.'

The fair boy was extremely handsome. His large eyes and smiling visage spoke of a fresh softness. He sported a soiled loin cloth and his bare body remained completely unadorned. It was as if some artist had fashioned with great care a flawless and attractive physique. In some past birth, he could have been a young ascetic and thanks to uncompromising, unstinting meditation, all that was excessive had been whittled away from his body and the result was the bearing and demeanour of a true Brahmin.

Very affectionately Motilal Babu responded, 'My dear, finish your bath, your meal will be of course here, with us'.

Tarapada answered, 'Just a moment,' and, unhesitatingly joined in the preparations for cooking. Motilal Babu's cook was not from Bengal and was not used to cutting and cooking fish with any degree of expertise; Tarapada took over from him and not only proved his culinary skills, but also some vegetarian dishes cooked with obvious habitual ease. The cooking complete, Tarapada bathed in the river and, clad in fresh clothes, with the sacred thread clearly visible, presented himself to Moti Babu.

Tarapada was taken inside the boat, where Moti Babu's wife and nine-year old daughter waited. Annapurna, Moti Babu's wife, was overwhelmed with fondness on seeing the fetching lad and thought to herself—'Oh—whose child could he be, from where has he appeared—how is his mother able to stay away from him?'

In due course two wooden-seats were laid side by side for Moti Babu and the young boy. The boy was not a particularly voracious eater; Annapurna assumed from the scanty quantity Tarapada put away that he was feeling awkward. She repeatedly requested him to partake of this, that or the other. However, once he had stopped eating, nothing could change his mind. It was observed that the young boy strictly followed the norms he had set for himself; but he did so in such an easygoing manner that not a trace of stubbornness or obstinacy was to be found in his behaviour. Neither could any hint be found of embarrassment in his conduct.

After everyone had eaten, Annapurna seated the young boy close and attempted to glean some personal information from him. No details could be extracted. All that could be wrested was—at the young age of eight or nine, Tarapada, of his own volition, had run away from home.

Annapurna asked, 'Don't you have a mother?'

'Yes, of course.'

'Does she not love you?'

Considering on such a question as being quite absurd, Tarapada laughed aloud and answered, 'Why would she not?'

Annapurna persisted, 'Then why did you leave her and come away?'

'She has four more sons and three daughters.'

Such a strange blasé attitude hurt Annapurna and she asked,

'What kind of a remark is that? If one has five fingers, does it mean one would cut-off and discard one?'

Tarapada was young and his past history proportionately sparse but the youngster was of an absolutely new ilk. He was the fourth son of his parents and had been rendered fatherless at a very young age. Even in a household of many children, Tarapada was quite a favourite of all; his mother, the siblings and all the people in his locality would shower him love and affection. As a matter of fact, even the teachers refrained from berating him harshly. Under such circumstances, it was practically unthinkable for him to take flight from home. The thin emaciated boy who unrestrainedly and continually stole fruit from neighbouring trees and more than amply was beaten remained behind in the village with his tyrannical mother, but the adored son and child with no compunction whatsoever took to his heels with a foreign touring theatre company!

A search was immediately organised and Tarapada was hauled back home. His mother clasped him to her chest and drenched him with tears; Tarapada's sisters too wept copiously. His elder brother—stepping into the role of male guardian—made a half-hearted attempt to chide him, but finally regretfully stopped and compensated by fulsome indulgence and rewards. All the women of the locality invited him and not only overwhelmed him with love, but also alluring promises. But no bonds—even those of love—could restrain him. It was his stars that rendered him homeless. Whenever he espied boats from foreign climes on the river, or some sage from afar who had taken shelter beneath the towering shady tree in the village, or vagabonds setting up temporary shelter in the abandoned field along the river line, Tarapada's innermost being would be in a turmoil. He hankered for the loveless independence of the outside world. After two or three consecutive attempts at escape, his relatives and people of the village gave up all hopes for him.

At first, he had joined an itinerant theatre troupe. The leader of the group began to look on him as a son and yet again he came to be the favourite of all—from the elderly to the youngsters. But, as a matter of fact, when the head of the house where the plays were staged, especially the women of the household began to ask after him and indulge him, suddenly, without telling a soul, he disappeared and could not be found.

Tarapada was chary about being tethered—just like an untrammelled fawn. And, further, the young lad was characteristically partial to music. It was the predilection for melody that first tore asunder his ties with his home. The strains of a song would make his nerves quiver and the rhythmic beat of any song would cause his entire body to shiver. When he was little more than an infant, the grave and engrossed manner in which he conducted himself at any musical soirée made restraining their laughter a tough task for the elderly people. Not only music—when rain poured down torrentially on the lush green trees, and thunder resounded in the sky and the wind shrieked and cried like an orphaned giant child in the forests, Tarapada's innermost being was thrilled in frenzy. Everything—from the shrill call of eagles in the boundless sky on a still afternoon, the noisy croaking of frogs on a rainy monsoon evening, the baying of foxes at the dead of night—all this evoked violent restlessness in him. It was this magnetic pull for music which made him join a musical troupe and the members with great care began to teach him the niceties and nitty-gritty of their genre of music. Like their own favourite bird, they taught him to sing in the manner they knew best. The bird learnt for a while and early one morning took flight for climes unknown.

The last time he had joined a gymnastics troupe. From the beginning of summer to almost the end of the rainy season, a number of fairs took place all around and a number of specialities were seen. The previous year a small gymnastics troupe from Kolkata had happened to join the activities and merriment. Tarapada had joined hands with the owner of the first boat and had engaged himself in selling betel leaves. Later, a sense of marvel and curiosity in the skill and adroitness of gymnastics had incited him into joining them. By dint of his own practice, Tarapada had become quite skilled in playing the flute. His only job was to play the flute to a very fast beat when the show was on.

The escapade from this troupe was his last. He had heard that the zamindars of Nandigram were starting an amateur theatre troupe with a lot of fanfare. Hearing this, he had readied his small bundle of belongings and was getting ready to leave when he came across Moti Babu and his family.

Thereafter, despite mingling with various troupes, Tarapada's naturally imaginative nature was not particularly influenced by any of them. He remained detached and free. There was a lot of ugliness in life that he had seen and even more ugliness that he had heard of. But, none of the dark degenerations he witnessed made any impact on him. This boy had no mind to anything. Neither was there any habit which held him in its coils. Life to him was like turbid waters in which he moved about regally like a pristine white swan. Out of curiosity, no matter how many times he took a quick dip, nothing sullied him. That was probably why this runaway shone with an unspoiled natural youth; it was that visage that had led the elderly worldly Moti Babu to welcome him affectionately, and without any suspicion or questions.

Chapter 2

At the end of the meal, the ferry set sail. With a great deal of affection, Annapurna began to question this Brahmin lad about his home and relatives. Somehow Tarapada escaped the tirade after some extremely terse replies. Outside, the monsoon river in full spate, overflowing to the last line of demarcation, remained self-engrossed in frenzied preoccupation, causing Mother Nature grave concern. In the cloudless sunlight by the riverside, half submerged grass flowers and the bamboo shoots and, further beyond, the boundary line of the forest... Like the fresh beauty awakened by the magical golden wand of some fairytale, beneath the mesmerised mute glance of the blue sky all had come to life; all appeared wondrously alive, pulsating, flooded with a kind of ethereal light and polished and glistening—replete in plenty.

Tarapada took shelter on the roof of the ferry. As the boat moved along, progressively—lush green expanses, flooded jute fields, deep green paddy fields, narrow paths leading from the ferry jetty towards the village and the village surrounded by thick shadowy forest all passed before his eyes—water all around, land, sky and vibrancy in the air. But there was no effort at all to hold this restless being in bonds of affection. On the river banks calves ran about, village horses chomped—the grass—all these familiar and yet novel sights Tarapada thirstily imbibed; there was no quenching—his passion for open nature.

Reaching the roof, Tarapada set up a conversation with the boatman and all his companions. As need arose, sometimes he voluntarily took up the oars from them and enthusiastically tried his hand at steering! Whenever the helmsman required taking a puff, he adroitly took over his task.

Before evening Annapurna sent for Tarapada and asked, 'What is your normal fare in the evening?'

'Whatever is available and sometimes nothing at all...'

The indifference of this Brahmin lad in accepting their hospitality began to trouble Annapurna. She keenly desired that by dint of feeding and clothing him, this run away from home would be made replete. In no way, however, she could gauge just what would satisfy him. Annapurna set up a hue and cry about sending servants to purchase sweets and milk. Tarapada graciously partook of them, but refused the milk. The generally taciturn Moti Babu also added his request, but the young boy abruptly replied, 'I do not like it'.

Two or three days passed on the river. Tarapada willingly participated in all activities—cooking, marketing or steering the boat. Whatever scene passed before his eyes, curiously he went in pursuit; whatever task befell—involuntarily he was attracted. His vision, hands and mind always remained active. That is probably why, like the eternally active Nature, he too remained passively uninvolved and yet always active. As a human, every individual has his own demarcated zone; but Tarapada remained outside the purview of it all. He appeared to have no links with the past or the future—he was only part of what was taking place at the moment.

Presently, having been involved with many troupes and organisations Tarapada was well-versed in the art of entertainment. Not being clouded with any mundane issues, he had a startling clear memory which could easily retain whatever and whenever required. Mythological stories, religious incantations or songs—he was well-versed in them all. One evening, as was his practice, Moti Babu was reading aloud from the religious text, the Ramayana. Unable to restrain his excitement Tarapada rapidly descended from the roof and asked Moti Babu to shut the book as he would sing aloud the verses from memory.

In a sweet and lilting voice the boy began—all listened mesmerised. All aboard stopped work and peered in through the door; an indescribable mingling of laughter, tragedy and melody resounded that evening on that serene and tranquil corner of the river. The silent banks on both sides resounded with curiosity, passengers in all the boats that passed by for a few seconds gazed with unabashed inquisitiveness and tried to take in what was being recited. When the impromptu soirée finally came to an end, all sighed unhappily, wondering—why did it have to end so soon.

The tearful Annapurna Devi wished that she could clasp him to her bosom and inhale his fragrance. Moti Babu began to ponder, 'If somehow this boy can be kept in close proximity, my hunger for a son will be fulfilled'. It was only the little girl Charusashi whose heart brimmed over with an acute envy and hatred.

Chapter 3

Charusashi was the only child of her parents and hence the only one privy to all their parental love and affection. She was not only whimsical, but extremely stubborn as well. The young girl had very strong opinions about her mode of dressing and attire, but there was no firmness associated with those opinions. Should there be any invitation, her mother would be tense in case she came up with some absurd demand which would be well nigh impossible to meet. If unfortunately her tresses were not dressed right the first time, no matter how many times opened and re-done, it would be impossible to gain her approval. The final and only outcome would be an abundance of tears. It was the same in everything else. On the other hand, when she was content and happy, she would not object to anything at all. Then, with an excessive show of love, she would embrace her mother and shower her with kisses and affection amidst laughter and smiles. This small girl was truly an enigma.

Projecting all the force of her incomprehensible heart, this child began to hound Tarapada with an intense hatred. Even her parents were not spared. In a flood of tears she would push away her food during meal, nothing that was cooked could please her, she would hit out at the servants all the time and for no reason at all there would be a continual volley of complaints. As Tarapada grew more adept at entertaining her and all the others, his popularity proportionately grew greater. It went absolutely against the grain for her to even acknowledge that Tarapada had any praiseworthy qualities; however, when there was undeniable proof of all his virtues, her acute ennui spiralled upwards even more. The day Tarapada sang aloud from the scriptures Annapurna thought to herself, 'After all, music tames even wild animals—perhaps my daughter will be appeased at long last'. She ventured to ask, 'Charu, how did you find this?' The girl made no answer, except to violently shake her head. If the gesture were to be analysed through the medium of language, the meaning would stand as—not a jolt of it was to taste and neither was there any chance of any favourable impression being made on her any time in the future.

Realising that Tarapada provoked strong feelings of jealousy, Annapurna refrained from any public display of affection for Tarapada in her daughter's presence. Fairly early in the evening, when Charu would retire for the day after her meal, Annapurna Devi would sit at the threshold of the door; with Moti Babu and Tarapada sitting outside, she would request Tarapada to begin singing. When the restful rustic silence of the river banks in the overwhelming darkness remained in stupefied calm and Annapurna's tender heart overflowed with affection and a sense of beauty, suddenly Charu would descend on them like a whirlwind. Angrily and brimming over with tears she would complain, 'Mother, what kind of furore have all of you set up—I cannot sleep'. It was impossible for her to tolerate the fact that sending her to sleep atone, her parents were enjoying Tarapada's company.

In turn Tarapada felt a strange curiosity for this bright, determined and vibrant young girl. Through narrating stories, singing songs, playing the flute he wasted no effort in overcoming her resistance—but to no avail. It was only at midday, when Tarapada went to swim in the river, she could not resist the fascination of the easy manner in which the healthy young lad frolicked in the water. She would wait impatiently for such a time, but let none know of this attraction. Apparently engrossed in knitting Charu would once in a while cast covert glances at the lad swimming in the water.

Chapter 4

When Nandigaon passed by, Tarapada made no movement or enquiry. The large boat moved sedately, sometimes with sails raised along the various tributaries of the river. Similarly, the days for all aboard—like the river and its tributaries—went by in beauteous diversity in easy gait and mild clamour. None was in any hurry; the midday meal was a leisurely and delayed affair. On the other hand, as evening fell, the boat would be anchored beside the river banks of a large village, amidst the pleasant verdant ambience of a forest.

In this manner, Kanthaley was reached in about ten days. At the advent of the zamindar, palanquins and horses were organised. Well-armed escorts firing blankly into the air and setting up an anxious furore amongst the crow community wound their way to their destination.

All these momentous events taking time, Tarapada rapidly descended from the boat and took a rapid survey of the village. Addressing all he met as some relative or the other, in a very short while the lad found a niche for himself in the heart of the entire village community. The very fact that he truly had no bonds at all led the young boy with astounding ease and rapidity to establish an acquaintance with all.

The reason behind so easily winning the hearts of all was simply that Tarapada mixed with all at their level and in the manner to which they were accustomed. He was not shackled by any particular convention—but he retained an abundant enthusiasm in all circumstances and in every situation. To a young boy he was simply a lad like them and yet completely individualistic and superior to them, he was no child to the elderly and yet disgustingly over-mature, to a cowherd he was of their ilk and, despite being a Brahmin, Tarapada would participate and intervene in the affairs of all like their ever-familiar compatriot. At the local sweetmeat shop, the owner would call out, 'Dadathakur, just stay here for a while—I'll be back very soon'. Tarapada would happily sit there swatting flies. He had a smattering knowledge of various skills and was reasonably skilled in them.

Tarapada conquered the entire village, but it was only the resentment of one little girl that he just could not overcome. Probably it was because he knew how ardently she craved his banishment to far off climes that he remained in the village for such a long while.

Even as a child Charusashi proved that it is well nigh impossible to gauge the heart of a woman.

Sonamoni, Bamunthakurun's daughter, had been widowed at five; she was the closest to Charu in age. Not keeping well, she had been unable to meet her friend who only recently returned home. On her recovery, the day she came to meet Charu an irreparable quarrel all but tore both friends asunder.

Charu with a lot of fanfare had started on an elaborate tale. She had assumed that a detailed description of the advent of the new arrival of Tarapada would stimulate her friend's curiosity and stun her with amazement. However, she came to learn from her friend that Tarapada was no stranger to them, rather, he was on very familiar terms. She was further told that not only had her parents been entertained with musical soirées, but on Sonamoni's request he had also fashioned a flute from bamboo reeds for her. Further, he had also gathered flowers for her many a day. All these tales stung and lacerated her with pain. Charu had taken for granted that Tarapada was their sole Tarapada—he was a secret treasure to be viewed guardedly from a distance by people in general, but would definitely have no access to him. They would marvel at his looks and admire his qualities from afar and repeatedly thank Charusashi and her family. Why had this astounding, divinely obtained Brahmin lad been so easily accessible? If we had not brought him here with so much care, tended to him so painstakingly—how would Sonamoni have caught sight of him? Now he was Sonamoni's brother! She fumed in rage.

Why such turbulent emotions centring on sole proprietorship over Tarapada—someone Charu had tried from her innermost being to shred into smithereens of hatred? Who was to understand the reason behind!

That very day, using a most trivial pretext as a cause, Sonamoni and Charu stopped all conversation and interaction with each other. Charu then marched to Tarapada's room and, finding his precious flute, broke it into tiny shreds.

When Charu was obsessively engaged in this wanton destruction, all of a sudden Tarapada entered the room. He was amazed at seeing this veritable tornado and asked, 'Charu, why are you breaking my flute?' With bloodshot eyes scarlet faced Charu retorted, 'Serves you right—I am glad,' and after unnecessarily kicking the flute a couple of time and weeping copiously all the while she rushed out of the room. Picking up the offending article Tarapada found that nothing was left of it. He could not contain his laughter at seeing the sorry plight of his old and favourite flute.

Each and every single day Charusashi became an object of insatiable curiosity for him.

Another point of interest and curiosity for him were the books on English paintings in Moti Babu's library. Tarapada was quite familiar with the outside world, but somehow was just not able to forge an entry into the world of paintings. Thanks to an extremely active imagination, he compensated himself somewhat, but somehow just could not find true satisfaction.

Observing Tarapada's avid interest in paintings, Moti Babu one day asked him, 'Do you want to learn English? You will then be able to understand the meaning of everything in the paintings'. Tarapada instantly agreed.

Very pleased Moti Babu then arranged for Ramratan Babu, the Headmaster of the Village Entrance School, to teach this lad English every evening.

Chapter 5

Tarapada thus began his English lessons, depending on his razor sharp memory and focused concentration. It was as though he had begun traversing through a remote, new kingdom—there remained no further connection with his old world. The people of the locality no longer saw him all around. In the evening, as he strolled rapidly along the river banks, focusing on learning his lessons by rote, the young lads who looked on him reverently would gaze at him with awe but none dared disturb him as he studied.

Charu too could barely see him. Previously Tarapada used to eat in the inner sanctum, under the watchful and affectionate care of Annapurna. However, because there would be an ensuing delay, Tarapada spoke to Moti Babu and other arrangements were made outside. Annapurna was a little upset at this and objected; Moti Babu, greatly pleased with the boy's enthusiasm, however, consented to the new schedule.

All of a sudden Charu too stubbornly demanded, 'I too want to learn English'. Initially her parents treated this as yet another absurd notion of their whimsical daughter and laughed indulgently; but the laughter was shortly set awash by their child's shower of tears. Finally, this affectionately weak couple was forced into taking their daughter's demand seriously. Charu began her lessons along with Tarapada under the tutelage of the Headmaster.

Studying seriously did not come naturally to the restless girl. She did not learn anything herself, instead persistently disturbed Tarapada. She would fall back, not work on the homework set—but adamantly refused to follow Tarapada in any manner. If Tarapada superseded her and attempted to go on to a new lesson, she would throw tantrums and did not stop short of copious tears. If Tarapada completed his books and new ones were bought, a new set also had to be bought for her. The envious girl could not tolerate the fact that during his leisure hours Tarapada would sit in his room and work on his lessons; in secret she would ensure ink was dropped all over his writing, his pen would be stolen and she would also tar the pages of the book from which lessons had to be prepared. Tarapada would tolerate all the tyranny with affectionate indulgence and, when it became intolerable, would smack her, but just could not manage to control her.

All of a sudden a solution suddenly presented itself. One day the dejected Tarapada—greatly irritated with tearing and throwing away his ink sodden books—was sitting alone; Charu coming to the door assumed that she would definitely get a beating. However, her expectations did not transpire. Tarapada did not speak a word and remained in absolute silence. The girl began to hover all around; she came so close that Tarapada could easily have reached out and given her a blow on the back, but instead he remained gravely silent. The girl was in an absolute quandary. She had never been particularly adept in the art of apologising; at the same time her tender young heart desperately sought her co-student's forgiveness. Finally, not seeing any other alternative, she picked up a shred of the copy and wrote on it in big bold letters, I WILL NEVER EVER MESS YOUR COPY. She then restlessly began to try and draw his attention to the notice in a series of restless movements. Tarapada could no longer control himself and burst out laughing. In rage and embarrassment the girl rapidly ran out of the room. If she could only have for all time and from the entire universe eradicated the humiliating emotions expressed therein, the searing regret of her heart would have known relief.

Sonamoni had for a couple of days peeped into the classroom and surreptitiously tiptoed away. She was on the best of terms with her friend Charusashi in every respect except for matters regarding Tarapada; in this instance, Sonamoni would look on her with fear and the gravest of suspicions. At a time when she was confident that Charu would be in the inner sanctum would she go with great trepidation to Tarapada's door. He would look up from his books and with extreme affection say, 'So Sona, what is happening? How is my aunt?'

'You have not come over for a number of days; mother has asked you to go over some time. Her hip is giving trouble and hence she cannot come.'

At such a juncture Charu would sometimes suddenly appear. Sonamoni would be thrown into a frenzy of panic—as though she was secretively trying to usurp her friend's property. Distorting her face and in a high pitched voice Charu would shrilly cry out, 'What, Sona! You have come here to cause problems during the study time. I will immediately complain to father'. One had the impression that she was Tarapada's senior and guardian; her only task was to ensure that at no hour of the day or night any disturbance was caused to his studies. But the purpose with which she herself had gone to his room at that hour did not remain unknown to the Almighty and Tarapada too was well aware of the situation. However, the timid Sonamoni in fright would present a whole tissue of lies; finally when she would be castigated as a liar, vanquished, ashamed and humiliated Sona would leave. The tender hearted Tarapada would call out, 'Sona, I will come by your place today evening'. Like a wounded serpent Charu would lash out, 'Definitely not! Don't you have studies to prepare? Won't I complain to our teacher?'

Not in the least intimidated by Charu's threats, Tarapada had gone across to Bamunthakurun's place once or twice in the evenings. The third or fourth time Charu made no further empty threats! She stealthily locked the door of Tarapada's room from the outside, hid the key in her mother's spice box—opening the door only when it was time for dinner. Enraged, Tarapada refused to eat and was about to leave when the repentant young girl wringing her hands began to repeatedly plead, 'I implore you, never will I do this again. I beg of you to please have your meal'. When even that did not melt the ice, Charu began to weep copiously. Feeling trapped, Tarapada sat down to eat.

Charu had solemnly promised innumerable times that she would behave well with Tarapada, not for an instant would she disturb him; but when Sonamoni and others turned up, her manner and intentions changed so diametrically that to retain any kind of control was virtually impossible. When for a prolonged consecutive period she would remain moderately gentle with decorum, Tarapada would remain tense and alert for some momentous and disastrous calamity. It was practically impossible to predict the reason for the furore or from which direction the attack would come. There would be a tumultuous storm followed by a torrential downpour of tears and, at the end, calm, peaceful tranquillity.

Chapter 6

Almost two years went by in this manner. Tarapada had never allowed himself to be tethered for such a long period anywhere. Perhaps the magnetic appeal of studies and education had succeeded in anchoring him. May be, with age, his innate nature was changing to some extent—his mind was gradually veering towards savouring the richness and bounty of life. Possibly the appeal behind his co-student's daily tyrannical mischief unknowingly had created strands of attachment.

With the passing of time, Charu was almost eleven years. Moti Babu, by dint of earnest looking around, located two or three promising matches for his daughter. Aware that his daughter had reached a marriageable age, Moti Babu stopped her English lessons and forbid her to step out of the house. At this sudden embargo Charu practically set up a revolt of sorts in the house.

One day Annapurna spoke to Moti Babu, 'Why are you searching so assiduously for a suitor? Tarapada seems to be a fine lad and your daughter too has taken quite a liking to him'.

Moti Babu was amazed, 'How can that be possible! Nothing is known of his family and background. Charu is my only daughter—I want to marry her into a good family.'

A family from Raidanga came to take a look at Charu, the proposed bride. Attempts were made to dress Charu and present her to the groom and his family. She locked the door of her room and refused to emerge. From outside Moti Babu entreated and chided her in no uncertain terms—but to no avail. Finally, he had no recourse but to lie and save face; he said that his daughter had suddenly taken ill and it was impossible for her to be brought out; the guests, however, assumed that there must be some marked flaw in the girl, which was why such an excuse was being presented.

Moti Babu then began to think, Tarapada is quite a handsome and presentable boy in every respect. We will be able to keep him at home and my only daughter will not have to be sent to her in-law's house. He also pondered on the fact that no matter how indulgently they might condone his unruly disobedient daughter, it would probably not be so forgivable in any in-law's home.

After consulting at length with his wife, messengers were sent to Tarapada's native village to find out about his religious and family background. The news came back to them that his family was not well off, but otherwise there was nothing objectionable. A marriage proposal was then sent to the boy's mother and brother. In euphoric joy, they lost no time at all in intimating their acceptance.

In Kanthaley, Moti Babu and Annapurna began to discuss wedding dates. But the naturally secretive Moti Babu chose to be very guarded about these plans.

Charu could not be restrained. Like a virtual marauder, she would sometimes raid Tarapada's room. Through rage, love, ennui—she would stir up a whirlwind. Thus these days, even the uninvolved free Brahmin lad would for just a few seconds be caught unawares and feel a lightening flash of some strange and sweet emotion. One who had all this while remained impassive and totally free of being buffeted by any emotion, sometimes grew absent-minded and enmeshed in some mesmeric daydream. Some evenings, he would even discard his studies and entering Moti Babu's library turn the pages of all the books on paintings; the spell that was woven around them and the hazy dreams that resulted were far different and much more colour-ful than in the past. Taking note of Charu's strange behaviour, he found it impossible to behave normally; when she misbehaved, he found it unthink-able to smack her. This deep-rooted change in himself, this enmeshment of emotions, appeared as a strange new dream to his own self.

Fixing a day in the month of *shravana* for the marriage to be solemnised, Moti Babu sent for Tarapada's mother and brothers, not, however, giving any inkling to Tarapada. Arrangements were also made as regards decora-tions and marriage after related fanfare.

Clouds heralding the arrival of the rainy season began to overcast the sky. The village which had been dry and had little more than a scanty flow of water suddenly overflowed the banks. All the village lads in glee and joy-ous merriment began to prance about and dive in and out of the puddles and ponds. A variety of boats, small and large, laden with goods of all kinds began to ply on the river; in the evenings the river banks began to resound with the melody of foreign boatmen. Villages located on either side lived and reined in solitary splendour and isolation through the year; but it was during the rainy season that the outside world with its abundance of diverse goods arrived via the watery pathway. For a short while, establishment of a relationship with the world momentarily eradicated their pettiness and all became living and vibrant and a silent sullen kingdom resounded all around with joyous laughter.

At about this time, in Kudulkata, at landlord Nag Babu's area, a popular fair took place. In the evening Tarapada went across to the landing jetty and noticed some boats laden with Ferris wheels, merry-go-rounds and vari-ous other means of entertainment—all moving rapidly with the current in the direction of the fair. The concert troupe from Kolkata had organised loud blaring music, the itinerant theatre group was singing to the accom-paniment of a musical instrument—and in short the entire surrounding resounded with raucous merriment and enjoyment. In no time thick dark clouds appeared to sail into the centre of the sky, the moon was overshad-owed—from the east a violent wind began to blow, clouds chased after clouds, the waters of the river bubbled in merriment and began to swell rap-idly and grow turbid. The forests along the river banks grew overcast with an even thicker darkness, the croaking of frogs began to be heard and the sound of crickets sawed through the darkness... Presently the entire world appeared to be a gigantic fairground—wheels turned around, flags fluttered wildly, the universe trembled; in no time at all clouds violently sounded, flashes of lightning streaked across the sky, tearing it asunder, from the far-away darkness the fragrance of a torrential downpour wafted across. It was just only on one bank of the river, on the dormant other bank, the village of Kanthaley barred its doors and, blowing out lamps, surrendered to sleep.

The next day Tarapada's mother and brother descended at Kanthaley and boats laden with goods for the wedding began to anchor at the landing jetty.

One morning Sonamoni very timorously and surreptitiously stood at the entrance to Tarapada's study room—but from the next day Tarapada could not be found. Before the petty bonds of affection, love and friendship could completely enmesh him, carrying away the heart of the entire village, on a dark and rainy overcast monsoon night, this Brahmin lad had gone into the arms of the detached, impassive universal mother.

Translated by **Malobika Chaudhuri** [*Tagore's best short stories*
(London: Frontpage Publications Ltd, 2011)]

False hope
(*Durasha*)

Darjeeling was swathed in rain and cloud when I arrived. I didn't want to go outside, but to stay indoors was even more unappealing. Straight after my hotel breakfast I put on heavy boots and a full-length mackintosh, and went out for a walk. It was drizzling intermittently, and the thick pall of cloud all around gave the impression that God was trying to erase the entire scene, mountains and all, with a rubber.

As I walked along the deserted Calcutta road, I hated these misty heights and wished I could grasp with all five senses Earth's busy variety and colour again. It was then that I heard the pathetic sound of a woman crying, not far off. Life is so tragic and troubled that the sound of crying is nothing out of the ordinary, and at any other time I doubt if I would have looked round; but here amidst the clouds the sound seemed like the cry of a whole vanished world. I could not ignore it.

I approached, and saw a woman sitting on a rock by the road, weeping. Her clothes were ochre-coloured, and her matted, light-coloured hair was scooped up into a top-knot. Hers was no recent grief: long suppressed exhaustion and misery had snapped under the weight of the clouds and desolation, and had burst out. 'This is odd,' I said to myself. 'I could base a brilliant story on this. I never thought to see a *sannyāsinī* sitting on a mountainside!' I could not tell which caste she was. I asked her kindly in Hindi, 'Who are you? What's happened to you?'

At first she did not answer, and merely glanced at me with fiery, tearful eyes. I spoke again: 'Don't be afraid—I'm a gentleman.' She smiled then and said in flawless Hindusthani, 'I've been beyond fear and terror for a long time now—shame, too. Once, Babuji, I lived in such purdah that even my own brother had to ask for permission to see me: But nothing hides me from the world now.'

I was rather annoyed. My clothes and manners were those of a *sāheb*. Yet this wretched woman addressed me, without hesitation, as 'Babuji'. I felt like ditching the story and stumping off in my best *sāheb's* manner, nose in the air and puffing cigarette-smoke like a train. But curiosity got the better of me. I asked her, tilting my head haughtily, 'Can I help you? Do you need anything?'

She stared straight at me, and after a pause replied briefly, 'I am the daughter of Golamkader Khan, Nawab of Badraon.'

I had not the slightest idea where Badraon was or who Golamkader Khan was or why his daughter should be sitting by the Calcutta Road in Darjeeling and weeping. I didn't believe her, either, but decided I would not spoil the fun, or the chance of such a good story. So I made a lengthy and solemn salaam before her and said, 'Bibisaheb, forgive me, I did not know who you were.' (There are many logical reasons why I did not know her, the chief one being that I had never seen her before, and on top of that the mist was so thick it was hard to see one's own hands and feet.) 'Bibisaheb' did not take offence, and pointing to a rock next to her said pleasantly, 'Sit down.'

I could see she was used to giving orders. I felt surprisingly honoured at being allowed to sit on a wet, hard, mossy rock beside her. The daughter of Golamkader Khan of Badraon, the Princess Nurunni Shah or Meherunni Shah or whatever she was called, had graciously given me a muddy seat by the Calcutta Road in Darjeeling, next to her and at about the same height! When I set out from the hotel in my mackintosh, I never dreamt of such a lofty possibility.

It might seem like poetry: a man and a woman mysteriously conversing on a rocky mountainside. Hot from the pen of a poet, it would rouse in the reader's heart the sounds of streams gurgling in mountain caves, or the Wonderful music of Kalidasa's *Meghadūta* or *Kumārasambhava*. Yet surely there must be few representatives of Young Bengal[1] who would *not* have felt ridiculous sitting in boots and mackintosh by the Calcutta Road on a muddy rock with a ragged Hindusthani lady! But we were wrapped in mist, there was no one to see us, no cause for embarrassment, no one but the Nawab of Badraon Golamkader Khan's daughter and I—a freshly minted

---

[1] Progressive-minded products of English education in nineteenth-century Calcutta were known collectively as 'Young Bengal'.

Bengali *sāheb*—two people on two rocks, like relics of a totally destroyed world. The great absurdity of our incongruous meeting concerned only *our* destinies, no one else's.

'Bibisaheb,' I said, 'who put you into this state?'

The Princess of Badraon struck her forehead. 'How can I know how things are caused? Who is it who hides these huge, harsh mountains in flimsy clouds?'

I agreed with her, not wishing to start a philosophic debate. 'Yes indeed, who knows the mysteries of Fate? We crawl like worms before them.'

I would have argued, I would not have let Bibisaheb off so lightly—but my Hindi was insufficient. The little I had learnt from dealing with watchmen and bearers did not permit me to discuss Fate and Free Will with a Princess of Badraon or of any other place, sitting by the Calcutta Road.

Bibisaheb said, 'The extraordinary story of my life has only just finished. At your command I shall tell it to you.'

'Command?' I said, rather flustered. 'If you *favour* me with it I shall be highly honoured.'

No one should think that I spoke exactly like this, but in Hindi. I wanted to, but I was not capable of doing so. When Bibisaheb spoke, it was like a delicate morning breeze stirring a dewy golden cornfield: there was such easy meekness in her flow of sentences, such beauty. And I could only reply in blunt, barbarous, broken phrases. I had never known such effortless excellence of speech; as I talked to Bibisaheb I felt, for the first time, my own inadequacy.

'My father,' she said, 'had the blood of the Emperor of Delhi in his veins, and in order to preserve the honour of his family went to great lengths to find me a suitable husband. A proposal came from the Nawab of Lucknow: my father was dealing with this when the fighting broke out between the British and the sepoys over cartridge-biting, and Hindusthan turned dark with the smoke of cannon-fire.'[2]

I had never before heard Hindusthani spoken by a woman, let alone by a high-born lady, and as I listened it was clear to me that this was aristocrat's language and that the days of this language were over. Everything today has been lowered, stunted, stripped by the railways and telegraph, by the hurly-burly of work, by the extinction of the nobility. As I listened to this nawab's language amidst the thick mists of British-built, modern,

---

[2] The Indian Mutiny of 1857 was sparked off by the use of animal fat in cartridges which had to be 'bitten off' before use. Hindus suspected cow-fat; Muslims suspected pig-fat (taboo in each case).

stony Darjeeling, an imaginary Mogul city arose in my mind, with huge white marble palaces soaring into the sky, with long-tailed liveried horses in the streets and elephants with gold-tasselled howdahs; a city whose people wore many-coloured turbans, baggy shirts and pyjamas of wool and silk and muslin, with brocade slippers curled up at the toes, and scimitars tied to their waists; a leisured, elegant, courteous way of life.

'Our fort,' said the Nawab's daughter, 'was on the bank of the Yamuna. Our army-commander was a Hindu Brahmin, called Keshar Lal.'

The woman seemed to pour all the music of her voice into that one name 'Keshar Lal'. I laid my walking-stick on the ground and settled myself into a bolt-upright position.

'Keshar Lal was a strict Hindu. When I got up in the morning I would look from the window of the zenana and watch him immerse himself up to the chest in the Yamuna, watch him circumambulating with hands cupped in an offering to the rising sun. He would sit with sopping clothes on the *ghāt*, recite mantras devotedly, and then sing a hymn clearly and smoothly in Rāg Bhairavī as he walked back to his house.

I was a Muslim girl, but I had never been told about my religion and I did not know its doctrines and practices. Among our menfolk, religious rules had been weakened by indolence, drinking and self-indulgence; and in the luxury of the zenana, too, religion was not much alive.

God probably implanted in me a natural thirst for religion—I cannot see how else it was caused. Be that as it may, at the sight of Keshar Lal performing his rituals in the pure dawn light on the bare white steps down to the calm blue Yamuna, my hitherto dormant feelings were seized by a sweet, unspoken devotion.

With his regular, disciplined piety, and his fair and supple body, Keshar Lal was like a smokeless flame: his Brahminical sanctity and grace chastened the ignorant heart of a Muslim girl with a strange reverence.

I had a Hindu maid who did obeisance before Keshar Lal every day and took the dust of his feet. The sight of this pleased me but also made me jealous. On days when special rites were observed, this maid would also sometimes lay on meals for Brahmins. I offered to help with the cost of this, saying, "Why not invite Keshar Lal?" She answered in horror, "Keshar Lal does not take food or gifts from anyone." It gnawed at my heart that I could not make any direct or indirect expression of devotion to Keshar Lal.

One of my ancestors had abducted a Brahmin girl and married her. As I sat inside the zenana, I felt her pure blood in my veins and found some comfort in thinking I was linked to Keshar Lal by that thread. I listened to everything my Hindu maid could tell me about Hinduism, its customs and rules, its amazing tales of gods and goddesses, its marvellous *Rāmāyana* and *Mahābhārata;* as I listened, a wonderful picture of the Hindu world unfolded before me. Statues and idols, the sounds of bells and conches, gold-topped temples, the smoke of incense, the scent of flowers and sandalwood, the unearthly powers of *yogīs* and *sannyāsīs,* superhuman Brahmins, the wiles and sports of gods in human disguise: all combined to create a realm that was supernatural, distant, vast and immeasurably old. My heart was like a bird without a nest, flying at dusk from room to room of a huge and ancient palace. To my girlish mind, the Hindu world was an enchanting fairy-tale kingdom.

It was at this time that the fighting broke out between the Company and the sepoys. Waves of revolt spread even to our small fort. Keshar Lal said, "The pale-skinned cow-eaters must be driven from Aryavarta! Hindu and Muslim kings must be free again to gamble for power!"

My father Golamkader Khan was a calculating man. "Those damned English can do the impossible," he said. "The people of Hindusthan can never match them. I'm not going to stake this little fort of mine on so slender a chance. Don't ask me to fight with the Honourable Company!"

At a time when the blood of both Hindus and Muslims was on fire, we were all enraged by my father's merchant-like prudence. Even my mother and step-mothers were stirred. Soon Keshar Lal came with an armed troop, and said to my father, "Nawab-saheb, if you don't join us I shall take you prisoner while the fighting lasts and command the fort myself."

"There is no need for that," said my father. "I'm on your side."

"Give us some money from your treasury," said Keshar Lal.

My father did not give much. "I'll give you more when you need it," he said.

I took my whole array of ornaments, tied them up in a cloth and gave them to my Hindu maid to take to Keshar Lal. He accepted them. I tingled with pleasure at this, all over my denuded body.

With the scraping and polishing of rusty guns and the sharpening of ancient swords, Keshar Lal began to get ready. But suddenly, one afternoon, the District Commissioner arrived: his red-shirted soldiers stormed into the fort, raising clouds of dust. My father Golamkader Khan had secretly given him news of the revolt.

Keshar Lal commanded such loyalty in the Nawab's guard that they fought to the death with their broken guns and blunt swords.

My traitorous father's house was like hell to me. I was bursting with grief and hatred, but I did not shed a single tear. I dressed in the clothes of my cowardly brother and escaped from the zenana, while no one was looking.

Dust, gunpowder smoke, the shouting of soldiers and the noise of guns died down, and the terrible stillness of death settled over land and water and sky. The sun set, turning the Yamuna red, and a nearly full moon hung in the evening sky. The battlefield was strewn with hideous scenes of death. At any other time my heart would have been pierced by the pity of it, but instead I wandered around as if in a trance, trying to find Keshar Lal—no other aim had meaning for me. I searched until, in the middle of the night, in bright moonlight, not far from the battle-field, on the bank of the Yamuna, in the shade of a mango-grove, I came across the dead bodies of Keshar Lal and his loyal batman. I could see that—appallingly wounded—either master had carried servant or servant had carried master from the battle-field to this place of safety, where they had quietly given themselves up to Death.

The first thing I did was fulfil the craving I had had for so long to abase myself before Keshar Lal. I fell to my knees beside him, loosed my long tresses, and fervently rubbed the dust from his feet. I raised his ice-cold soles to my feverish forehead, and kissed them; months of suppressed tears welled up. But then his body moved, and a weak groan emerged from his lips. I drew back in alarm at the sound. With closed eyes and parched voice he murmured, "Water."

I ran to the Yamuna—returned with my clothes soaking wet. I wrung the water out over Keshar Lal's half-open lips, and tore wet strips of cloth to bind the ghastly wound that had destroyed his left eye. I brought him water a few more times in this way, and as I moistened his face and eyes he slowly regained some consciousness. "Shall I give you more water?" I asked.

"Who are you?" said Keshar Lal.

I could not hold back any more and said, "I am your humble, devoted servant. I am the daughter of Golamkader Khan, the Nawab." At least he would die knowing my devotion to him! No one could deprive me of the joy of that feeling.

But as soon as he heard who I was he roared out like a lion, "Daughter of an arch-traitor! Heretic! You, a Muslim, have profaned my religion by giving me water at my time of death!" He struck me a heavy blow on my cheek with his right hand: everything swam before my eyes and I nearly fainted.

I was sixteen years old and this was the first time I had been out of the zenana; the greedy heat of the sun had not yet stolen the luscious pink of my cheeks; but this was the first greeting I received from the outside world, from my one idol in the world!'

My cigarette had gone out. All this time I had sat like a figure in a paint-ing—so engrossed that I knew not whether it was words or music that I heard. I had said nothing myself. But now at last I burst out, 'Animal!'

'Animal?' said the Nawab's daughter. 'Would a dying animal refuse a drop of water?'

Embarrassed, I said, 'Maybe not. He was a god, then.'

'What sort of god?' said the Princess. 'Would a god reject the service of an eager and devoted heart?'

'Indeed not,' I said, and fell silent again.

'At first,' continued the Princess, 'I was devastated. I felt as if the world had collapsed over my head. But I quickly recovered myself, bowed from a distance before that harsh, cruel, high-minded Brahmin, and said to myself, "O Brahmin, you accept neither the service of the wretched, nor food from another's hand, nor the gifts of the wealthy, nor the youth of a girl, nor the love of a woman: you are separate, alone, aloof, distant. I have no right at all to offer my soul to you."

I cannot say what Keshar Lal thought when he saw the daughter of the Nawab bowing down before him till her head touched the dust, but there was no surprise or change of expression in his face. He looked at me calmly; then, very slowly, stood up. I anxiously stretched out my arm to support him, but he silently refused it, and with great difficulty staggered to the bank of the Yamuna. A ferry was moored there. There was no one to cross and no one to take anyone across. Keshar Lal boarded the boat and untied the mooring-rope: the boat quickly drifted to the middle of the stream and gradually faded from view. I longed with all the force of my feelings, youth and unrequited devotion to make a last obeisance before that boat and drown: to end this futile life of mine in the waveless, moonlit Yamuna, in the still night, like a bud shed before it could bloom.

But I could not do that. The moon in the sky, the dense black woods on the bank, the inky-blue unruffled waters, the towers of our fortress glit-tering above the mango-grove in the moonlight, sang together a silent, solemn song of death; heaven, earth and the nether world that night, by their moon-and-star-studded stillness, told me with one voice to die. But a frail invisible boat, on the calm breast of the Yamuna, dragged me from the moonlit night's soothing, ever-bewitching spell of death and back to the path of life. I followed the bank of the river like a sleep-walker, some-times through clumps of reeds, sometimes over sandbanks, sometimes over rugged broken-up beaches, sometimes through scarcely penetrable thickets.'

She fell silent here. I also said nothing. After a long pause the Nawab's daughter said, 'What happened after this was very complicated. I don't know how to break it up and describe it clearly to you. I wandered through a thick forest, but I can't remember which path I took when. Where shall I begin? Where shall I end? What shall I leave out? What shall I keep in? How can I make the whole story clear so that it won't seem impossible or preposterous or unnatural?

During this period of my life I realized that nothing is impossible or unattainable. To a young girl from a nawab's zenana the outside world might seem totally forbidding, but that is an illusion: if one once steps out, a way through will be found. This path is not a nawab's path; but it is a path by which people have always come. It is rugged, weird and uncharted, full of branchings and divisions, fraught with agony and ecstasy, obstacles and obstructions; but it *is* a path.

An account of a princess's long, solitary journey along this inevitable path would not be pleasant to listen to, and even if it was I have no wish to tell it. In a word, I endured many trials and dangers and indignities; yet life was not unbearable. Like a firework, the more I burned the more wildly I moved; so long as I kept moving I did not feel I was burning. But now at last the flame of my pain and joy has gone out, and I find myself lying like a dumb thing in the roadside dust. My journey is over; my story is finished.'

With this the Nawab's daughter stopped. I mentally shook my head: the story was surely *not* yet over. I was silent for a while, then said in broken Hindi, 'Forgive my rudeness, but if you would speak a little more openly about the last part of your story my impudent curiosity would be greatly eased.'

The Nawab's daughter smiled. No doubt my broken Hindi helped. If I had been able to speak Hindi properly, she would not have been so frank with me: the fact that I knew so little of her mother tongue created a space between us, a protective veil.

She began again. 'I often got news of Keshar Lal, but in no way could I get to meet him. He had joined Tatya Tope's army, and kept appearing and disappearing like a bolt of thunder from a sky that was still dark with revolt: sometimes to the east, sometimes to the west, sometimes to the north-east, sometimes to the south-west.

I was by then dressed as a *yoginī*, and studying the Sanskrit Shastras in Benares with Shibananda Swami, my spiritual father. News from all over India reached him: I devotedly learnt the Shastras, and at the same time eagerly lapped up news of the war.

Gradually the British Raj stamped out the flames of revolution in Hindusthan. There was no more news of Keshar Lal. All the heroic figures, right across India, who had been glimpsed in the bloody light of battle, were eclipsed. I could hold myself no longer. I left the protection of my guru, and went out in the world again, dressed as a devotee of Shiva. I wandered from road to road, shrine to shrine, to ashrams and temples, but found no news of Keshar Lal anywhere. Some who knew his name said, "He must have died in the fighting or been executed." My heart said, "That can never be: Keshar Lal cannot die. He is a Brahmin; that blazing invincible fire can never be put out; it is still burning brightly on a lonely, remote, ritual hearth, waiting for me to sacrifice myself to it."

It is said in the Hindu Shastras that through meditation and austerity a Shudra can become Brahmin; there is no mention of a Muslim becoming a Brahmin, for the simple reason that there were no Muslims at that time. I knew it would be a long time before I could be united with Keshar Lal, because first I had to become a Brahmin. Thirty long years went by. I became a Brahmin inside and out; in habit and behaviour; in body, mind and speech. The blood of my Brahmin grandmother flowed through my body with unmixed energy; I acquired a strange mental fire, by abasing myself totally before the first and last Brahmin of my adolescence and youth, for me the only Brahmin in the world.

I had heard a lot about Keshar Lal's heroism in the revolutionary war, but that was not what imprinted itself on my heart. What I saw was Keshar Lal floating out alone in a little boat into the calm central stream of the Yamuna, in the silent moonlight: *that* was the picture that obsessed me. I saw nothing but this, day and night: a Brahmin floating away on the empty stream towards some undefined mystery—with no companion, no servant, no need of anyone; immersed in the purity of his soul, complete in himself; with the planets, moon and stars watching him silently.

Then I heard that Keshar Lal had escaped execution and taken refuge in Nepal. I went there. After living there for many months I heard that he had left Nepal a long time before and had gone nobody knew where.

I wandered through the mountains. This was not a Hindu land: it was a land of Bhutanese and Lepchas with their weird beliefs; there was no orthodoxy in their diet and behaviour; their gods and styles of worship were completely alien; I was terrified of the slightest desecration of the holiness I had acquired through years of spiritual endeavour. I took great pains to avoid being touched by anything unclean. I knew that my boat was nearly at the shore, that my life's supreme goal was not far off.

What shall I say of what happened next? The end of the story is very brief. When a lamp is about to go out it can be extinguished with a single puff. I need not elaborate. After thirty-eight years, I have arrived in Darjeeling. I saw Keshar Lal this morning.'

She fell silent again, so I asked her eagerly, 'What did you see?'

'I saw,' said the Nawab's daughter, 'an aged Keshar Lal in a Bhutanese village with his Bhutanese wife, sitting in a filthy yard with their grandchildren born of her, picking grain out of maize.'

Her story was finished. I thought I ought to offer some word of consolation. 'How can anyone,' I said, 'who has had to survive amidst strangers for thirty-eight years, stick to his religious rules?'

'You think I don't understand that?' said the Nawab's daughter. 'But why was I so deluded for so long? Why didn't I know that the Brahminism that stole away my young heart was nothing but custom and superstition? I thought it was *dharma*, unending and eternal. How else could I—after being so shamefully rejected when I offered on that moonlit night my freshly bloomed body and heart and soul, trembling with devotion, after leaving my father's house for the first time at the age of sixteen—how else could I have silently accepted the insult as a kind of initiation by a guru, and meekly dedicated myself to him with redoubled devotion? Alas, Brahmin, you exchanged one set of habits for another, but I gave away my life and youth, and how can I get them back again?'

The woman stood up and said, '*Namaskār*, Babuji!' Then a moment later she said, as if correcting herself, 'Salaam Babu-saheb!' With this Muslim valediction she took her leave, as it were, of the Brahminism whose foundations had crumbled to the dust. Before I could say anything, she disappeared like a cloud into the mists that swirled round these icy mountain-tops.

I shut my eyes for a while and let all she had described roll through my mind. I saw the young, sixteen-year-old Nawab's daughter sitting on a fine carpet in her room overlooking the Yamuna; I saw the statuesque figure of a *yoginī* rapt in ecstatic devotion during evening worship in a place of pilgrimage; and then I saw also an image of heart-broken disillusionment in an older woman, shrouded in mist, on the edge of the Calcutta Road in Darjeeling; and the poignant music of beautiful, pure Urdu, formed by the clash of Brahmin and Muslim blood flowing through this woman in opposite ways, reverberated in my mind.[3]

I opened my eyes. The clouds had parted, and the clear sky was bright with gentle sunshine. Englishwomen in hand-pushed carts and Englishmen

---

[3] There is a large area of overlap between Hindi and Urdu. Hindi uses the *devanāgarī* script and draws from Sanskrit for its higher vocabulary. Urdu uses the Persian script and a more Perso-Arabic vocabulary. In British India 'Hindusthani' was the name given to the colloquial language common to Hindi and Urdu; but the Princess's Hindusthani is clearly a highly refined hybrid, i.e. Urdu.

on horseback were out taking the air. There were one or two Bengalis too, casting amused glances at me from faces swathed in scarves.

I got up quickly, and in the bright light of this sunny world I could no longer believe in the stormy story I had heard. My imagination had made it up, out of mist mixed with ample tobacco-smoke. That Muslim-Brahmin woman, that Brahmin hero, that fort on the bank of the Yamuna, had perhaps no truth in them at all.

Translated by **William Radice**
[*Rabindranath Tagore: Selected short stories*
(London: Penguin Books, 2005, ed.)]

The wife's letter
(*Streer patra*)

My submission at your lotus feet—

We have been married for fifteen years, but to this day I have never written you a letter. I have always been at hand—you have heard so many words from my lips, and I too have listened to you—but there has never been an interval in which a letter might have been written.

Today I have come on a pilgrimage to the seat of Lord Jagannath in Puri, while you remain tied to your work in your office. Your bond with Calcutta is like that of a snail with its shell; the city has grown into your body and soul. That is why you did not apply for leave from the office. Such was the wish of the Almighty; he granted *my* application for leave.

I am the second daughter-in-law of your father's house. Today, after fifteen years, standing by the ocean's shore, I have learnt that I have a different relation as well with the world and the Lord of the world. That is why I have taken courage to write this letter; it is not a letter from the second daughter-in-law of your family.

In infancy—when no one but God, who had fated my relation with your family, knew of its possibility—my brother and I were struck down together by typhoid. My brother died; I survived. The women of the neighbourhood began to say, 'Mrinal lived because she's a girl; if she'd been a boy, would she have been spared?' The god of death is skilled in the art of theft; he covets what is precious.

Death will not come for me. It is to explain this properly that I have sat down to write this letter.

When a distant uncle of yours came with your friend Nirad to our house to inspect the prospective bride, I was twelve years old. We lived in an inaccessible village, where you could hear the jackals howl by day. To reach it you had to take a carriage from the railway station for fourteen miles, and cover the last three miles of dirt road in a palanquin. How sorely were they harassed that day! And on top of that, our East Bengal cooking—your uncle has still not forgotten the farce of that meal.

Your mother was determined that her second daughter-in-law's looks should make good the elder one's deficiency in beauty. Otherwise why should you take so much trouble to visit our village? In Bengal, no one has to hunt out diseases of the spleen, the liver, or the stomach, nor need you search for a bride; they come and fasten on you themselves, they will not let you go.

My father's heart began to quake, my mother called on the goddess Durga. How was a rustic worshipper to appease the gods of the city? Their hope lay solely in the beauty of their daughter. But their daughter took no pride in that beauty—it was priced at whatever the buyer offered. It is for this reason that women never lose their diffidence, whatever their beauty or virtues.

The anxiety of the entire household, indeed of the entire neighbourhood, lay on my heart like a stone. That day it seemed as though all the light in the sky and all the powers of the universe were joint bailiffs firmly holding up a twelve-year-old country girl for the scrutiny of her two examiners' two pairs of eyes. I had nowhere to hide.

The whole sky wept to the strains of flute-music as I entered your house. Even after a minute scrutiny of my imperfections, the crowd of housewives acknowledged that on the whole I was indeed beautiful. This verdict made my elder sister-in-law grave. But I wonder what use my beauty was! If some ancient pedant had created beauty out of holy Ganga silt, then you would have valued it; but as it is, it was created by God for His own pleasure, and so it has no value in your righteous household.

It did not take long for you to forget that I had beauty—but you were forced to remember at each step that I had brains. This intelligence is so much a part of my nature that it has survived even fifteen years in your household. My mother feared for this cleverness of mine; for a woman it was an impediment. If one who must follow the limits laid down by rule seeks to follow her intelligence, she will stumble repeatedly and come to grief. But what was I to do? God had carelessly given me much more intelligence than I needed to be a wife in your household; to whom was I now to return it? Your family have abused me daily as an over-clever female. Harsh words are the consolation of the weak—so I forgive them.

I had one possession beyond your household, which none of you knew about. I used to write poems in secret. Whatever rubbish they were, the walls of your women's quarters had not grown round them. In them lay my freedom—I was myself in them. You and your family never liked, never even recognised, whatever in me exceeded the 'second daughter-in-law' of your household. In fifteen years, you never discovered that I am a poet.

The most vivid of my first memories of your house is of the cattle-shed. The cattle were housed in a shed just next to the stairs leading to the women's quarters; they had no room to move in except for the courtyard in front. In a corner of that courtyard stood the wooden trough for their fodder. The servant had much to do in the mornings; meanwhile the starving cows would lick and chew the sides of the trough to a pulp. My heart wept for them. I was a country girl—when I first entered your house, those two cows and three calves seemed to me as my only familiar relatives in the whole city. When I was a new bride, I would feed them secretly out of my own food. When I grew up, my evident fondness for the cows led those of my in-laws on jesting terms with me to express doubts about my lineage.

My daughter died almost immediately after she was born. She called to me, too, to go with her. If she had lived, she would have brought to my life whatever is great and true: from being the second daughter-in-law, I would then have become a mother. A mother, even within the confines of her own family, belongs to the family of the world. I suffered only the pain of motherhood; I never experienced its freedom.

I remember that the English doctor was astonished at the sight of our women's quarters, and scolded us angrily about the state of the lying-in room. There is a garden to the front of your house; your outer rooms lack nothing by way of furniture and ornaments. The inner rooms are like the reverse of a piece of work in wool; they have neither decorum, nor grace, nor ornament. There lights burn dimly; the air enters by stealth, like a thief; the courtyard is immovably choked with rubbish; the stains on the walls and floors reign undisturbed. But the doctor made a mistake: he thought that this caused us constant suffering. In fact the reverse was true. Neglect is like the ashes which cover a fire: perhaps keeping it alive, but preventing its heat from being outwardly felt. When self-respect dwindles, neglect does not seem unjust; for this reason, it causes no suffering. That is also why women are ashamed to fee! pain. I say, therefore, if it is your decree that women must suffer, then it is best to keep them in as neglected a state as possible; in comfort, the pain of suffering becomes greater.

Whatever the condition in which you kept me, it never occurred to me that there was any suffering involved. In the lying-in room, death came and stood at my head, yet I felt no fear at all. What is life to us, that we should fear death? Death is unwelcome only to those whose hold on life has been strengthened by love and care. If death, that day, had pulled me by the hand, I would have come away roots and all, like a dump of grass from loose earth. A Bengali woman speaks of dying in every second utterance. But where is the glory in such death? I am ashamed to die, so easy is death for the likes of me.

My daughter was like the evening star, appearing briefly only to fade away. I became occupied again with my daily chores and the cows and their calves. Life would have rolled on in this way to the very end, and there would have been no need, today, to write you this letter. But a tiny seed is blown by the wind to take root as a peepal shoot in a mortared house; in the end its ribs of brick and timber are cracked apart by that tiny seed. From somewhere a little speck of life blew into the firmly mortared arrangements of my household existence, and from that day the cracks began to appear.

After the death of their widowed mother, my elder sister-in-law's young sister Bindu was driven by her cousins' ill-treatment to seek refuge in her elder sister's house. All of you thought: what a nuisance! So vexatious is my nature that there was no helping it, the moment I saw all of you growing irritated and angry, my whole heart ranged itself to do battle by the side of the helpless girl. To have to take shelter with strangers against their wishes—how immense a humiliation! Is it possible to push aside one who has been forced to submit even to this?

I then became aware of my sister-in-law's situation. The claim of affection alone had prompted her to give shelter to her sister. But when she realised her husband's unwillingness, she began to pretend that the whole matter was a great nuisance—that she would do anything to be rid of this burden. She lacked the courage to show her love openly, from the heart, to her orphaned sister. She is an obedient wife.

Her dilemma grieved me still further. I saw that she made a point of demonstrating to everyone the coarseness of the clothes and food she provided for Bindu, as well as the fact that Bindu was put to work at the most menial of household chores. At this I felt not only pain but shame. My sister-in-law was anxious to prove to everyone that our household, by some fluke, had secured Bindu at a bargain price. She yielded much labour but cost very little.

My elder sister-in-law's family had little to boast of beyond its lineage: they possessed neither wealth nor good looks. You know how they pleaded with and importuned your father to agree to the marriage. My sister-in-law had always thought of her marriage as a great offence to your family. For this reason she tried, in every way, so to restrict herself as to take up very little space in your house.

But her wise example makes life difficult for us women. It is impossible for me to so limit myself in every point. When I decide that something is right, it is not my nature to be persuaded for someone else's sake that it is wrong. You too have had many proofs of this.

I drew Bindu to my rooms. Sister-in-law said: 'Meja Bou is simply spoiling a poor man's daughter.' She went around complaining to everyone as though I had brought about some terrible disaster. But I know that in her heart, she was relieved. Now the burden of blame would fall on me alone. Her heart was at peace in the knowledge that I was providing her sister with the love she herself could not show her.

My sister-in-law had tried to strike a few years off her sister's age. But it would not have been wrong to say, if only in secret, that she was no younger than fourteen. You know that the girl was so ill-favoured that if she fell and hurt her head, people would be worried that the floor had suffered some damage. As a result, in the absence of her parents, there was no one to arrange a marriage for her, and who would be so hardy as to want to marry such a girl?

Bindu came to me in great trepidation of heart, as if she thought that I would not survive the contagion of her touch: as though there was no need for her to have been born at all in this world, as though she must pass by unobtrusively, avoiding people's eyes. In her father's house, her cousins had been unwilling to give up to her even a corner where some unwanted thing might lie forgotten. Inessential rubbish can easily find a place around our houses, because people forget it, but an inessential girl is in the first place unwanted, and moreover impossible to overlook; hence she does not find a place even in the rubbish-heap. One cannot say that Bindu's cousins are utterly necessary to this world either; but they do well enough.

So when I called Bindu to my rooms, there was a trembling in her heart. Her fear filled me with sadness. I conveyed to her in many loving ways that there was a little place for her in my household.

But my household, after all, was not mine alone, and so my task was not easy. After a few days with me she developed a red rash on her skin: perhaps a heat rash, perhaps something else. All of you said it was small-pox—because it was Bindu. An inexperienced doctor from the neighbourhood came and said that he could not tell what it was until a day or two had passed. But who was prepared to wait that day or two? Bindu herself was ready to die of shame at her illness. I said, 'Never mind if she has smallpox, I'll stay with her in the lying-in room. No one else need be troubled.' When all of you were in a fury at me over this, and even Bindu's sister was putting on a show of extreme irritation and proposing to send the poor girl to hospital, suddenly the rash disappeared completely. At this you became even more concerned. You said that undoubtedly the smallpox had settled deep into her. For she was Bindu.

One great virtue of being reared in neglect is that one's constitution becomes virtually indestructible. Ailments refuse to visit you—the highways to death are wholly shut off. So illness mocked at Bindu and passed on—nothing happened to her. But it grew abundantly clear that the most insignificant person in the world was the one that was hardest to give shelter to. One who has most need of shelter finds the greatest obstacles to it.

When Bindu lost her fear of me, she tied herself in yet another knot. She developed so great a love for me that it made me afraid. I had never seen such an image of love in my household. I had read of such love in books, but that was love between men and women. For a long time, there had been no occasion for me to recall that I was beautiful—now, after so many years, this ugly girl became obsessed with my beauty. It was as if her eyes could never have enough of gazing on my face. She would say, 'Didi, no one but me has ever seen this face of yours.' On the days when I braided my hair myself, she would be hurt and offended. She loved to handle the weight of my hair. I did not need to dress up unless we were invited out; but Bindu would plague me to dress up every day. The girl was infatuated with me.

There is not even the smallest patch of earth in the women's quarters in your house. A gab tree has somehow taken root by the north wall near the gutter. When I saw the leaves of that tree flush red, I would realise that spring had come to the earth. In the midst of my household cares, when I saw this unloved girl's heart one day glow with colour, I realised that in the heart's world too, there is a breeze of spring-time—a breeze which comes from some far-off heaven, not from the end of the lane.

The unbearable force of Bindu's love made me restless and uneasy. I confess that sometimes I felt angry with her. Yet that love made me glimpse a true image of myself, one that I had never seen before. This was the image of my free self.

Meanwhile, all of you thought it excessive that I should lavish such care on a girl like Bindu. As a result, there were endless complaints and objections. When my armlets were stolen from my room, you were not ashamed to suggest that Bindu was somehow involved in the theft. When the police started searching people's houses during the Swadeshi Movement,[†] you began to suspect that Bindu was a female informer in the pay of the police. There was no other proof of this than that she was Bindu.

The maids in your house refused to do any work for her. Bindu herself would grow rigid with embarrassment if I asked any of them to do something for her. As a result, my expenditure on her behalf went up. I had to keep a maid especially for her. You did not like this. When you saw the clothes I gave her, you became so angry that you stopped my allowance. From the very next day, I began to wear the coarsest mill-produced dhotis† at twenty annas a pair. I also forbade Mati's mother to take out the dishes after my meal; I would myself feed the leftover rice to the calves and scrub the dishes at the pump in the courtyard. You were not very pleased by the sight when you saw me at these tasks one day. Yet I never learned this wisdom: whether I was pleased or not did not matter, but you had to be pleased at all costs.

Meanwhile, as your anger increased, so did Bindu's age. This natural event made you unnaturally concerned. I am still amazed at one thing: why did you not send Bindu away from your house by force? I know very well that you are secretly afraid of me. Inwardly, you cannot but respect the intelligence that God gave me.

In the end, unable to get rid of Bindu by your own means, you had recourse to Prajapati, the god of marriage. A bridegroom was arranged for Bindu. My sister-in-law said, 'Thank heavens, Mother Kali has saved the reputation of our family.'

I did not know what the groom was like; I heard from you that he was eligible in every respect. Bindu clasped my feet and wept, saying 'Didi, why need I get married?'

I tried to persuade her, telling her, 'Bindu, don't be afraid, I've heard he's a good groom.'

Bindu answered, 'If he's so eligible, what have I got that might please him?'

The groom's family did not even come to see Bindu. My sister-in-law was greatly relieved at this.

But Bindu's tears continued incessantly, day and night. I know what she suffered. I had fought many battles for Bindu in my household, but I did not have the courage to say that her marriage must be stopped. How should I say this? What would happen to her if I died?

In the first place she was a girl, and on top of that she was dark-complexioned. It was better not to think of where she was going or what might happen to her. The thought sent shudders through my heart.

Bindu said, 'Didi, there are still five days to the wedding. Mightn't I die in this time?'

I scolded her severely, but God knows that I would have been relieved if there had been an easy means of death for Bindu.

The day before the wedding, Bindu went to her sister and asked her, 'Didi, I'll live in your cattle-shed, I'll do whatever you ask of me. I beg of you, don't throw me away like this.'

Her sister had been shedding tears in secret for the past few days; she wept then as well. But we do not have hearts only, we have the scriptures too; she said, 'Bindi, you know that a husband is the sole end of a woman's life. If you are fated to suffer, no one can avert it.'

The truth was that there was no escape anywhere. Bindu must marry, whatever befell her.

I had wanted the wedding to take place in our house. But you announced that it must be held in the groom's house—this was the custom in their family.

I realised that your household deity would never endure it if your family were forced to spend on Bindu's wedding. So I had to fall silent. But there is one thing you did not know. I had wanted to tell my sister-in-law, but I did not, because she would have died of fear. I adorned Bindu with some of my jewellery. Perhaps my sister-in-law saw this but pretended not to notice. I beg you in the name of righteousness, forgive her for this.

Before leaving, Bindu embraced me, asking, 'Didi, are you all abandoning me?'

I answered 'No, Bindu, whatever happens to you, I'll never abandon you.'

Three days passed. In one corner of the coal-shed on the ground floor of your house, I had reared a lamb which one of your tenants had sent as a gift for your table, and which I had rescued from the flames of your appetite. Every morning I would feed it gram with my own hands; for a few days I had tried relying on your servants, but found that they were more interested in eating it than in feeding it.

That morning, when I entered the coal-shed, I found Bindu crouched in a corner. On seeing me she collapsed on the floor, clasped my feet and began to weep silently.

Bindu's husband was mad.

'Are you telling the truth, Bindi?'

'Could I tell you such a big lie, Didi? He is mad. My father-in-law did not want this marriage; but he is mortally afraid of my mother-in-law.

He left for Varanasi before the wedding. My mother-in-law had set her heart on marrying her son off; she went ahead with it.'

I sat down, overcome, on the heap of coal. Women have no pity for women. They say, 'She's only a woman. So what if the groom's mad, he's a man, isn't he?'

One could not tell at first sight that Bindu's husband was insane; but he would sometimes grow so violent that he had to be locked up in a room. He had seemed normal on the night of the wedding, but staying up at night and all the excitement had brought on an attack the next day. In the afternoon, Bindu had sat down to her meal of rice, served on a brass platter, when suddenly her husband snatched the platter and threw it, rice and all, into the courtyard. He had got it into his head that Bindu was Rani Rasmani; the servant must have stolen her golden plate and served her on his own brass platter. This was the reason for his anger.

Bindu was terrified. On the third night, when Bindu's mother-in-law commanded her to sleep in her husband's room, she shrivelled up in fear. Her mother-in-law had a vicious temper; in a rage, she lost control of her senses. She too was insane, though not so completely as her son, and therefore she was more terrible. Bindu was forced to enter her husband's room. That night he was quiet, but Bindu's entire body grew stiff with fear. Very late at night, when he had fallen asleep, Bindu found a means to flee the house and come here. I need not describe in detail how she managed this.

My whole body burned with anger and disgust. I said, 'Such a fraudulent marriage isn't a marriage at all. Bindu, stay with me as you used to. Let me see who dares take you away.'

You said, 'Bindu is lying.'

I answered, 'Bindu has never lied.'

You asked, 'How do you know?'

I answered, 'I'm certain of this.'

You tried to frighten me by saying that if Bindu's in-laws lodged a case with the police, we would be in trouble.

I answered, 'They deceived us by marrying her to a madman. Will the court not listen to us?'

You said, 'Must we go to court, then? What obligation is it of ours?'

I replied, 'I'll sell my jewellery and do what needs to be done.'

You asked. 'So are *you* going to go to the lawyer's chambers?'

There was no answer to this. I could beat my forehead in despair, but what more could I do?

Meanwhile, Bindu's brother-in-law had arrived and was kicking up a great row in the outer rooms. He was threatening to go to the police.

I do not know where I got the strength; but I could not bring myself to send back to the slaughter-house the calf that had run away from there to take shelter with me. I said defiantly, 'Let him go to the police, then!'

Saying this, I decided to take Bindu to my bedroom, lock the door, and stay there with her. But when I looked for her, Bindu was gone. While I had been exchanging words with you, she had gone out of her own accord and turned herself over to her brother-in-law. She had realised that if she stayed in this house, I would be in great trouble.

By running away Bindu had simply added to her suffering. Her mother-in-law's argument was, that her son had not after all tried to eat Bindu up. The world had many instances of bad husbands; compared to them her son was pure gold.

My sister-in-law said, 'She's an ill-fated girl. What's the point of being sorry for her? He might be a madman or a stupid goat, but he's her husband all the same.'

You recalled the supreme instance of wifely devotion: how a wife carried her leprosy-stricken husband herself to his whore's house. You never felt the least embarrassment about proclaiming this tale of the greatest cowardice in the world. Hence being born a human being never prevented you from being angry at Bindu's behaviour: you felt no shame. My heart burst with pity for Bindu, but I could not contain my shame for you. I was a village girl, and cast moreover into your household: through what crack had God filled me with such sense? I could not bear this righteous talk of yours.

I knew for certain that Bindu would die rather than come back to our house. Yet had I not given her my word, the day before she was married, that I would never abandon her? My younger brother Sharat was at college in Calcutta. You know that he was so enthusiastic a volunteer for every kind of social mission, from killing rats in the plague quarter to relief work in the Damodar floods, that even two successive failures in the First Arts Examination had not curbed his zeal. I called him and said, 'You must arrange to bring me news of Bindu, Sharat. Bindu will not dare write to me—and even if she does, the letter would never reach me.'

Rather than this, if I had told him to abduct Bindu from her house and bring her to me, or to beat her mad husband's head, Sharat would have been better pleased.

As I was talking to Sharat, you came into the room and asked, 'What trouble are you starting now?'

I said, 'It's the same trouble that I began when I entered your house-hold—but that was your doing.'

You asked, 'Have you brought Bindu here again and hidden her somewhere?'

I answered, 'If Bindu came, I would certainly hide her here. But she won't come: you need have no fear.'

Your suspicion grew at seeing Sharat with me. I knew that you had never liked Sharat's visits to our house. You were afraid that the police were watching him; some day he would get involved in a political case, and drag the lot of you into it as well. For this reason I was even forced to send him my blessings through a messenger on Brothers' Day; I did not invite him to the house.

I heard from you that Bindu had run away again, and so her brother-in-law had come to enquire at your house. It was as though I had been pierced to the heart. I realised how terrible was the unfortunate girl's suffering, yet there was nothing I could do about it.

Sharat hurried off to bring news. He returned in the evening and told me, 'Bindu had gone to her cousins' house, but they flew into a terrible rage and took her back immediately to her in-laws. They still haven't got over the sting of the expense and carriage-hire she cost them.'

Your aunt was staying in your house on her way to Puri on pilgrimage. I said to you, 'I'll go with her.'

You were so delighted by this sudden evidence of piety in me, that you made not the least objection. The thought was also in your mind that if I remained in Calcutta, I would again create a problem over Bindu someday. I was myself a terrible problem.

We were to leave on the Wednesday; by Sunday it had all been decided. I called Sharat and told him, 'By whatever means, you must put Bindu on the train to Puri on Wednesday.'

Sharat's face lit up; he said, 'Never fear, Didi, I'll put her on the train and go to Puri myself as well. I'll get to see Lord Jagannath into the bargain.'

That evening Sharat came again. The look on his face stopped my heart. I asked, 'What is it, Sharat? Couldn't you manage it?'

He said, 'No.'

I asked, 'Weren't you able to persuade her?'

He said, 'There's no need any longer. Yesterday night she set her clothes on fire and killed herself. I got word from one of the nephews of the house, with whom I'd struck up a friendship, that she'd left a letter for you, but they've destroyed it.'

Peace at last!

Everyone in the land was annoyed. They began to say, 'It's now the fashion for girls to set their saris on fire[†] and kill themselves.'

You said, 'This is all play-acting.' That may be so. But one should reflect why this play-acting takes its toll only of the saris of Bengali women, not of the dhotis of brave Bengali gentlemen.

Bindi was always unlucky! So long as she was alive, she was never known for beauty or talent; even in dying, it never occurred to her to work out some novel means of dying which all the men in the land could applaud! In death, too, she made people angry.

My sister-in-law hid herself in her room and. wept. But there was some consolation in her tears. Whatever befell, the family was saved; Bindu had only died. If she had lived, who knows what might have happened!

I have come on pilgrimage. Bindu did not need to come after all, but for me there was need.

I did not suffer in your household, as suffering is commonly understood. In your house there is no lack of food or clothes. Whatever be your elder brother's character, you have no vices of which I can complain to the Almighty. Even if your nature had been like your brother's, I might have passed my days somehow or other, and like that devoted wife my sister-in-law, might have tried to blame not my lord and husband but only the Lord of the Universe. And so I have no complaint to make against you—that is not the purpose of my letter.

But I will never again return to your house at number 27, Makhan Baral Lane. I have seen Bindu. I have learnt what it means to be a woman in this domestic world. I need no more of it.

And I have also seen that though she was a woman, God did not abandon her. Whatever the powers you exercised over her, there was a limit to them. She was greater than her wretched human birth. Your feet were not long enough to tread her life underfoot for ever, at your wish and by your custom. Death is more powerful than you. In that death, she has attained greatness. There, she is no longer simply the daughter of a Bengali household, the young 'sister' of her tyrannical cousins, the deceived wife of an unknown, mad husband. There she is infinite.

When the flute-call of that death sounded through the broken heart of a young girl to the Yamuna-bank of my own life, it seemed at first as though I had been struck by an arrow. I asked God, 'Why should the most petty things in life prove the most difficult? Why should the fragile bubble of a joyless life, immured in this little lane, be so terrible an obstacle? When Your whole earth beckons me, holding out the nectar-bowl of the six seasons, why can I not, even for a moment, cross the tiny threshold of these women's quarters? In this universe You have created, with this life I have been given, why must I die inch by inch in this petty shelter of brick and wood?

How trivial is this daily commerce of my life, how trivial are its set rules, set habits, set phrases, set blows—yet in the end, must the stranglehold of this pettiness triumph, and Your creation, this universe of joy, be defeated?'

But death sounded its flute-call: 'What are these walls of masonry, these thorny hedges of your domestic laws? By what suffering or humiliation can they still imprison human beings? See, the triumphal flag of life waves in the hands of death! O second daughter-in-law, you need have no fear! It takes not even a second to cast off your wifely slough.'

I am no longer afraid of your lane. The blue ocean is before me today, and the rain-clouds of Asharh are gathered overhead.

You had shrouded me over in the darkness of your habits and customs. For a short space, Bindu came and stole a glimpse of me through the rents in that shroud. And it was this very girl who, through her death, tore my shroud to tatters. Today, having come out, I find no vessel to contain my glory. He who found my slighted beauty pleasing, that Beauteous One is gazing at me through the whole sky. The second daughter-in-law is dead at last.

Do you think I am going to kill myself? Have no fear, I shan't indulge in such a stale jest with you. Mirabai[†] too was a woman like me. Her fetters were not light either, but she did not need to die in order to live. Mirabai said in her song, 'Let father, mother, everyone abandon her, O Lord, but Mira will never let you go, whatever befalls her!' It is this holding on which is life.

I too shall live. At last, I live.

Bereft of the shelter of your family's feet,
Mrinal.

Translated by **Supriya Chaudhuri**
[Sukanta Chaudhuri, trans. and ed., *Rabindranath Tagore:
Selected short stories* (Oxford: Oxford University Press, 2000)]

Haimanti
(*Haimanti*)

The bride's father could have waited, but the groom's father did not want to wait. In his view the girl had already crossed the right age for marriage; any further delay, and the time to cover it up with proper or improper means would also be lost. It was true that the girl's age had gone up beyond the acceptable limit. But in relation to it, the standing of the cash dowry was still a trifle higher. Therefore, his impatience.

I was the groom. Quite naturally, it was not necessary to seek my view on the marriage. I had done my work, passed F.A., and won a scholarship. So, the God of marriages, the butterfly, its two wings, the bride's wing and the groom's wing, began to flap restlessly.

In our country, a man who has married once is free of any apprehension about marriage. His attitude towards a wife is akin to that of a tiger's towards man after having got the taste of human flesh. Regardless of his age and worldly circumstances, he does not hesitate to fill the loss of one wife immediately with another. All the wavering and brooding I have noticed is the lot of our young students. With repeated marriage proposals, the grey hairs of their fathers become black again and again with the blessed help of dye, and the black hair of our young men, at the first hint of a marriage proposal, tends to turn grey overnight with worry.

To tell you the truth, I was not greatly alarmed. On the contrary, with the talk of marriage, spring's gentle south wind drifted through my mind and a whispering seemed to erupt amongst the tender shoots of my ever-curious fantasies. This feeling was wrong in one who had to memorise the six or seven exercise books of notes on Burke's French Revolution. If this present piece of my writing was in any danger of being approved by the textbook committee, I would have been careful.

But what on earth am I up to? Is this the plot of a story, that I have sat down to narrate it like a novel? How would I know that my piece of writing would begin in this vein. I had thought that like one of the sudden blustery showers of a *Baishakhi*[1] evening, I would in one torrential downpour, empty out the dark pain-laden clouds that have amassed in the last few years. But neither have I been able to write a Bengali textbook for children—I am quite without the basics of grammar—nor have I been able to write poetry. My own language has not blossomed in me in such a way that I can give an outer expression to my innermost feelings. That is why, the cremation-ground-roaming mendicant in me, laughing uproariously, has sat down to make a mockery of himself. What else can he do? His tears have all dried up. The harsh sunlight of *Jaishtha*[2] is really its tearless sob.

I need not give the real name of the girl I married, for there is no reason to fear that in the world's history there will be a controversy amongst the archeologists over her name. The copper plate on which her name has been engraved is my heart. I refuse to think that the name and the plate will one day disappear. But historians don't traverse the deathless land in which her name has been preserved.

Nevertheless, she requires a name for this piece of prose. All right, I shall call her Shishir (dew), because in a drop of dew, iridescent smile and grieving tear blend into one, and the dawn's saga coming into the morning sadly dries up.

Shishir was only two years younger to me. It was not that my father was not in favour of child marriage. His father had been a passionate social rebel. He had no faith in the country's prevailing religious and social conventions. He had studied English with a vengeance. My father, on the other hand, was a zealous conformist. It was difficult to find anything in our society, governing our men and women, in the lanes of our public and private lives that he hesitated to accept—he too had studied English with a vengeance. My grandfather's and father's opinions were the two different faces of rebellion—neither was simple or natural. Even so, that my father had agreed to my marriage with a girl whose age was higher than what was considered correct was because the dowry was big since the girl was big. Shishir was my father-in-law's only daughter. My father's expectation was

---

[1] The first half of summer—mid-April to mid-May.

[2] The hot summer month in Bengal—between mid-May and mid-June.

that the entire wealth of the bride's father would one day fill the belly of the son-in-law's future.

My father-in-law did not bother to stick to any opinion inflexibly. He was in some high post under a *raja* in the western hills. Shishir's mother had died when she was a baby, and he did not notice that his daughter was adding to her age every year. There was also no one of his community there to point it out to him.

Shishir duly reached the age of sixteen. But that was her natural age, not the society-defined age. Nobody cautioned her to heed her age. She too didn't give it a second thought.

I had just stepped into the third year in college; I was nineteen when I got married. Whether my age was appropriate in the view of society or its reformists, let them fight a bloody battle over it. But let me tell you this: if my age was right for passing an examination, it was no less so for receiving a marriage proposal.

The dawn of my marriage arrived with a tantalizing glimpse at a photograph. I was busy with my studies when a woman relative, in a position to tease me, put Shishir's picture on the table and said, 'Now you can get down to some true and proper lessons, with your nose to the grindstone.'

The photograph was the work of an amateur photographer. There was no mother, so no one had combed her hair back and tied it into a bun with a *zari* ribbon intricately wrapped around it, or put her into a tawdry jacket of a Mullick or Saha company. In short, nothing had been done to trick the eyes of the groom's side. Instead, it was a beautiful simple face, two innocent eyes and a plain sari. Yet I will not be able to tell you how sublime she looked. She had been made to sit on an ordinary stool. A striped rug had been hung behind her. A bunch of flowers had been placed next to her in a vase on a *teepoy*. And on the carpet, below the curve of her sari's border, peeped a pair of bare feet.

My heart touched the photograph, as if with a magic wand, and she came alive in my life. Her two dark eyes gazed through all my day's musing. And the bare feet below that sinuous border turned my heart into their own lotus-seat.

The pages of the almanac went on turning; two or three auspicious dates were given up because my father-in-law couldn't get leave. Four or five arid inauspicious months stretched ahead, conspiring to push the limit of my bachelorhood from the nineteenth to the twentieth year. I became annoyed with my father-in-law and his *raja*.

However, the wedding was fixed on the last auspicious day before the months of drought. I remember clearly every strain of the tune played on the *shehnai* that day. I touched every moment of that day with my very soul. May that nineteenth year of my life remain with me forever.

Amidst the din and bustle of the marriage hall, the girl's fragile hand came to rest on mine. Can anything be more electrifying? My heart began to sing repeatedly, 'I've got her. At last I've got her.'

But whom did I get? She was the unobtainable, the eternal woman. Was there an end to her mystery?

My father-in-law's name was Gaurishankar. He was a friend of the Himalayas amongst whom he lived. At the very pinnacle of his reserve sparkled a steady pristine smile. Those who had discovered the warm stream of affection that coursed through him did not want to deny themselves his company. Before returning to his place of work, he called me aside and said, 'Son, I know my daughter for seventeen years and you for two or three days. Even so, I leave her in your care. May you know the value of the treasure I have given you. No blessing can be greater than this.'

My parents reassured him again and again, 'Don't burden your mind with worries. Though your daughter is leaving her father today, she will get both a father and a mother here.'

After this, my father-in-law, taking leave of his daughter, smiled and said, '*Buri*, I am off. This is your one and only father. From now on, if anything of his is lost or stolen or damaged I should not be held responsible.'

His daughter said, 'So you think! If anything is lost, you'll have to compensate for it.'

She alerted him about the little problems he was prone to run into everyday. My father-in-law showed little restrain about his food. He had a special liking for those very things he was forbidden to eat. An important part of her responsibility was to keep him from his temptations. She took his hand and said anxiously, '*Baba*, please do what I have told you. Promise, you will?'

Her father smiled and said, 'We promise in order to feel the relief of breaking it. Therefore, it is safer not to promise.'

After he left, she went into her room and closed the doors. No one knows what happened afterwards.

The tearless parting between father and daughter was observed by prying eyes from the inner quarters. Amazing! These two have become as dry as the land they live in. There is no tender feeling at all!

My father-in-law's friend, Banamali Babu, had been our match-maker. He was also known to our family. He told my father-in-law, 'Your daughter is all you have in this world. You should take a house in the same neighbourhood and live the rest of your life near her.'

His reply was, 'What I have given, I have given without stinting. To look back will only bring grief. Nothing can be more frustrating than trying to retain one's claim after having given it up.'

Finally he told me diffidently, like one full of guilt, 'My daughter is fond of reading and loves to feed people. I don't want to trouble your father on this account. I will send you money. Will your father be annoyed if he comes to know?'

I was a little astonished by his question. I had not known my father's temper to be so foul that he would get angry if some money came to him from somewhere.

In the manner of giving me a bribe, he pushed a hundred rupee note into my hand, and quickly walked away. He didn't wait for me to touch his feet. Observing him from the back I saw, only now a handkerchief came out from his pocket.

I sat in silence, thinking; I could very well see that they were made of a different fibre.

I have seen many of my friends get married. No sooner the chanting of the *mantras* are done with, the wife is swallowed in one big gulp. Once the substance, so to say, settles in the stomach, its good and bad qualities begin to manifest themselves and every once in a while, there are some inner discomfort also, but that seldom hinders the process of further intake.

I realized at the time of the ceremony that the small portion of the wife that one can lay claim on through the sanction of the *mantras,* may be enough for running a household but all that is most essential in her eludes the husband. I suspect, most men only marry their wives, do not get them, and don't even know they have not got them. Their wives are also denied this knowledge all their lives. But to me she was God's gift to my ardent prayer; she was my fortune, not my property.

Shishir—no, the name won't do any longer. For one, it's not her name; then, it does not describe her. She was constant like the sun, not the ephemeral dawn's parting teardrop. There is no point in keeping it a secret; her name was Haimanti.

This seventeen-year-old girl possessed all the radiance of youth, but still slept in the lap of adolescence. Just like the snow on the mountaintop that shimmers in the morning light but has not melted under it. I know how fresh and flawless she was, how intensely pure.

I had one anxiety. She was a fairly educated, grown up girl. How should one win her? But within a few days I discovered that there was no conflict between the road to her heart and the road to the bookshop. I won't be able to say though, when exactly her virgin white heart flushed with a touch of colour, when her body and mind became keen.

This is one side of the story. It has another side, and it is time to dwell on it.

My father-in-law was a member of the state administration. There were many rumours about the amount of his money accumulating in the bank but none of it was put at less than a lakh of rupees. The consequence was that with every rise in her father's assumed bank balance, the affection Haimanti received from our family also went up. She was eager to learn the ways of the household, but my mother did not let her do any work out of love for her. So much so, the hill woman who had come with her as her personal maid, though not allowed to enter my mother's rooms, was never asked about her caste lest her answer made matters awkward.

Things would have gone on in this manner but one day my father's face looked ominously dark. The reason was this: my father-in-law had given 15,000 rupees in cash and 5,000 rupees in jewellery for the marriage. My father had come to know through an agent friend of his that the entire 15,000 rupees had been borrowed, and at not a low rate of interest either. The rumours about the lakh of rupees were empty.

Although there had been no discussion about the size of my father-in-law's wealth between him and my father, I don't know by what logic my father decided that he had been intentionally misled. He had also carried the impression that my father-in-law held a position something like that of the prime minister's, but found out that he was director of the education department. 'In other words,' my father said, 'the headmaster of a school.' His position was the lowest in the scale of respectable posts. My father had secretly nurtured the fond hope that when my father-in-law retired, I would be made a minister.

About this time, some of our relatives came to our house from the village on the occasion of the *Raash Leela* festival. When they saw the bride, a whispering campaign was started by them. After a while, the hushed whispers became loudly vocal. One distantly related grandaunt burst out, 'My goodness! Our bride's age seems to be even more than mine.'

Another old lady said, 'If she does not have something more than we do, why would Apu travel so far to get himself a wife?'

My mother countered emphatically, 'What on earth are you saying? My daughter-in-law is not more than eleven. She will be twelve in *Phalgun*. She has grown up eating the simple healthy food of that place, that's why she looks big for her age.'

The old cronies said, 'My dear, our eyesight is not that bad yet. The bride's people must have concealed her real age.'

My mother said, 'But we saw the horoscope.'

The statement was true enough. But the age shown there was seventeen. The elders said in one voice, 'As if horoscopes can't be faked.'

The argument became heated, then there was a quarrel. Haima walked into the scene. One old woman asked, 'Come my child, can you tell us your age?'

My mother tipped her a wink, but Haima did not understand the meaning of it. She said, 'Seventeen.'

My mother became agitated; she said, 'You don't know.'

Haima said, 'I know I am seventeen.'

The old women snickered.

Infuriated by her stupidity, my mother said, 'You know everything. It was your father who said you were eleven.'

Haima gave a start. She said, 'He did? It can't be.'

My mother said, 'In front of me he himself said it, and his daughter says, "It can't be"'!

She again winked at her.

Now Haima took in the meaning of the wink. She hardened her voice to say, 'My father could not have said that.'

My mother raised her voice, 'Are you calling me a liar?'

Haima said, 'My father never tells a lie.'

After this, the more my mother raved and ranted, the more the ugliness of the incident was spattered all around. My mother reported to my father about his daughter-in-law's stupidity and stubbornness. My father sent for Haima and told her, 'A girl has remained unmarried till the age of seventeen; is that something to be proud of? And should you therefore announce it by beating the drum? I warn you, such things will not be tolerated.'

Alas! How did my father's honeyed tenor that once resonated on the fifth octave when he spoke to his daughter-in-law change to this stentorian tone? Hurt, she said 'If someone asks my age, what should I say?'

My father said, 'There is no need to tell a lie. Say you don't know, your mother-in-law knows.'

When Haima heard his advice on how not to tell a lie, she became so silent that my father understood that his judicious advice had been wasted.

More than feeling sorry for her plight, I hung my head in shame before her. Some misgiving had dimmed her artless forlorn eyes that were like the autumn's morning sky. She looked at me like a frightened doe. She was probably thinking, 'I don't know these people.'

I had brought for her a beautifully bound book of English poetry. She took the book and put it slowly on her lap without opening it. I lifted her hand and said, 'Haima, don't be angry with me. I will never go against your truth. I am bound to you by ties of truth.'

She did not say anything, only smiled a little. One gifted with that smile, has no need to speak.

Ever since my father began to prosper, religious activities in our house had been taken up with a new fervour, to make stable God's favour. Up to this time, the family's new bride had not been called upon to actively participate in these functions. One day she was asked to make arrangements for the *puja*. She said, '*Ma*, please tell me what I should do.'

At this, the heavens should not have fallen. Everybody knew that she had been brought up motherless and away from her cultural mooring. The only reason to tell her to make the arrangements was to humiliate her. In utter amazement, with their hands on their cheeks, they said, 'Good heavens! What is this now? What sort of an atheist's daughter is she? The Goddess Lakshmi will soon desert this family.'

They also said the most unspeakable things about Haima's father. Since the time rude words had started to fly, Haima had borne them in complete silence. Not once did she shed tears before anybody. Today, tears rolled down flooding her two large eyes. She stood up and said, 'Do you know, there, people call my father a saint?'

What? A saint? Rolls of laughter reverberated all around. After this, when they talked about her father, they invariably said, 'Your saint of a father.' My family had found out where lay this girl's most tender spot.

Actually, my father-in-law was not a *Brahmo*,[3] not a Christian, perhaps not even an atheist. He had never given thought to ritual prayers. He had encouraged his daughter to read. He had talked to her much but had not held forth on the idea of God. Banamali Babu had spoken to him about this. His answer had been, 'If I try to teach her what I myself don't understand, I would be giving her a lesson in falsehood.'

Haima had a true admirer in the inner quarters—my sister Narani. Narani was often scolded for loving her sister-in-law. I used to hear from her the degrading role Haima was being made to play in the daily drama of our family. Not once did I hear about it from Haima. Out of embarrassment, she could not bring herself to tell me, and the embarrassment was not on account of her own humiliation.

---

[3] A break-away reformist branch of Hinduism.

She used to give me all her father's letters to read. They were short but full of humour. She also showed me all her letters to her father. If she had not shared with me her relationship with her father, her life with me would not have been complete. In what she wrote, there was not even a suggestion of a complaint against her in-laws. Otherwise, there could have been trouble for her because, as I came to know from Narani, they sometimes opened her letters to find out what she was writing about them.

It was not that their mind was at peace after not finding anything they could blame her with. Sorely disappointed and extremely displeased they began to say, 'Why such frequent letters? As if her father is everything to her and we are nothing.' This became the subject of a lot of malicious gossip. I became angry and said to Haima, 'Instead of giving the letters to somebody else, give them to me. I'll post them on my way to college.'

Surprised, Haima asked, 'Why?'

I did not tell her out of shame.

Now, they started to say, 'Apu's head has been properly turned. He can forget about his B.A. degree. Who can blame him?'

But of course, the fault was all Haima's. Her fault was that she was seventeen. Her fault was that I loved her. Her fault was that it was God's will that the sky should pour its impassioned music into me through every single pore of my body.

I could have happily dumped any B.A. degree into the fire. But, for Haima's sake, I swore that I would pass, and pass well. There were two reasons to make me think it possible even in that state of my mind. One was that, in her love there was the sweep of the sky which did not stifle my mind with the narrowness of desire. The air that swirled around her love was exhilarating; the other was that, the books that I was required to read for my examination, I could read with her.

I began in earnest to get ready to pass the examination. On a Sunday afternoon I was sitting in the front room and, with a blue pencil, furrowing through certain important portions of Martino's psychology, when I looked out. There in front, at the northern end of the courtyard, were the stairs that went up to the inner quarters. On one side, on the wall, were windows fitted with iron bars. Haima was sitting quietly at one of them and looking out westwards. On that side, in the garden of the Mullicks, a *kanchan* tree teemed with pink flowers.

The sight of her jolted me. The veil of insensitivity dropped away. I had not seen before such a silent expression of profound grief. It was a small thing, only her posture. Her hands were on her lap, one on the other, still.

Her head was tilted against the wall. Her hair was loose, draped over her left shoulder and fell over her breast. My heart went out to her.

I was myself so full to the brim that I had not noticed any emptiness anywhere. Suddenly, very close to me, I saw an abyss of despair. How, and with what, could I ever fill it up?

I had to give up nothing; my family, my way of life, nothing at all. Haima had to drop everything before coming to me. I had not considered before the extent of her sacrifice. In our house, she had been sitting on a bed of thorns; I had shared the bed with her. Our bond was forged in that suffering, it did not divide us. But this seventeen-year-old daughter of the mountain had grown up in complete inner and outer freedom. What pristine truth and generous clime must have shaped her nature to make it so upright, so pure and strong. Hitherto I had not sensed with what finality and cruelty she had been torn away from all that, because we did not share a similar background.

Every moment, bit by bit, Haima was dying inside. I could give her everything except freedom. Where did I have it myself? That is why in one of Calcutta's narrow lanes, through the iron bars, she held a mute conversation with a mute sky. Sometimes I woke up at night to find her not in bed. She had gone up to the rooftop to lie with her head on her arm, her gaze lost amongst the stars.

Martino was forgotten. I began to think; what should I do? From childhood, I had been wary of my father. I didn't have the courage nor was I in the habit of approaching him for anything. But I couldn't hold myself back anymore. Abandoning my usual diffidence I went and told him rather bluntly, 'Your daughter-in-law is not well. She should go to her father for a while.'

My father sat stunned. He had no doubt in his mind that Haima had put me up to this piece of impertinence. He went at once to the inner quarters and asked her, 'Now tell me *bou-ma*, what is this illness that you have?'

Haima replied, 'I have no illness.'

My father detected arrogance in her answer. We, who saw her everyday, couldn't make out that she was wasting away. Banamali Babu, who saw her one day, was shocked: 'What's this? Haimi? You look awful; not ill I hope?'

Haima said 'No.'

About ten days after this, my father-in-law arrived without prior information. Banamali Babu had probably written to him about Haima's health. After the wedding, she kept her tears in check at the time of parting with her father. Now, on this day of reunion, when he held her chin and raised her face, Haima could not hold back her tears. Her father did not say a word, not even to ask her, 'How are you?' He had seen something on her face that had broken his heart.

Haima led her father to her room. There was so much to ask; he was not looking too well, either.

Her father asked, '*Buri* will you come with me?'

Like a beggar, hungrily she answered, 'Yes. I will.'

Her father said, 'All right. I'll make all the arrangements.'

If my father-in-law had not been blind with worry, he would have at once seen on entering this house that his position here had changed. Taking his sudden arrival as an inconvenience, my father didn't speak to him properly. My father-in-law had not forgotten that my father had once assured him he could take his daughter with him when he wished. He could not imagine that word once given could be taken back.

Puffing at his tobacco, my father said, 'I can't tell you anything. Those in the inner quarters...'

I knew what was meant by passing the buck to the inner quarters. Nothing would happen; and nothing did.

Their daughter-in-law was not keeping well! Such a false accusation?

My father-in-law brought a well-known physician to examine her. He said, 'A change is necessary. Otherwise she might come down with a serious illness.'

My father smirked. He said, 'Anyone can suddenly come down with a serious illness. What a statement!'

My father-in-law said, 'As you know, he is a leading physician. His opinion... .'

My father said, 'I have seen many doctors like him. For money, *any pundit* will lay down any law, and any doctor will certify any illness.'

My father-in-law was shocked into silence. Haima realized, her father's proposal had been rudely rejected. Her mind stiffened like a block of wood.

I could not stand it anymore. I told my father, 'I'll take Haima away to some place.'

My father thundered, 'How dare you...,' and so on.

Some of my friends have asked me, why didn't I do what I had said I would. I could have taken my wife away. Why didn't I? Why! If I had not put social duty before moral duty, if I had not been able to sacrifice the person closest to me at the altar of the family, then what was the use of carrying the age-old doctrines in my blood? Do you know, the day the people of Ayodhya demanded that Sita must be sacrificed, I was amongst them! And those who have, through the ages, sung to the glory of that sacrifice, I have been one of them! Only the other day, I wrote an article in a monthly magazine on the nobility of giving up one's wife to satisfy public sentiment. Who knew then that I would have to write—the saga of a second sacrifice of Sita with my own blood.

Another moment of parting arrived between father and daughter. This time too there was a smile on both their faces. Still smiling, the daughter scolded, 'Baba, if you come running again to see me, I'll lock the door on you.'

Her father, also smiling, said, 'If I come again, I'll bring a lock-picker with me.'

I did not see that ever present gentle smile on Haima's face again. I will not be able to relate what happened after that.

I hear my mother is looking for a suitable bride. Perhaps, I will not be able to ignore her request—even that is possible. Because... let it be, what is the point?

Written in May–June, 1915 (*Jaishtha*, 1321)

Translated by **Joyasree Mukerji**

[*She: A collection of short stories of Rabindranath Tagore* (UBSPD, 2004)]

The story of a Muslim woman
(*Musalmanir galpa*)

At that time the perpetrators of anarchy had complete control over the state administration. Days and nights were rocked by unexpected tyranny. Daily activities were enmeshed in nightmares; common people turned to gods for succor and their minds were filled with apprehensions of evil. It was difficult to believe either in man or God; the only consolation was tears. The dividing line between good and evil deeds was tenuous. At every walk of life, men stumbled into troubles.

In such circumstances the presence of a beautiful girl in a family was rather a curse of providence. The relatives would say, 'Sooner this unlucky woman is married off the better.' Such a trouble came to Banshibadan, the landlord of three estates.

Kamala was very beautiful, though her parents were dead. The family would have welcomed her death too; but that did not happen. Her uncle Banshi brought her up with great affection and extreme caution till now.

However, her aunt would often complain to her female neighbours, 'Look, her parents left her to add to my burden. Nobody knows what can happen to her any moment. I've children of my own, and among them she's like a burning torch of destruction. She can't escape the evil gaze of wicked fellows. She alone will sink my boat. For this reason I can't sleep at night.'

Somehow days passed in this manner; then came a proposal for matrimony. She could not be hidden from the public gaze by the pomp and splendour of marriage ceremonies. So her uncle said, 'For this reason I'm looking for a bridegroom whose family can protect her.'

The bridegroom was the second son of Paramananda Seth of Mochakhali. He was destined to inherit huge wealth which would evaporate in no time as soon as his father died. The boy was very extravagant; he found a facile way of splurging money on hawk-flying, gambling, bulbul-fights. His wealth was huge and so was his pride. Famous musclemen from Bhojpur with stout sticks were on his payroll. He used to brag—in his locality no man worth his salt could dare to touch him. He was a habitual womanizer though he had a wife at home, and he was now looking for a younger one. He came to know about the attractiveness of Kamala. The Seth family was very rich and very powerful. They vowed to take her as his bride.

Kamala cried, 'Uncle, where are you packing me off?'

'You know, my child, if I had the power to protect you, I'd have held you to my heart forever!'

The groom came proudly, to the marriage ceremony, accompanied by endless extravaganza including musical bands. The uncle said humbly with folded hands, 'My son it isn't good to show off. It's bad time now!'

Hearing this, he challenged the audacity of any opponents, 'Let me see if anyone dares approach me.'

The uncle replied, 'Our responsibilities end with the marriage ceremonies. Then the bride would be yours—you should escort her home safely. It's not within our power to take such responsibility. We're weak.'

With an inflated chest the groom said, 'There's nothing to fear.'

Twirling their moustaches, his *Bhojpuri* guards stood up with their big sticks.

The bridegroom set out with his bride through the infamous field of Taltori. The leader of the brigands was Madhu Molla. Around midnight he attacked the wedding party with his gang with torches in hand. None of the strongmen of Bhojpur were traceable. Madhu was a notorious brigand; none could escape his onslaught.

Rushing out from the palanquin, Kamala was about to hide in a bush. Then old Habir Khan emerged behind her. Everybody revered him like a *Paigambar*. Standing erect, Habir Khan warned, 'Sons, move away. I am Habir Khan.'

The brigands said, 'Khan Saheb, we can't refuse you anything, but why have you spoiled our business?'

Nevertheless, they had to quit.

Habir told Kamala, 'Don't be afraid. You're my daughter. Now, let's leave this dangerous place.'

Kamala became very embarrassed. Habir said. 'I understand—you're a daughter of a Hindu Brahman, so you're hesitating to go to a Muslim's house. But remember, those who are true Muslims know how to respect a pious Brahman. You'll stay in my house as a girl of a Hindu family. My name is Habir Khan. My house is very near. Come with me, I'll keep you safe.'

Kamala was a Brahman girl; she could not give up her reservations. Habir noticed it and said, 'Look, none can touch your religion in this area. Come with me. Don't be afraid.'

Habir Khan took Kamala to his house. Surprisingly, one of the eight *mahals* of this Muslim mansion had a Shiva temple with complete arrangements for observing Hindu rituals and ceremonies. An old Hindu Brahman came and assured her, 'My child, it's just like a Hindu household. Your caste is in safe custody.'

Kamala cried, 'Please inform my uncle; he'll take me back.'

Habir said, 'Child, you're mistaken. Nobody from your family will take you back now. They will desert you on the road. However, you may try.'

Habir Khan took her to the backdoor of her uncle's house and said, 'I'll be waiting here.'

Inside the house Kamala embraced her uncle and said, 'Uncle, please, don't desert me.'

Tears rolled down her uncle's cheeks.

Her aunt came and shouted, 'Drive out—drive out this vicious woman. Are you not ashamed of returning from the house of the casteless?'

The uncle said, 'I'm helpless. We are a Hindu family. Nobody will accept you. On the other hand, we'll lose our caste.'

For some time Kamala stood with her head bent down. Then slowly she left through the rear door and set out with Habir. Now, the doors of her uncle's house were closed forever.

Arrangements were made for the observance of her religion. Habir Khan said, 'No male member of my family will enter your chamber. With the help of this old Brahman priest, you can perform *puja* and other Hindu rituals.'

This house had an historical background. This particular chamber was known as *Rajputani's mahal*. In the past a Nawab of this family had brought a Rajput woman but allowed her to lead the life of her caste. She worshipped Shiva, and sometimes went on pilgrimage. In those days the aristocratic Muslims used to respect the devoted Hindus. That *Rajputani's mahal* sheltered many deserted Hindu wives whose cultures and customs remained intact. According to the legend, Habir was the son of that Rajput woman. Though he did not embrace the religion of his mother, he worshipped her from the core of his heart. His mother was now dead, but to perpetuate her memory, he made it a mission of his life to shelter the oppressed and the outcast Hindu women.

The kind treatment Kamala received there was unknown to her even in her family. There her aunt always nagged and abused her—she had to hear that she was unlucky and brought with her destruction and misfortune to the family. The family would prosper only when she died. Her uncle sometimes bought her new clothes, but she had to keep it a secret for fear of her aunt. In the Rajputani's chamber she was treated like a queen. Abundant care and affection were showered on her. She was attended to by female servants who came from Hindu families.

At last, youthful passion got the better of her body. A boy of the family began to visit her *mahal* secretly, and she became emotionally involved with him.

Then one day she told Habir Khan, 'Father, I've no religion of my own. The man I love is my religion. I could not find the grace of God in the religion which deprived me of all love and dumped me to the garbage heap of neglect. The deity there humiliated me every day. I can't forget such insults. Father, I discovered love for the first time in your house. I realized that the life of a destitute like me has some value. I worship the deity which has sheltered me through the respect of such love. He's my God—he's neither Hindu nor Muslim. I've accepted your second son Karim; my life and my religion have mingled with him. You can convert me to Islam, I've no objection—maybe, I belong to two faiths.'

Thus she passed her time. There was no possibility of keeping in touch with her former relatives. On his part, Habir Khan tried to establish that Kamala no longer belonged to her former family—she was renamed Meherjan.

In the meantime her uncle's second daughter reached the marriageable age. Arrangements were made as before, and the danger came in the same way. On the road the brigands attacked with a war-cry. Once repulsed, they nursed a grudge for losing their prey; now they were bent on revenge.

But next came another shout, 'Beware!'

'Look, the followers of Habir Khan have spoiled it again.'

When the companions of the bride ran helter-skelter leaving the bride in her palanquin, the tip of Habir Khan's spear with a crescent-moon flag came into view. It was a woman who bravely held the spear.

She addressed Sarala, 'You need not be afraid, my sister. For you I've brought the offer of shelter from the One who provides shelter to all. He doesn't bother about one's caste...'

'Uncle, my *pranam* to you. Don't be afraid, I won't touch your feet. Now take your daughter back home. Nothing has made her untouchable. Tell my aunt I had to take her grudging food and clothes for long, and never thought I could repay your debt like this. I've also brought for Sarala a red silk sari and this brocade sitting mat. If my sister is ever in trouble, let her remember that she has a Muslim elder sister to protect her.'

June 24–25, 1941

Translated by **Swapan Kumar Banerjee** [www.parabaas.com]

Essays, Lectures and
Letters to the Editor

The Indian ideal of marriage

A request has come to me from Europe to say something about the Indian idea of marriage. This puts me in mind of the difference between the European and the Indian idea,—a difference which is not merely of outer method, but of inner purpose.

Like all distinctive features of civilized societies, the marriage system is an attempt at compromise between the biological purposes of Nature and the sociological purposes of Man; and both its outer form and inner aim depends upon the divergence between these two. For, in his individual as well as in his social life, man is governed by this Diarchy.

Thus, where society is complex with a net-work of widely-ramified relationships, the natural propensities have to be kept in check by social pressure from every side. While, where wants are numerous and their supply difficult, and man is compelled to venture forth to distant places to make a living, there the social obligations need must be light, and the nature and extent of the mutual claims of individuals over one another cannot be rigidly prescribed by society, but must be left to be adjusted by the individuals themselves.

It is a matter of comment by Europeans that we use no word like 'thanks' in our own language, for expressing gratitude; and they jump to the conclusion that our character must be free from that troublesome feeling. But the fact is, that in our society the obligation of the giver of help is held to be stronger than that of the recipient. On him who has acquired learning is cast the duty of giving to others,—that is not taken as a favour done by teacher to student. The offering of hospitality even to the casual visitor, is incumbent on the householder for his own sake. Each of the domestic ceremonies, from the birth-celebration to the funeral, is but an expression of the debt which each member owes to his community. From this it becomes evident that our society is not like a stream on which its members float in comparative freedom, but like the earth in whose depths their root-system is held secure.

The Aryans of India were at first forest dwellers. Then as the dense screen of forest was lifted off the stage of their history, India's broad, river-served plains were converted from sylvan shelters of patriarchal communities into monarchical territories; and agriculture became the mainstay of her growing settlements. On the one hand, the close neighbourhood of peoples, racially different, giving rise to perpetual cultural conflict; and, on the other, the agricultural civilization claiming co-operation and the complex regulations of stable life,—these are the two forces that moulded Hindu society and still guide its course. Such a society can never exist and perform its functions unless peace is maintained amongst its members by a perfect system of mutual adjustment of rights.

In the beginning of India's history, of which we gain glimpses in the Rāmāyana, three different parties are to be distinguished,—the Aryans, the barbarians (variously called monkeys, bears, etc.) and the powerful, cultured Rākshasas. While all these were at daggers drawn, their constant dissensions precluded the establishment of any common social polity. Then as the conquering Kshatriyas extended their sway, and populous settlements grew up in their wake, the need for peace was felt and its merits were exalted. So, broadly speaking, the establishment of relationships between the Aryans, the barbarians and the Rākshasas, form the main theme of the Rāmāyana.

Courage, in the ethics of Peace, means the courage of self-sacrifice; there, bravery has for its object the triumph Renunciation. And, in societies where such sacrifice and renunciation are cultivated, not the individual but the household is the primary unit, and such household is broad, not narrow conception and content. That is why, as the Rāmāyana evolves from a collection of ballads into an epic, its main function is transformed from a narration of struggles against the outrages offered to the cult of tillage (*sītā*) into the exaltation of the Ethics of the Household. The unfaltering strength of self-renunciation which is needful for keeping true the varied relations between king and subject, father and son, brother and brother, husband and wife, master and servant, and among neighbours different in colour and character,—that is what it really glorifies.

Wherever many men have congregated, not for the purpose of attacking others, but for mutual benefit, there is evolved a mentality which eventually transcends all considerations of expediency and envisages Supreme Good as an absolute fulfilment. And so, in our country, there was a day when the household was glorified, not as a comfortable home, not as the enjoyment of proprietary right, but as the means of living the fullest communal life, and through it of attaining supreme liberation at the end.

The intimacy of relationship with wife and child is but natural, and so may hardly help to loosen the bonds of self,—rather it serves to strengthen them. But the household wherein even the most distant of kinsmen have a recognized right, where one's own earnings have to be shared by those who are almost strangers, where it is a matter of shame and censure if differences be made between near and distant relations,—there the claims of moral welfare override those of natural affection, and give rise to certain special qualities of heart. These gradually grow so powerful that both the individual as well as the social conscience refuse to tolerate any personal claims when these conflict with those of the household *dharma*.

Therefore the home of the Indian has never been looked upon as his castle, the place where he is lord and master. No doubt the duty, there cast on him, of considering the rights of others on any and every occasion, has involved him in expenditure of time and money but his accounts have ever been cast up, not in terms of self-interest, but of social and spiritual welfare.

In societies where the household is founded on the comfort and convenience of the individual, his acceptance or non-acceptance of the householders' estate remains optional. If any such should say that he does not care for domestic joys, but prefers the freedom of irresponsibility, no room for objection is left. But in Hindu India, because the household is an essential element in its social structure, marriage is almost compulsory,—like conscription in Europe on the threat of war.

According to our Lawgivers, anyone making gifts to, or taking gifts from, a Brahmin who remains a householder, but does not marry, goes to hell. Says Atri: 'No hospitality should be accepted from an unmarried householder.' The household has been compared, in our *shāstras*, to a great tree; for, just as the roots of the latter support its branches, twigs and foliage, so does the life of the household maintain the different institutions of society; and the Lawgiver lays it down that the King should do honour to the upholder of the householders' estate. But the mere fact of setting up a household, anyhow, does not constitute that estate according to our *shāstras*:

Grihasthopi kriyāyukto na grihena grihāsrami,
Na chaiva putradārena svakarma parivarjita.

Not by the house is made the household but by the performance of the householders' duties,—nor even by wife and children, if the householder be wanting in his own *karma*.

Karma here does not mean the looking after his family interests, but the performance of his specific duty,—the fulfilment of his obligation to society.

> *Tathā tathaiva kāryāni na kālastu vidhīyate,*
> *Asminneva prayuñjáno hyasminneva tu liyate.*

With society are we connected, in it do we terminate this life, therefore should we do our duty as it arises, and not await our own convenience.

To perform the duties of a householder is in fact looked upon as a spiritual discipline. Says Vasistha:

> *Grihastha eva yajate grihasthastapyate tapah,*
> *Chaturnāmāsramānāntu grihasthastu vishishyate.*

That is to say, because the life of a householder is a life of self-abnegation having its manifold obligations to gods and men therefore of all the four *āsramas*, the *āsrama* or estate of the householder is specially distinguished.

In societies where the household is but the means of ensuring the comfort and security of the individual, the notion of property also becomes intensely individualistic; for the right of property is at the base of the householders' estate. And when property is viewed as dedicated to individual enjoyment, it ceases as such to be a joy to the others who own it not, but becomes rather an object of their envy. Not only that, but in the process of its acquisition the question of social or moral welfare is lost sight of, and the spirit of rivalry and competition acknowledges no limit. And so, in ancient India, the class of merchants whose object in life was to acquire wealth in excess of the requirements of their livelihood, were held in contempt. Even to-day, water touched by such is deemed to be impure.

A school of thought has arisen in Europe which looks upon property as inherently vicious, and would advise its forcible extirpation. For, there, the irresponsible ownership of property is a potent factor in maintaining the antagonism between the claims of universal humanity and of individual man. And, so far, Western Politics has devoted its forces to the protection of the rights of the proprietor. Hence the need for this counter-movement.

But many substances which are now good food, were once unpalatable or even poisonous. Man, however, did not reject those at the outset, but made them wholesome and toothsome by a long process of culture.

India, likewise, cultivated the viciousness out of property by converting the household into a field for spiritual discipline. And thus society in India stably maintained itself for centuries on the basis of the individual ownership of property; in fact India's wealth of food and clothing, education, morals and religion were all so acquired,—by virtue of that original precautionary measure.

When the welfare of society is left to depend on the voluntary generosity of its wealthy members, then is the vicious aspect of property brought out; for the indiscriminate acceptance of charity spoils the recipient. But, in India, expenditure by the householder for social welfare was not a matter of generosity, but of primary duty in the interests of his own fulfilment. Such duty was cast not only on the rich, but also on the poor, according to their means. Manu says: 'The *rishis,* the forefathers, the gods, the guests, and all living creatures, expect to be maintained by the house-holder. Knowing this, he should act accordingly.' By many such injunctions and in diverse other ways, are the Indian people kept reminded that the *dharma* of the householder consists in fulfilling the various claims of humanity. And further, in Manu's opinion, those who are of weak character and have no control over their passions,—they are not worthy of the householders' high estate.

In order to understand the principle underlying Hindu marriage, it is necessary first to come to a true appreciation of this principle underlying the Hindu social system. It will then become clear that, in this type of society, having for its object the perfection of communal life, there is danger in allowing marriage to pursue the path of self-will. Such a society can only withstand the encroachments of Nature, if its marriage system is walled round with a protective embankment. So the Hindu ideal of marriage has no regard for individual taste on inclination,—it is, rather, afraid of them.

If any European would really understand the psychology behind this, let him bethink himself of the state of things that obtained during the last war. Ordinarily, in Europe, there is no bar to international marriages. But, when the one objective of the war overshadowed all other considerations, marriage with the subject of an enemy country became an impossibility; so much so, that European society felt no compunction in cruelly severing even long-standing marriage ties of this description. Not only was the marriage question so affected, but during war conditions, food and all other amenities of life had to be cut down to a uniform standard. The personal liberty and elasticity of occupation, so characteristic of Western civilization, tended wholly to disappear.

These war conditions afford a good parallel to the permanent conditions which govern Hindu society, where the encroachment of alien cultures has always been a constant danger to be guarded against. This vital objective of the twice-born leaders, who practically represented the whole people, therefore runs as a steady undercurrent through our society. The problem of keeping its civilization pure having been acknowledged as all-important, and its solution thus sought by India, her society has had to claim of its members the severe and permanent curbing of their individual liberty of choice and action.

Indian society, however, did not reach this stage all at once. It was gradually evolved through successive adaptations to changing circumstances. Meanwhile many relics of earlier stages survived into the later. Therefore Manu had to recognize, in his treatise, different other forms of marriage, such as the *Gāndharva* (by mutual choice), *Rākshasa* (by conquest), *Asur* (by purchase), *Paishācha* (by taking advantage of helplessness). In none of these is the social will manifest, but only the desire of the individual; for force whether of arms, or money, or circumstances, is arrogant and passion refuses to submit to extraneous considerations. But, while recording these forms, Manu censured them.

Though the Gāndharva marriage, founded on mutual attraction, was also one of those which did not find favour with the Lawgiver, it nevertheless long persisted in Indian society, as our epics and other literature make clear. This only shows that, however conservatively stable a society may be, the principle of stability cannot be equally strong amongst all the classes which it comprises. In the Kshatriya character, especially, the cultivation of self-suppression was least likely to attain its fullest development. It is not possible to keep confined in a complex net of social obligations the warrior spirit which ever seeks fresh fields for expansion. It is for this reason that our *shāstras* prohibited the crossing of the sea. Any adventurous activity whatsoever, that may loosen our mind from its mooring and disturb the fixed habit of our thought and belief and behaviour, is bound to undermine the very foundation of our society.

Not only sea voyage, but also residence in foreign countries with antagonistic social ideals, was prohibited and penalised. In the West we find now-a-days all kinds of forcible attempts being made to prevent the intrusion of Bolshevic ideas. This is comparable with our prohibition of foreign travel. No penalty is deemed too severe if it but keep in check the propaganda which, it is apprehended, may destroy the elements essential for the stability of the orthodox Western social system. The liberty of the people [to] form their own opinions, to regulate their own conduct, is here no longer respected. The terrorist organization called Fascism, which seems to be daily gaining ground in Europe, is the exact counterpart of our rigorous social injunctions. There was a day in India when for the Sudra to aspire to the path of the Brahmin entailed the death penalty. The same psychological phenomenon is seen in the West in the cruel forms of Lynching, Fascism, Ku-Klux-Klanism, and the like.

It is no doubt conducive to a certain strength if all the members of a society are, in the main, moulded in accordance with some uniform standard. That may be a bar to the fullest development of its individuals, but it certainly does help to keep the society, as a whole, in a state of stable equilibrium. And, if any society, on the cessation of its growth, should come to pride itself on being, not like a growing tree, but like a temple of which its securely established immovableness is its glory, it will inevitably feel the moving of a single one of its bricks to be a loss. Nevertheless it is not possible to keep all the members of any society uniformly bound in such unalterable fixity—that is against the nature of man and destructive of the principle of life itself. So that, so long as any people is vigorously alive, they or some of them cannot but keep breaking through the rules and prohibitions imposed by their society. Both in its biological and sociological phases, these opposing forces of conservation and experimentation, are characteristic of Life.

Anyhow, so long as the Kshatriyas were real Kshatriyas it was not found possible to keep them rigorously bound down to the habitual performance of the prescribed rules for daily observance. That is why, in the history of ancient India, at the bottom of all the social and religious revolutions, were the Kshatriyas. We must remember that Buddha was a Kshatriya, that Mahāvīra was a Kshatriya; and that the clan, to which Srīkrishna himself belonged, was not famous for observing the precepts and prohibitions most esteemed by the Lawgivers. As we read through the Mahābhārata, we are reminded at every turn that, however determined may have been the endeavour to protect society behind a permanent embankment, there was not a single kingly clan of note which did not break through the walls. It was only in comparatively recent times, when the Kshatriyas had lost their virility and the Brahmins had gained almost unquestioned ascendancy, that it became possible to make the social bonds so rigorously inert.

Manu gives the name of *Gāndharva* to marriage by mutual choice, and signifies his disapprobation by stigmatising it as 'born of desire'. The way to marriage, which is shown by the torchlight of passion, has not for its goal the welfare of society, but the satisfaction of desire. Even in Europe, where the obligation of the individual to society is much lighter, it is well known how the mingling of the sexes under the impulse of passion often gives rise to antisocial difficulties; but there, society being mobile, the effects are not so deep as with us. In our *shāstras*, therefore, the *Brāhma* marriage is considered to be the best. According to this, the bride should be given to a man who had not solicited her. If the institution of marriage has to be regulated strictly from the social standpoint, room cannot be found for the personal wishes of the people concerned. So, the system which obtains in the case of the Royal Houses of Europe, is the system which prevails throughout Hindu society.

Another way for the better understanding by the European of the mentality underlying our marriage system, would be by reference to the discussions on eugenics, which are a feature of modern Europe. The science of Eugenics, like all other sciences, attaches but little weight to personal sentiment. According to it, selection by personal inclination must be rigorously regulated for the sake of the progeny. If the principle involved be once admitted, marriage needs must be rescued from the control of the heart, and brought under the province of the intellect, otherwise insoluble problems will keep on arising; for passion recks not consequences, nor brooks interference by outside judges.

To return to our Kshatriyas, they were, as I have indicated, not in the habit of observing with any strictness the social rules relating to marriage. But it becomes clear from the poems of Kalidas, that there was a struggle of protest in his mind against this laxity of their observance. The Poet keenly felt the value of the eugenic restrictions which were directed towards maintaining the racial ideals pure, and yet his heart could not fail to be moved by the beauty of the play of the natural loves of man and woman against the background of the exuberance of the Universal Life. In most of the great works of Kalidas are treated the conflict of these opposites. The coming of the line of the Bhāratas was a great event in the History of India. But though the prelude of unbridled desire, which ushered in the founder of the line, has been viewed by the Poet in its aspect of Beauty in the first part of the play, he has corrected it from the standpoint of the Good towards the conclusion.

Amidst the natural beauty of the forest hermitage, Sakuntalā's youth blossoms out in prodigal curves of body and mind, along with the ecstasy of form and movement in the flowering trees and creepers around her. Everywhere in this retreat does Nature beckon, but Society, as yet, has found no loophole through which to obtrude the warning of her uplifted finger. Sakuntalā's secret union with King Dushyanta, which takes place amidst these surroundings, is not in harmony with the rest of society. So, according to the Poet, the curse comes upon her. She overlooks, in her self-absorption, the duty of hospitality; for when Nature is busy securing any special purpose, she throws all other purposes into the background. Society thereupon exacts its penalty and, in the Kings' audience hall, the inevitable thunderbolt of insult and rejection falls upon Sakuntalā.

In the seventh Act, the picture which the Poet draws of the hermitage, in which is consummated King Dushyanta's final union with Sakuntalā, now purified by discipline, is everywhere full of the rigour of renunciation, eclipsing the life-play of Nature. In the opening scene, the King is informed that the *Rishi* is busy expounding the *dharma* of the wifely estate Sakuntalā, here, is seen as the emblem of devotion, the Mother. It is clear that the Poet's object was vividly to contrast these two pictures of the relations of woman to man, the one carrying the bondage of desire, the other the detachment of *dharma*.

Motherhood, in so far as it is concerned with the physical nurture of offspring, is not essentially different in man and the lower animals, being a function of biological, not of sociological life, governed by instincts which are of nature, not by man's own creative power. But where the mother undergoes voluntary penance for the elevation of the human race, keeping her natural instincts in rigorous subordination to the dictates of mind and soul, there indeed is her own creative power at work. Now-a-days in the West, we often find women feeling a certain degradation in becoming subject to Maternity; that is to say, they feel the insult of having to submit to this tyranny of Nature over their sex. But the way for woman to avoid such insult is not by abjuring Motherhood, but by making it subserve her ideal, by bringing it under the control of her own intellect and conscience. How far India's conscious activity in the past—this striving of hers for the best possible progeny—was fully consonant with the conclusions of modern science, is not the question here. The point is, that just by such intellectual and spiritual vigilance can the human Mother achieve her true dignity.

In his Kumāra-sambhava it is the same thing that the Poet tells us. There he has shown the divine aspect of the eternal love of man and woman. When the Titans have won paradise, and banished the gods therefrom, the love of man and woman, transformed into ascetic striving, wins back heaven from the insult of defeat. The gods are eternally awaiting the birth of Kumāra, the conqueror of evil. And, in order to achieve this birth, the passion of desire must be transmuted into pure, disciplined endeavour. The rigorous aspect of such achievement is the truth which is beauty. The beauty of Illusion is gorgeous in its adornment, the beauty of Freedom is naked.

In all the three of his works, the Raghu-vamsa, the Kumāra-sambhava and Sakuntalā, India's Poet has looked upon marriage as a state of discipline, not intended for gaining individual happiness but of which the method is the control of desire and the object to bring about the birth of the Slayer of Evil, the super-man who will make possible the achievement of heaven on earth. The agony of the Poet which we glimpse in each of these, springs from his consciousness of the degeneracy which was overtaking society through the flagrant disregard by the Kshatriya kings of the Aryan ideal of marriage. And the Poet sends out his call to bring away the union of man and woman from the realm of Kandarpa (*Eros*) into the hermitage of Shiva, the Good. This Indian ideal of marriage can be much more vividly understood from the works of the Poet than from any Dharma-shāstra.

Here the question arises that, if desire be banished from the very threshold of marriage, how can love find any place in the wedded life? Those who have no true acquaintance with our country, and whose marriage system is entirely different, take it for granted that the Hindu marriage is loveless. But do we not know of our own knowledge how false is such conclusion?

If we accept the institution of marriage, we must also admit that no system can be devised to ensure that its original object shall remain true throughout the long period covered by the life of the wedded couple. That is why, both law and public opinion have to keep such vigilant watch from the outside. But when external compulsion tries to bind together those whom only mutual love can truly unite, it makes their relations inherently impure,—in fact, no greater insult can be offered to man. Yet, all over the civilized world, man submits even to this for the sake of the welfare of his children. So far, no society has been able to claim that it has arrived at a faultless solution of the difficulty. In entering the married state we have all to make our plunge into the doubtful and leave it to providence whether we shall sink, or swim through.

The 'desire', however, against which India's solution of the marriage problem declared war, is one of Nature's most powerful fighters; consequently, the question of how to overcome it was not an easy one. There is a particular age, said India, at which this attraction between the sexes reaches its height, so if marriage is to be regulated according to the social will, it must be finished with before such age. Hence the Indian custom of early marriage.

This brings to my mind the conversation I once had with an Agriculturist. I was complaining to him of the lack of common grazing grounds in our villages, whereupon he told me that it was a mistake to suppose that a cow would thrive best if allowed to graze at will. Scientific feeding with specially cultivated fodder-crops could only yield the best results. These must have been the lines of argument, in regard to married love, pursued in our country. For the purpose of marriage, spontaneous love is unreliable, its proper cultivation should yield the best results,—such was the conclusion,—and this cultivation should begin before marriage. Therefore from their earliest years, the husband as an idea, is held up before our girls, in verse and story, through ceremonial and worship. When at length they get this 'husband', he is to them not a person but a principle, like Loyalty, Patriotism, or such other abstractions which owe their immense strength to the fact that the best part of them is our own creation and therefore part of our inner being.

There is also in our society the glorification of the *Sati,* the ideal wife; and, accordingly, a real reverence for woman, as the embodiment of house-wifely virtues, is not rare in our country. The idea was, in both cases, to replace the natural passion of sexual love by the cultivated emotion of wed-ded love. But, it must be admitted that woman being emotional by nature, it has not been as easy for man thus to idealise the married state as it has been for her. It must also be admitted that the restraints and restrictions prescribed in the case of the man have not been so rigorous as those for the woman.

Therefore, in coming to our judgement on the marriage system of India, we must not fail to recognize the fact that therein the man and the woman are not on a footing of equality. Such inequality would have utterly humili-ated her, but that, for the wife, the husband is an idea. She has not sur-rendered herself to the brute force of another, but voluntarily consecrated herself to the service of her own ideal. And if the husband is a man of sensi-tive soul the flame of this ideal love is transmitted to his own life also. Such mutual illumination it has often been our lot to witness.

There is yet another vital element in India's culture which we must keep in mind. In spite of her exaltation of the household estate, India did not look upon this as man's ultimate stage. According to India's ideal, even the home must be given up in due course, in quest of the Infinite,—the house-hold, in fact, is only to be set up as an important stage in this quest. Even to-day, we see our householders, when their children are grown up, leaving their home to spend the rest of their life in some place of pilgrimage. Here is another pair of opposites which India attempted to reconcile. On the one hand, her civilization is essentially bound up in the home, albeit a home in which a wide circle of relationships find their place. On the other, its endeavour is, one by one, to snap all earthly ties in its pursuit of the lib-eration of the soul. In fact, it recognizes the social bonds because it is only through their acceptance that they can be transcended. In order to get rid of the natural desires of man, they must be used up; that is to say, guided by the spirit of renunciation to their own extinction. Here we find the dif-ference between Hinduism and Buddhism. In its relations with Nature, Buddhism is uncompromisingly anarchist from the very outset.

The weakness of the Hindu system lies in the fact that its complex web is too closely knit, and that the least loosening of its fibre, in any of its parts, tends to its disruption. It is afraid of the contact of the outside because the bond which holds it together is that of external regulation, whose strength depends upon habitual conformity. But self-segregation for any society is no longer practicable in this age. For, while it may be possible to prevent the man on this side of the sea from crossing to the other, what about preventing those on the other side from coming over here?

So have alien ideas, alien systems, alien customs, breaking in through her embankments, dashed upon India in a multitudinous flood, making visible breaches in all the habits and beliefs which were the pillars of her social system. Further, apart from this disturbance of her inward life, there has been the more effective attack of an alien economic system; for without a sufficiency of food, it is impossible for the various relationships of her complex society to be kept together. And, just as foreign ideas come pouring in on our mental world, so do our foodstuffs, caught up in various currents of commerce, keep flowing away towards foreign lands. So that the people of our country, in their social dealings, are now compelled to keep careful count of their meagre resources. Lastly, there is the nemesis of the unrealized ideal, which overtakes any civilization when, by reason of flagging vitality, it fails in the earnestness of its pursuit, and lapses into the stagnation of mechanical habits. Every living organism is constantly confronted with the waste products of its own fatigue, for which its vital forces, while active, find natural means of elimination. The adoption of complex external devices is of no avail when vitality is on the wane, for they only tend to weaken the natural functions still further, if not to create new forms of weakness and disease. The civilizations which flourished for a time, and have disappeared, are those which committed suicide, clinging on to their own toxic products, by suppressing, under the urgency of their special purposes, the cleansing impulses provided by Nature.

Anyhow, the special qualities of head and heart, which once found varied support in our broad social system, are now dying out for lack of opportunity for their exercise; meanwhile it has not been possible to effect a corresponding change in the structure of our society; with the result, that while all its restrictions keep on hampering us, their original object and justification have become impossible of acknowledgement. And so, on every side, are the members of this vast society overwhelmed with futility. In particular, the very basis of our marriage system having been undermined, there is no longer any harmony of adjustment between the underlying ideals and the actual facts of our modern marriages. One section of our people keeps crying out for a return of the *Satya-yuga,* but that golden age refuses to respond to their call. The time has, therefore, come for us to think out our problems afresh, to correlate our thoughts and conclusions with those of all humanity.

The gulf of separation, which Nature has contrived between the sexes, has preserved in its atmosphere the varied play of a powerful mutual attraction. This force which is creative,—but destructive as well,—continually sends its awakening message to our souls from behind the veil. If we screen off society from its forceful activity, that may conduce to its own safety, but will surely reduce it to passivity. In our language we call the power of woman over man by the name of *shakti.* Deprived of *shakti* the creative process in society languishes, and man, losing his vitality, becomes mechanical in his habits. In such case, though he may still retain many a passive quality, all energy of activity forsakes him. The manner in which the relations between the sexes have been regulated in our country, has left no room for the action of this *shakti*; for, as we have seen, our society, with immovable stability as its objective, has been busy cultivating the passive qualities, ever in dread of individual forcefulness. Now that our country has awakened to outside influences, she finds herself powerless to resist alien aggression. She has even lost the faculty of recognizing that her weakness proceeds from within her own social system, and is not the outcome of any outward accident.

In every society, its civilization is the territory conquered in its contest with Nature. And since in our country this contest was long and bitter, everywhere we find its fences more in evidence than its roads. But because there was once a good reason for this state of things, it does not help to save her when the reason has ceased to exist. Her barriers which kept the outsider off, now keep herself confined.

It seems that in the age which has now come upon us, man is thinking of giving up the desperate hope of victoriously keeping up this constant struggle. He would now make his peace with Nature,—and that duty has been entrusted to Science. But the marriage system of every society belongs to an age when, in the Parliament of Life, man was sitting on the opposition benches against Nature's government. And Nature has ever retaliated against his obstructive tactics. Up to now they have nowhere come to any satisfactory agreement. That is why these ubiquitous attempts at the external regulation of man's most intimate relations, have been insulting his best feelings and degrading the greatest of his institutions, all over the world.

Let me, as an individual Indian, offer in conclusion my own personal contribution to the discussion of the marriage question generally.

There are two parallel activities in the human world, the one which carries forward the stream of population: the other, the civilization of man. The first chiefly belongs to the realm of Life, and the second to that of Mind. In the creation of progeny, man's part though essential, is secondary. After he has once roused the passive seed, in woman's keeping, to vital activity, all the travail of child-hearing and parturition are hers alone. It is because of this comparative lightness of the male function in the propagation of the species, that we find instances of the killing off of superfluous males in the insect world, and of the keeping down of the number of male beasts by internecine struggles due to the savage jealousy which is their characteristic; showing the minor importance of this sex for the purpose of biological creation.

But, when Mind evolved itself into greatness, man found the opportunity to gain glory for his sex in the scheme of human development. For, while woman remained entangled in the specific duties which Life had assigned to her, man, with his greater freedom therefrom, was able to respond to the call of his intellect and engage in various work of creation in the world of Mind,—in fact he created the sphere of his own usefulness. In this, the first chapter of civilization, when Mind was in the ascendant, woman in her turn dropped into the second place, not only as less useful, but even as an actual impediment; for the world which was her special creation, constantly sought to throw its toils round the adventurous spirit of man as well. This comparative unimportance of woman in the birth stage of civilization, clings to her still. That is why the rebellious section of womankind would curtail her responsibilities in the region of Life, in order to enable her to claim equality with man in the work of his creation of society.

Opportunities, however, cannot be artificially created. The propensities of heart, strongly ingrained in woman's nature, cannot be dislodged by attacks from the outside. The tendency of these propensities of hers are towards holding fast, and not progressing onwards. So it is only by adherence to the cult of preservation that woman can attain her true welfare. If she desperately engages in adventurous pursuits, she will at every step come into conflict with her own inner nature, and thus constantly distracted, she can never succeed in competing with man in his own special sphere. But just as man, after a long period of subordination during the ascendancy of Life, was enabled to get rid of his disabilities in a subsequent stage, so woman too may look forward to a yet higher regime whereunder she will have the right to emerge from her present subjection. It is difficult to decide what to call this next stage; for the word '*spiritual*' is so beset with controversy regarding its true meaning. However, let me for my present purpose give it that name.

The inner qualities of the woman's heart, result in an important by product, which may be called *charm*. This charm like light, is a force. Intangible, imponderable though it be, the strivings of our intellect may not attain fruition if deprived of its life-giving touch. The nourishment which the tree draws though its roots may be classified and measured,—not so the vitality which is the gift of the sunlight, and without which its functioning becomes altogether impossible.

This ineffable emanation of woman's nature has, from the first, played its part in the creations of man, unobtrusively but inevitably. Had man's mind not been energised by the inner working of woman's vital charm, he would never have attained his successes. Of all the higher achievements of civilization,—the devotion of the toiler, the valour of the brave, the creations of the artist,—the secret spring is to be found in woman's influence. In the clash and battle of primitive civilization, the action of woman's *shakti* is not clearly manifest; but, as civilization becomes spiritual in the course of its development, and the union of man with man is acknowledged to be more important than the differences between them, the charm of woman gets the opportunity to become the predominant factor. Such spiritual civilization can only be upheld if the emotion of woman and the intellect of man are contributed in usual shares for its purposes. Then their respective contributions may combine gloriously in ever-fresh creations, and their difference will no longer make for inequality.

Woman, let me repeat, has two aspects,—in one she is the Mother; in the other, the Beloved. I have already spoken of the spiritual endeavour that characterises the first, viz., the striving, not merely for giving birth to her child, but for creating the best possible child,—not as an addition to the number of men, but as one of the heroic souls who may win victory in man's eternal fight against evil in his social life and natural surroundings. As the Beloved, it is woman's part to infuse life into all the aspirations of man; and the spiritual power that enables her to do so I have called *charm,* and was known in India by the name of *shakti.*

There is a poem called *Ānanda-laharī* (The stream of delight), attributed to Shankarāchārya. She who is glorified therein is the *shakti* in the heart of the Universe, the Giver of joy, the Inspirer of Activity. On the one hand, we know and use the world; on the other we are related to it by ties of disinterested joy. We can know the world because it is a manifestation of Truth: we rejoice in it because it is an expression of Joy. 'Who would have striven for life,' says the *Rishi*, 'if this *ānanda* (joy) had not filled the sky.' It seems to me that the 'Intellectual Beauty', whose praises Shelley has sung, is identical with this *Ānanda*. And it is this same *ānanda* which the poet of *ānanda-laharī* has visualised as the woman; that is to say, in his view, this Universal *Shakti* is manifest in human Society in the nature of Woman. In this manifestation is her charm. Let no one confuse this *shakti* with mere 'sweetness', for in this charm there is a combination of several qualities,— patience, self-abnegation, sensitive intelligence, grace in thought, word and behaviour,—the reticent expression of rhythmic life, the tenderness and terribleness of love; at its core, moreover, is that self-radiant Spirit of Delight which ever gives itself up.

This *shakti*, this joy-giving power of woman as the Beloved, has up to now largely been dissipated by the greed of man, who has sought to use it for the purposes of his individual enjoyment, corrupting it, confining it, like his property, within jealously-guarded limits. That has also obstructed for woman herself her inward realization of the full glory of her own *shakti*. Her personality has been insulted at every turn by being made to display its power of delectation within a circumscribed arena. It is because she has not found her true place in the great world, that she sometimes tries to capture man's special estate as a desperate means of coming into her own. But it is not by coming out of her home that woman can gain her liberty. Her liberation can only be effected in a society where her true *shakti*, her *ānanda*, is given the widest and highest scope for its activity. Man has already achieved the means of self-expansion in public activity without giving up his individual concerns. When, likewise, any society shall be able to offer a larger field for the creative work of woman's special faculty, without detracting from her creative work in the home, then in such society will the true union of man and woman become possible.

The marriage system all over the world, from the earliest ages till now, is a barrier in the way of such true union. That is why woman's *shakti*, in all existing societies, is so shamefully wasted and corrupted. That is why, in every country marriage is still more or less of a prison house for the confinement of woman,—with all its guards wearing the badge of the dominant male. That is why man, by dint of his efforts to bind woman, has made her the strongest of fetters for his own bondage. That is why woman is debarred from adding to the spiritual wealth of society by the perfection of her own nature, and all human societies are weighed down with the burden of the resulting poverty.

The civilization of man has not, up to now, loyally recognized the reign of the Spirit. Therefore the married state is still one of the most fruitful sources of the unhappiness and downfall of man, of his disgrace and humiliation. But those who believe that society is a manifestation of the spirit, will assuredly not rest in their endeavours till they have rescued human marriage relations from outrage by the brute forces of society,—till they have thereby given free play to the force of Love in all the concerns of humanity.

1925
Source: The English writings of Rabindranath Tagore
(New Delhi: Sahitya Akademi, 2004)

Woman
(from *Personality*)

When male creatures indulge in their fighting propensity to kill one another Nature connives at it, because, comparatively speaking, females are needful to her purpose, while males are barely necessary. Being of an economic disposition she does not specially care for the hungry broods who are quarrelsomely voracious and who yet contribute very little towards the payment of Nature's bill. Therefore in the insect world we witness the phenomenon of the females taking it upon themselves to keep down the male population to the bare limit of necessity.

But because greatly relieved of their responsibility to Nature, the males in the human world have had the freedom of their occupation and adventures. The definition of the human being is said to be that he is the tool-making animal. This tool-making is outside of Nature's scope. In fact, with our tool-making power we have been able to defy Nature. The human male, having the most part of his energies free, developed this power, and became formidable. Thus though in the vital department of humanity woman still occupies the throne given to her by Nature, man in the mental department has created and extended his own dominion. For this great work detachment of mind and freedom of movement were necessary.

Man took advantage of his comparative freedom from the physical and emotional bondage, and marched unencumbered towards his extension of life's boundaries. In this he has travelled through the perilous path of revolutions and ruins. Time after time his accumulations have been swept away and the current of progress has disappeared at its source. Though the gain has been considerable yet the waste in comparison has been still more enormous, especially when we consider that much of the wealth, when vanished, has taken away the records with it. Through this repeated experience of disasters man has discovered the truth,—though not fully utilized it, that in all his creations the moral rhythm has to be maintained to save them from destruction; that a mere unlimited augmentation of power does not lead to real progress, and there must be balance of proportion, must be harmony of the structure with its foundation to indicate a real growth in truth.

This ideal of stability is deeply cherished in woman's nature. She is never in love with merely going on, shooting wanton arrows of curiosity into the heart of darkness. All her forces instinctively work to bring things to some shape of fullness,—for that is the law of life. In life's movement though nothing is final yet every step has its rhythm of completeness. Even the bud has its ideal of rounded perfection, so has the flower, and also the fruit. But an unfinished building has not that ideal of wholeness in itself. Therefore if it goes on indefinitely in its growth of dimensions, it gradually grows out of its standard of stability. The masculine creations of intellectual civilization are towers of Babel, they dare to defy their foundations and therefore topple down over and over again. Thus human history is growing up over layers of ruins; it is not a continuous life growth. The present war is an illustration of this. The economic and political organizations, which merely represent mechanical power, born of intellect, are apt to forget their centres of gravity in the foundational world of life. The cumulative greed of power and possession which can have no finality of completeness in itself, which has no harmony with the ideal of moral and spiritual perfection, must at last lay a violent hand upon its own ponderousness of material.

At the present stage of history civilization is almost exclusively masculine, a civilization of power, in which woman has been thrust aside in the shade. Therefore it has lost its balance and it is moving by hopping from war to war. Its motive forces are the forces of destruction and its ceremonials are carried through an appalling number of human sacrifices. This one-sided civilization is crashing along a series of catastrophes at a tremendous speed because of its one-sidedness. And at last the time has arrived when woman must step in and impart her life rhythm into this reckless movement of power.

For woman's function is the passive function of the soil which not only helps the tree to grow but keeps its growth within limits. The tree must have life's adventure and send up and spread out its branches on all sides, but all its deeper bonds of relation are hidden and held firm in the soil and this helps it to live. Our civilization must also have its passive element broad and deep and stable. It must not be mere growth but harmony of growth. It must not be all tune but it must have its time also. This time is not a barrier, it is what the banks are to the river; they guide its current into permanence, which otherwise would lose itself into the amorphousness of morass. It is rhythm, the rhythm which does not check the world's movements but leads them into truth and beauty.

Woman is endowed with the passive qualities of chastity, modesty, devotion and power of self-sacrifice in a greater measure than man is. It is the passive quality in nature which turns its monster forces into perfect creations of beauty—taming the wild elements into the delicacy of tenderness fit for the service of life. This passive quality has given woman that large and deep placidity which is so necessary for the healing and nourishing and storing of life. If life were all spending, then it would be like a rocket, going up in a flash and coming down the next moment in ashes. Life should be like a lamp where the potentiality of light is far greater in quantity than what appears as the flame. It is in the depth of passiveness in woman's nature that this potentiality of life is stored.

I have said elsewhere that in the women of the Western world a certain restlessness is noticed which cannot be the normal aspect of her nature. For women who want something special and violent in their surroundings to keep their interests active only prove that they have lost touch with their own true world. Apparently, numbers of women as well as men in the West condemn the things that are commonplace. They are always hankering after something which is out of the common, straining their powers to produce a spurious originality that merely surprises though it may not satisfy. But such efforts are not a real sign of vitality. And they must be more injurious to women than to men, because women have the vital power more strongly in them than men have. They are the mothers of the race, and they have a real interest in the things that are around them, that are the common things of life; if they did not have that, then the race would perish.

If, by constantly using outside stimulation, they form something like a mental drag habit, become addicted to a continual dram-drinking of sensationalism, then they lose the natural high sensibility which they have, and with it the bloom of their womanhood, and their real power to sustain the human race with what it needs the most.

A man's interest in his fellow-beings becomes real when he finds in them some special gift of power or usefulness, but a woman feels interest in her fellow-beings because they are living creatures, because they are human, not because of some particular purpose which they can serve, or some power which they possess and for which she has a special admiration. And because woman has this power, she exercises such charm over our minds; her exuberance of vital interest is so attractive that it makes her speech, her laughter, her movement, everything graceful; for the note of gracefulness is in this harmony with all our surrounding interests.

Fortunately for us, our everyday world has the subtle and unobtrusive beauty of the commonplace, and we have to depend upon our own sensitive minds to realize its wonders which are invisible because spiritual. If we can pierce through the exterior, we find that the world in its commonplace aspects is a miracle.

We realise this truth intuitively through our power of love; and women, through this power, discover that the object of their love and sympathy, in spite of its ragged disguise of triviality, has infinite worth. When women have lost the power of interest in things that are common, then leisure frightens them with its emptiness, because their natural sensibilities being deadened, there is nothing in their surroundings to occupy their attention. Therefore they keep themselves frantically busy, not in utilizing the time, but merely in filling it up. Our everyday world is like a reed, its true value is not in itself,—but those who have the power and the serenity of attention can hear the music which the Infinite plays through its very emptiness. But when they form the habit of valuing things for themselves, then they may be expected furiously to storm your mind, to decoy your soul from her love-tryst of the eternal and to make you try to smother the voice of the Infinite by the unmeaning rattle of ceaseless movement.

I do not mean to imply that domestic life is the only life for a woman. I mean that the human world is the woman's world, be it domestic or be it full of the other activities of life which are human activities, and not merely abstract efforts to organize.

Wherever there is something which is concretely personal and human, there is woman's world. The domestic world is the world where every individual finds his worth as an individual, therefore his value is not the market value, but the value of love; that is to say, the value that God in His infinite mercy has set upon all His creatures. This domestic world has been the gift of God to woman. She can extend her radiance of love beyond its boundaries on all sides, and even leave it to prove her woman's nature when the call comes to her. But this is a truth which cannot be ignored, that the moment she is born in her mother's arms, she is born in the centre of her own true world, the world of human relationships.

Woman should use her power to break through the surface and go to the centre of things, where in the mystery of life dwells an eternal source of interest. Man has not this power to such an extent. But woman has it, if she does not kill it,—and therefore she loves creatures who are not lovable for their uncommon qualities. Man has to do his duty in a world of his own where he is always creating power and wealth and organizations of different kinds. But God has sent woman to love the world, which is a world of ordinary things and events. She is not in the world of the fairy-tale where the fair woman sleeps for ages till she is touched by the magic wand. In God's world women have their magic wands everywhere, which keeps their hearts awake,—and these are not the golden wands of wealth nor the iron rods of power.

All our spiritual teachers have proclaimed the infinite worth of the individual. It is the rampant materialism of the present age which ruthlessly sacrifices individuals to the bloodthirsty idols of organization. When religion was materialistic, when men worshipped their gods for fear of their malevolence, or for greed of wealth and power, then the ceremonies of worship were cruel and sacrifices were claimed without number. With the growth of man's spiritual life, our worship has become the worship of love.

At the present stage of civilization, when the mutilation of individuals is not only practised, but glorified, women are feeling ashamed of their own womanliness. For God, with his message of love, has sent them as guardians of individuals, and, in this their divine vocation, individuals are more to them than army and navy and parliament, shops and factories. Here they have their service in God's own temple of reality, where love is of more value than power.

But because men in their pride of power have taken to deriding things that are living and relationships that are human, a large number of women are screaming themselves hoarse to prove that they are not women, that they are true where they represent power and organization. In the present age they feel that their pride is hurt when they are taken as mere mothers of the race, as the ministers to the vital needs of its existence, and to its deeper spiritual necessity of sympathy and love.

Because men praise with pious unctuousness the idolatry of their manufactured images of abstractions, women in shame are breaking their own true God, who is waiting for His worship of self-sacrifice in love.

Changes have been going on for a long time underneath the solid crust of society on which woman's world has its foundation. Of late, with the help of science, civilization has been growing increasingly masculine, from which the full reality of the individual is more and more ignored. Organization is encroaching upon the province of personal relationship, and sentiment is giving way to law. In some societies, too much dominated by masculine ideals, infanticide prevailed, which ruthlessly kept down the female element of the population as low as possible. The same thing in another form has taken place in modern civilization. In its inordinate lust for power and wealth it has robbed woman of the most part of her world, and the home is every day being crowded out by the office. It is taking the whole world for itself, leaving hardly any room for woman. It is not merely inflicting injury but insult upon her.

But woman cannot be pushed back for good into the mere region of the decorative by man's aggressiveness of power. For she is not less necessary in civilization than man but possibly more so. In the geological history of earth the periods of gigantic cataclysms have passed when the earth had not attained her mellowness of maturity which despises all violent exhibition of force. And the civilization of competing commerce and fighting powers must also make room for that stage of perfection whose power lies deep in beauty and beneficence. So long it has been ambition which was at the helm of our history, and therefore every right of the individual had to be wrenched by force from the party in power and man has had to invoke the help of evil to attain what was good for him. But such arrangement cannot last for long, it must give way time after time; for the seeds of violence lie in wait in its cracks and crevices, and roots of disruption spread in the dark and cause breakdown when it is least expected.

Therefore although in the present stage of history man is asserting his masculine supremacy and building his civilization with stone blocks, ignoring the living principle of growth, he cannot altogether crush woman's nature into dust or into his dead building materials. Woman's home may have been shattered, but woman is not, and cannot, herself be killed. It is not that woman is merely seeking her freedom of livelihood, struggling against man's monopoly of business, but against man's monopoly of civilization where he is breaking her heart every day and desolating her life. She must restore the lost social balance by putting the full weight of the woman into the creation of the human world. The monster car of organization is creaking and growling along life's highway, spreading misery and mutilation, for it must have speed before everything else in the world. Therefore woman must come into the bruised and maimed world of the individuals; she must claim each one of them as her own, the useless and the insignificant. She must protect under her care all the beautiful flowers of sentiments from the scorching laughter of the science of proficiency. The growing impurities, born of life's deprivation of its normal conditions imposed upon it by the organized power of greed, she must sweep away. The time has come when woman's responsibility has become greater than ever before, when her field of work has far transcended the domestic sphere of life. The world with its insulted individuals has sent its appeal to her. These individuals must find their true value, raise their heads once again in the sun, and renew their faith in God's love through her love.

Men have seen the absurdity of to-day's civilization, which is based upon nationalism,—that is to say, on economics and politics and its consequent militarism. Men have been losing their freedom and their humanity in order to fit themselves for vast mechanical organizations. So the next civilization, it is hoped, will be based not merely upon economical and political competition and exploitation, but upon world-wide social cooperation; upon spiritual ideals of reciprocity, and not upon economic ideals of efficiency. And then women will have their true place.

Because men have been building up vast and monstrous organizations they have got into the habit of thinking that this turning out power has something of the nature of perfection in itself. The habit is ingrained in them, and it is difficult for them to see where truth is missing in this present ideal of progress.

But woman can bring her fresh mind and all her power of sympathy to this new task of building up a spiritual civilization, if she will be conscious of her responsibilities. Of course, she can be frivolous or very narrow in her outlook, and then she will miss her great mission. And just because woman has been insulated, has been living in a sort of obscurity, behind man, I think she will have her compensation in the civilization which is waiting to come.

And these human beings who have been boastful of their power, and aggressive in their exploitation, who have lost faith in the real meaning of the teaching of their Master, that the meek shall inherit the earth, will be defeated in the next generation of life. It is the same thing that happened in the ancient days, in the prehistoric times, to those great monsters like the mammoths and dinosaurs. They have lost their inheritance of the earth. They had the gigantic muscles for mighty efforts but they had to give up to creatures who were much feebler in their muscles and who took up much less space with their dimensions. And in the future civilization also, the women, the feebler creatures,—feebler at least in their outer aspects,—who are less muscular, and who have been behindhand, always left under the shadow of those huge creatures, the men,—they will have their place, and those bigger creatures will have to give way.

Source: The English writings of Rabindranath Tagore
(New Delhi: Sahitya Akademi, 2004)

Woman and home

Creative expressions attain their perfect form through emotions modulated. Woman has that expression natural to her—a cadence of restraint in her behaviour, producing poetry of life. She has been an inspiration to man, guiding, most often unconsciously, his restless energy into an immense variety of creations in literature, art, music and religion. This is why, in India, woman has been described as the symbol of Shakti, the creative power.

But if woman begins to believe that, though biologically her function is different from that of man, psychologically she is identical with him; if the human world in its mentality becomes exclusively male, then before long it will be reduced to utter inanity. For life finds its truth and beauty, not in any exaggeration of sameness, but in harmony.

If woman's nature were identical with man's, if Eve were a mere tautology of Adam, it would only give rise to a monotonous superfluity. But that she was not so was proved by the banishment she secured from a ready-made Paradise. She had the instinctive wisdom to realize that it was her mission to help her mate in creating Paradise of their own on earth, whose ideal she was to supply with her life, whose materials were to be produced and gathered by her comrade.

However, it is evident than an increasing number of women in the West are ready to assert that their difference from men is unimportant. The reason for the vehement utterance of such a paradox cannot be ignored. It is rebellion against a necessity, which is not equal for both the partners.

Love in all forms has its obligations, and the love that binds women to their children binds them to their homes. But necessity is a tyrant, making us submit to injury and indignity, allowing advantage over us to those who are wholly or comparatively free from its burden. Such has been the case in the social relationship between man and woman. Along with the difference inherent in their respective natures, there have grown up between them inequalities fostered by circumstances. Man is not handicapped by the same biological and psychological responsibilities as woman, and therefore he has the liberty to give her the security of home. This liberty exacts payment when it offers its boon, because to give or to withhold the gift is within its power. It is the unequal freedom in their mutual relationships which has made the weight of life's tragedies so painfully heavy for woman to bear.

Some mitigation of her disadvantage has been effected by her rendering herself and her home a luxury to man. She has accentuated those qualities in herself which insidiously impose their bondage over her mate, some by pandering to his weakness, and some by satisfying his higher nature, till the sex-consciousness in our society has grown abnormal and overpowering. There is no actual objection to this in itself, for it offers a stimulus, acting in the depth of life, which leads to creative exuberance. But a great deal of it is a forced growth of compulsion bearing seeds of degradation. In those ages when men acknowledged spiritual perfection to be their object, women were denounced as the chief obstacle in their way. The constant and conscious exercise of allurements, which gave women their power, attacked the weak spots in man's nature, and doing so added to its weakness. For all relationships tainted with repression of freedom must become sources of degeneracy to the strong who impose such repressions.

Balance of power, however, between man and woman was in a measure established when home wielded a strong enough attraction to make men accept its obligations. But at last the time has come when the material ambition of man has assumed such colossal proportions that home is in danger of losing its centre of gravity for him, and he is receding farther and farther from its orbit.

The arid zone in the social life is spreading fast. The simple comforts of home, made precious by the touch of love, are giving way to luxuries that can only have their full extension in the isolation of self-centred life. Hotels are being erected on the ruins of homes; productions are growing more stupendous than creations; and most men have, for the materials of their happiness and recreation, their dogs and horses, their pipes, guns, and gambling clubs.

Reactions and rebellions, not being normal in their character, go on hurting truth until peace is restored. Therefore, when woman refuses to acknowledge the distinction between her life and that of man, she does not convince us of its truth, but only proves to us that she is suffering.

All great suffering indicate some wrong somewhere. In the present case, the wrong is in woman's lack of freedom in her relationship with man, which compels her to turn her disabilities into attractions, and to use untruths as her allies in the battle of life, while she is suffering from the precariousness of her position.

From the beginning of our society, women have naturally accepted the training which imparts to their life and to their home a spirit of harmony. It is their instinct to perform their services in such a manner that these, through beauty, might be raised from the domain of slavery to the realm of grace. Women have tried to prove that in the building up of social life they are artists and not artisans. But all expressions of beauty lose their truth when compelled to accept the patronage of the gross and the indifferent. Therefore when necessity drives women to fashion their lives to the taste of the insensitive or the sensual, then the whole thing becomes a tragedy of desecration. Society is full of such tragedies. Many of the laws and social regulations guiding the relationships of man and woman are relics of a barbaric age, when the brutal pride of an exclusive possession had its dominance in human relations, such as those of parents and children, husbands and wives, masters and servants, teachers and disciples. The vulgarity of it still persists in the social bond between the sexes because of the economic helplessness of woman. Nothing makes us so stupidly mean as the sense of superiority which the power of the purse confers upon us.

The powers of muscle and of money have opportunities of immediate satisfaction, but the power of the ideal must have infinite patience. The man who sells his goods, or fulfils his contract, is cheated if he fails to realize payment, but he who gives form to some ideal may never get his due and be fully paid. What I have felt in the women of India is the consciousness of this ideal—their simple faith in the sanctity of devotion lighted by love which is held to be divine. True womanliness is regarded in our country as the saintliness of love. It is not merely praised there, but literally worshipped; and she who is gifted with it is called Devi, as one revealing in herself Woman, the Divine. That this has not been a mere metaphor to us is because, in India, our mind is familiar with the idea of God in an eternal feminine aspect. Thus the Eastern woman, who is deeply aware in her heart of the sacredness of her mission, is a constant education to man. It has to be admitted that there are chances of such an influence failing to penetrate the callousness of the coarse-minded; but that is the destiny of all manifestations whose value is not in success or reward in honour.

Woman has to be ready to suffer. She cannot allow her emotions to be dulled or polluted, for these are to create her life's atmosphere, apart from which her world would be dark and dead. This leaves her heart without any protection of insensibility, at the mercy of the hurts and insults of life. Women of India, like women everywhere, have their share of suffering, but it radiates through the ideal, and becomes, like sunlight, a creative force in their world. Our women know by heart the legends of the great women of the epic age—Savitri who by the power of love conquered death, and Sita who had no other reward for her life of sacrifice but the sacred majesty of sorrow. They know that it is their duty to make this life an image of the life eternal, and that love's mission truly performed has a spiritual meaning. It is a religious responsibility for them to live the life which is their own. For their activity is not for money-making, or organizing power, or intellectually probing the mystery of existence, but for establishing and maintaining human relationships requiring the highest moral qualities. It is the consciousness of the spiritual character of their life's work, which lifts them above the utilitarian standard of the immediate and the passing, surrounds them with the dignity of the eternal, and transmutes their suffering and sorrow into a crown of light.

I must guard myself from the risk of a possible misunderstanding. The permanent significance of home is not in the narrowness of its enclosure, but in an eternal moral idea. It represents the truth of human relationship; it reveals loyalty and love for the personality of man. Let us take a wider view, in a perspective truer than can be found in its present conventional associations. With the discovery and development of agriculture there came a period of settled life in our history. The nomad ever moved on with his tents and cattle; he explored space and exploited its contents. The cultivator of land explored time in its immensity, for he had leisure. Comparatively secured from the uncertainty of his outer resources, he had the opportunity to deal with his moral resources in the realm of human truth. This is why agricultural civilization, like that of India and China, is essentially a civilization of human relationship, of the adjustment of mutual obligations. It is deep-rooted in the inner life of man. Its basis is co-operation and not competition. In other words, its principle is the principle of home, to which all its outer adventures are subordinated.

In the meanwhile, the nomadic life with its predatory instinct of exploitation has developed into a great civilization. It is immensely proud and strong, killing leisure and pursuing opportunities. It minimises the claims of personal relationship and is jealously careful of its unhampered freedom for acquiring wealth and asserting its will upon others. Its burden is the burden of things, which grows heavier and more complex every day, disregarding the human and the spiritual. Its powerful pressure from all sides narrows the limits of home, the personal region of the human world. Thus, in this region of life, women are every day hustled out of their shelter for want of accommodation.

But such a state of things can never have the effect of changing woman into man. On the contrary, it will lead her to find her place in the unlimited range of society, and the Guardian Spirit of the personal in human nature will extend the ministry of woman over all developments of life. Habituated to deal with the world as machine, man is multiplying his materials, banishing away his happiness and sacrificing love to comfort, which is an illusion. At last the present age has sent its cry to women, asking her to come out from her segregation in order to restore the spiritual supremacy of all that is human in the world of humanity. She has been aroused to remember that womanliness is not chiefly decorative. It is like that vital health, which not only imparts the bloom of beauty to the body, but joy to the mind and perfection to life.

Source: The English writings of Rabindranath Tagore
(New Delhi: Sahitya Akademi, 2004)

Travelogues

Epistles from Europe
(*Europe-probashir patra*)

Selected portion from *The seventh letter*

Allow me a few words on the affluent, fashionable women here in London. If they are to be trained, they should be entrusted to the supervision of our native mothers-in-law and widowed sisters-in-law. They are daughters and wives of big men. They have servants; they don't need to do any work. A housekeeper is there to supervise all the household work, a nurse who rears the children and a governess who monitors the lessons of the children and looks after other sundry activities. What is then left to strive for? The only 'work' that is left, then, is adornment. But there's a lady's maid for this; so even this one task doesn't need to be accomplished fully on one's own. From dawn to dusk, the entire day is free. Some of them shorten the day by lingering in bed in the morning, and by avoiding the sunlight by shutting all the doors and windows. They even have breakfast in bed and feel that they have risen too early in the morning if they happen to emerge from the bedroom before eleven. Then comes adornment, of which I can't tell you much. It's being heard that very recently taking a bath has become fashionable here, but it's not very common yet. Married women clean their face and neck and the bare parts of their arms with great care a number of times; as for the rest of their body, they don't see much need to clean it, because it's enough to keep the face, the main 'tool' of enticing the mind, from tarnishing. They think it enough to have a sponge-bath twice a month. Once I went to live with an English family; they were perturbed to hear that I am in the habit of bathing regularly. They had no bathing implements, and, therefore, had to borrow a shallow, round tub for my sake.

If any visitors arrive in a house, it is the responsibility of the lady of the house to make conversation. If a lot of people arrive together, her duty is to distribute the sweetness of her words and smiles equally to all; it is deemed impolite to talk exclusively to a particular guest. The task is complicated, and is gradually perfected through practice. I have noticed that they utter a sentence looking at somebody but the moment they finish they give a smile to all and sundry. Again, sometimes they start talking facing someone but as they go on they cast a smile or manage to throw a glance at everybody. Sometimes, again, they distribute the words in a sentence among the visitors so swiftly and skilfully that it is quite comprehensible that they have many cards ready in their hands, in the manner of card players in our country who shuffle cards during the game. To one she said, 'Lovely morning, isn't it?', and immediately turned towards another and remarked, 'Madam Neilson sang last night at the concert hall, it is exquisite!' Each of the women visitors present started contributing one adjective in response; one said, 'Charming'; another said, 'superb'; yet another said, 'something unearthly'. One was left and she came up with, 'Isn't it?' I feel that it is something like a dumb-bell exercise in the morning.

Be that as it may, visitors keep coming like this. She subscribes to the Moody's library. From there, the short-lived novels come and go. She devours them incessantly. And then she has to enact love—exchange of sweet smiles and words, or feigned reproach at a trivial issue, such as this: A tease from a man is met by a sweet reprimand with a raised fist, 'Oh you naughty, wicked, provoking man!' This fills the 'naughty man' with a sense of complete satisfaction. Reception of visitors, cancellation of visits, reading of new novels, creation of new fashions or emulation of those already in vogue, and flirtation with an added flavour of sweetness in all these, and 'love'—these are their daily activities. Just as the girls in our country are trained for marriage since their childhood without enough education, because it is taken for granted that they won't have to become office-goers, here too the girls are polished from their early days to make them market-worthy. The amount of education that they need to become marriageable is thought to be sufficient. A little training in music and piano, some good dancing, a bit of French with a broken pronunciation and some idea of sewing and knitting make an appropriate doll for display in the shop-window of a wedding stall. In this, the difference between the girls here and the girls in our country is just that which exists between the dolls in these two lands. The girls in our country don't need to learn piano and a few other things;

the girls here have to study a little; but both are products for sale in the market. Here also, it is the men who are masters; wives are subservient to them. Men think that it is their God-ordained right to reign over and direct the minds of their women.

However, apart from the stylish women, there are other women here too, without whom the world won't go on. The women of the middle-class households have to toil hard; they can't afford to indulge in frivolity. They have to mind the kitchen in the morning—whether it's clean or not, whether the provision is enough for the day, whether everything is in the right place. Then they have to arrange for meals and other kitchen supplies, make some clever wifely pretensions to save money, prepare soup from the leftover meat of the previous day—and many other such wifely duties are there. Then they sew socks and garments for their children, and sometimes even prepare clothes for themselves. Reading a novel is not in the fortune for all of them. At best, they read the newspapers, and many don't even do that. Reading and writing for many of them is restricted to letters, bills from shopkeepers and minding the family budget. They say, 'Let men deal with politics and other heavy topics; our duty and work space are different.' Women seem to take pride in appearing weak. Therefore, many women simply lie down even if they are not tired. It is the same with knowledge and intellect. They proudly say, 'We do not understand all this.' Lack of knowledge and lack of intellect become a thing of public boast.

Middle-class women here do not devote much attention to their studies, and neither are the husbands too upset about this. Their lives are a sum total of trivial activities. When the husband returns from work in the evening, the wife earns a warm kiss. (Needless to say, there are families which are exceptions to this general rule.) The furnace is lit, and the food is laid out for him. In the evening, the wife sometimes sits with some sewing, and the husband reads out loudly to her from a novel—the furnace burning before them, the room fairly warm, a downpour outside, the doors and windows closed. Sometimes the wife plays the piano and sings a song to her husband.

The middle-class women here are very simple. Although they are not properly educated, they know many things, and their intellect is flawless. Here one can acquire knowledge through conversation. These women are not cooped up in the home. They interact with friends; they listen to some lofty topic being discussed in a family gathering and can voice their own opinions about it. They can understand the many facets of a single issue in the same way as wise men. Therefore, when a topic is raised, they don't have to ask some vague, childish questions or sit dumb-founded. They talk to their friends in a normal way, and in a party they don't have to either put

up a gloomy countenance or remain shyly nervous. There is no unnecessary closeness with their acquaintances, nor do they maintain any unsocial
distance from them. Publicly, she would sport a happy and smiling expression; she may not be very jocose herself, but nevertheless she appreciates
humour, can praise something she likes with an open heart and can laugh
heartily at some joke.

Translated by **Soham Pain**

Travel diary from Japan

(Japan jatrir diary)

Extract from Letter 13

There's one more thing to say in this context [of Japanese customs]. I do not see any prohibition in the closeness between men and women here; the veil of shyness and reserve between men and women, visible elsewhere, is absent here. It appears that the trap of physical obsessions is a shade less among these people. The main reason behind such a conclusion is the prevalence of a custom of men and women bathing in nudity in Japan. That there isn't the slightest discomfiture about this custom is known by the fact that even the nearest kin does not feel any inner resistance to such participation. In this way, men and women do not harbour any illusions about each other's bodies. Both parties have a normal attitude towards the human form. This tradition is gradually fading in the cities due to the tainted gaze and wicked thoughts of those coming from other countries. But it still holds ground in the rural areas. Among all the civilised countries in the world, it is only Japan that is free from an obsession about the human body—this is something striking for me.

But it is surprising that the naked woman is portrayed nowhere in Japanese painting. This has been possible only because the secrets of nudity haven't cast a mysterious aura over their minds. One thing more. Here, not the least attempt is made on the part of the women to advertise themselves as female through their attire. Almost everywhere in the world, there is some gesture in women's garments which reveals that they demand the bemused gaze of men. Here, the attire of the women is beautiful, but there is no attempt in it to identify the female form through subtle hints. I am not claiming that there is no weakness in character among the Japanese at all, but in Japan, there is absent the artificial and illusory veil constructed around the relation between men and women that prevails in all civilised nations. The relation here is relatively normal and free from obsessions.

Translated by **Soham Pain**

Epilogue

The path of your creation

(*Tomar srishtir path*)

You have spread the path of your creation
With nets of varied wiles,
O guileful one.
You have laid the snare of false belief
With skilful hands, in simple lives.
By this deceit you have marked greatness out:
Not for him the secret night.
The path your star shows him
Is the path of his heart.
It is ever-clear,
It makes him ever-radiant with simple faith.
Tortuous outside, inwardly it is straight.
In this lies his glory.
People think he is deceived;
He gains truth
In his heart of hearts, washed in its own light.
Nothing can deceive him.
He takes into his store
The last reward.
He who has with ease endured deception,
Gains from your hand
The imperishable right to peace.

Translated by **Supriya Chaudhuri**
[Sukanta Chaudhuri, ed., *Rabindranath Tagore: Selected poems*
(Oxford: Oxford University Press, 2004)]

ABOUT THE EDITOR AND CONTRIBUTORS

Editor

Malashri Lal is currently the Dean of Colleges, and also the Dean, Academic Activities and Projects at the University of Delhi. She has held other senior administrative positions in the same university, including that of the Head, Department of English (2000–03), Director, Women's Studies (2000–06) and Joint Director, South Campus (2006–11). As a recipient of fellowships from the Fulbright, the British Council, the Rockefeller Foundation and the Shastri-Indo Canadian Institute, she has conducted research in prestigious institutes, including Harvard University, USA, Bellagio, Italy, and Newcastle, UK. Malashri Lal's academic specialisation is in Women and Gender Studies, a subject on which she has written ten books. Her book *The law of the threshold: Women writers in Indian English* was widely acclaimed. Recently, she has co-edited *In search of Sita: Revisiting mythology* and *Chamba–achamba: Women's oral narratives*. She has served on international book award committees, including the Commonwealth Writers Prize and the DSC Prize for South Asian Literature.

Contributors

Swapan Kumar Banerjee is Associate Professor of English, Narasinha Dutta College, Howrah.

Aruna Chakravarti taught in Delhi University for many years and retired as the Principal of Janki Devi Memorial College. Aruna Chakravarti's translation of Sharatchandra Chattopadhyay's *Srikanta* fetched her the prestigious Sahitya Akademi Award. She has also introduced the works of the Bengali novelist Sunil Gangopadhyay to the English-speaking world through her translations of *Pratham alo* and *Sei samay*.

Radha Chakravarty teaches English Literature at Gargi College, University of Delhi. She is a reputed Tagore scholar and translator. Her most recent book, *The essential Tagore*, was published jointly with Fakrul Alam.

Malobika Chaudhuri is the translator of the book *The scarlet dusk*.

Sukanta Chaudhuri is Professor Emeritus, Jadavpur University. He is a renowned scholar and translator. The most challenging translation of his is that of Sukumar Ray's nonsense verse collection, *Abol tabol*.

Supriya Chaudhuri is a scholar of English Literature. She is Professor Emeritus at Kolkata's Jadavpur University. Tagore's novel, *Jogajog*, was translated by her.

Charu Chowdhury (1895–1987) was a legal and constitutional expert with a varied range of literary interests. The most famous of all his translations is Tagore's *Purabi*.

Sanjukta Dasgupta, Professor and Former Head, Department of English and currently Dean, Faculty of Arts, University of Calcutta, is a critic, translator and poet.

Uma Dasgupta is Former Professor, Social Sciences Division, Indian Statistical Institute, Kolkata. A scholar of Tagore's biographical writings, she has written extensively from source documents.

Dipannita Datta is an independent researcher, international academic and the author of several books on 19th and 20th century literature. She has translated Tagore extensively.

Krishna Dutta was born in Calcutta and has lived many years in London where she teaches. She is an author and translator specialising in the cultural history of Bengal. Her book, *Calcutta: A cultural and literary history*, was published to critical acclaim.

Ketaki Kushari Dyson's research-based books include a study of the journals and memoirs of the British in India in 1765–1856, the relationship of letters between Tagore and Victoria Ocampo, and a study, done jointly with other scholars, of the effects of protanopic colour vision on Tagore's writings and art.

Mary Lago (1919–2001) was on the University of Missouri Department of English faculty from 1977 to 1991. From 1989 until her retirement, she held the endowed professorship, the Catherine Paine Middlebush Chair of English. *Biographical passages: Essays on Victorian and modernist biography honoring Mary M. Lago* (2000) describes her as a distinguished biographer, editor, translator and scholar of Victorian and Edwardian literature.

Joyasree Mukerji is a freelance translator. She published a translation of Tagore's women-centric short stories under the title *She: Short stories of Rabindranath Tagore*, and is currently working on the poet's lyrics and songs.

Soham Pain is Ph.D. Research Scholar at the Centre for English Studies, Jawaharlal Nehru University, New Delhi, and currently a Fulbright scholar at the University of Texas at Austin.

William Radice is a poet, writer and translator. He is Senior Lecturer in Bengali at the School of Oriental and African Studies, University of London. He has done challenging translations of Kaliprasanna Singha's satire, *Hutom pyanchar naksha*, and Michael Madhusudan Dutt's epic, *Meghnadvadh*.

Andrew Robinson is the author of more than fifteen books, including *The art of Rabindranath Tagore* and two books published by I.B. Tauris: *Satyajit Ray: The inner eye* and *Satyajit Ray: A vision of cinema* (with Nemai Ghosh). He is the former literary editor of *Times higher education supplement*, and is now a visiting fellow of Wolfson College, Cambridge, and a full-time writer.

Jadu Saha, a scientist by education and training, is a former Senior Executive in the Government of Canada. After his retirement, he began his literary career in 2001. His poems in English were published in American anthologies. Shipra Publications, Delhi, has published five books of English translations of Rabindranath Tagore's songs, poems, short stories and writings for children.

Reba Som is an academic, historian, writer and classical singer. She is the former Director of Indian Council for Cultural Relations' Rabindranath Tagore Centre in Kolkata.

INDEX